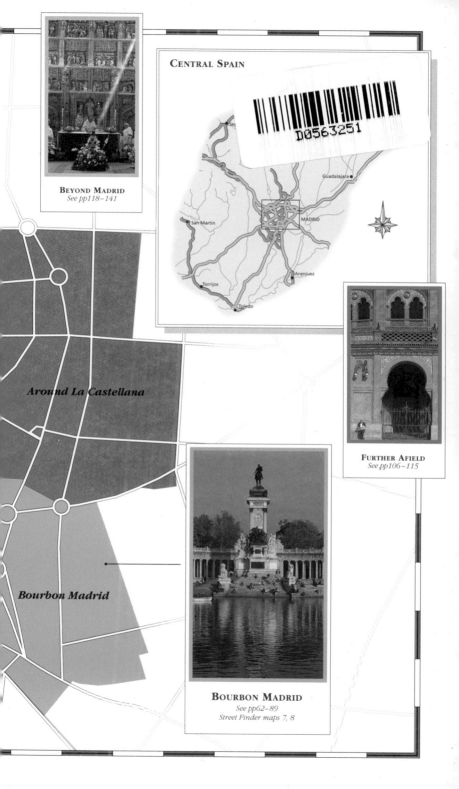

BEYOND MADRID
See pp118–141

CENTRAL SPAIN

Guadalajara

MADRID

San Martín

Torrijos

Aranjuez

Toledo

Around La Castellana

FURTHER AFIELD
See pp106–115

Bourbon Madrid

BOURBON MADRID
See pp62–89
Street Finder maps 7, 8

EYEWITNESS *TRAVEL GUIDES*

MADRID

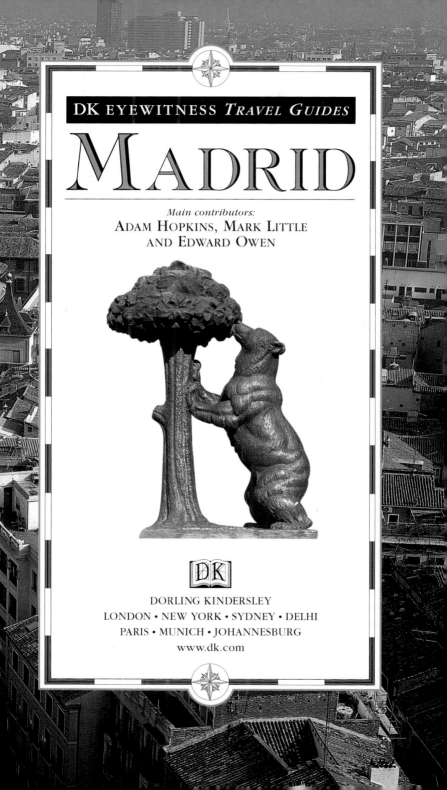

DK EYEWITNESS *TRAVEL GUIDES*

MADRID

Main contributors:
ADAM HOPKINS, MARK LITTLE
AND EDWARD OWEN

DORLING KINDERSLEY
LONDON · NEW YORK · SYDNEY · DELHI
PARIS · MUNICH · JOHANNESBURG
www.dk.com

A DORLING KINDERSLEY BOOK

www.dk.com

PROJECT EDITOR Helen Townsend
ART EDITOR Gillian Andrews
EDITORS Elizabeth Atherton, Sophie Warne
DESIGNERS Carolyn Hewitson, Nicola Rodway
MAP CO-ORDINATOR David Pugh
DTP DESIGNER Pamela Shiels
PICTURE RESEARCHER Monica Allende

MAIN CONTRIBUTORS
Adam Hopkins, Mark Little,
Edward Owen

PHOTOGRAPHERS
Peter Wilson and Kim Sayer

ILLUSTRATORS
Richard Bonson, Stephen Gyapay, Claire Littlejohn, Isidoro González-
Adalid Cabezas (Acanto, Arquitectura y Urbanismo S.L.), Maltings
Partnership, Chris Orr & Associates

Reproduced by Colourscan (Singapore)
Printed and bound by L Rex Printing Company Limited (China)

First published in Great Britain in 1999
by Dorling Kindersley Limited
9 Henrietta Street, London WC2E 8PS

Copyright 1999, 2001 © Dorling Kindersley Limited, London

Reprinted with revisions 2000, 2001

CONTENTS

**Winged Victory on the dome of
the Edificio Metrópolis** *(see p74)*

INTRODUCING MADRID

PUTTING MADRID ON THE MAP
8

THE HISTORY OF MADRID *12*

MADRID AT A GLANCE
22

MADRID THROUGH THE YEAR *34*

***Madrileños* enjoying the May-time
Fiesta de San Isidro** *(see p34)*

Restaurant inside the historic Hotel Reina Victoria *(see p47)*

The 13th-century church of San Esteban in Segovia *(see p128)*

Selection of Madrid's cakes

Street-by-street map of Paseo de Recoletos *(see pp92–3)*

INTRODUCING
MADRID

Putting Spain on the Map

Sᴘᴀɪɴ, ɪɴ sᴏᴜᴛʜᴡᴇsᴛᴇʀɴ Europe, covers the greater part of the Iberian Peninsula. The third largest country in Europe, it includes the Canary Islands in the Atlantic and the Balearics in the Mediterranean, and two small territories in North Africa. Its capital, Madrid, lies geographically in the centre of the country, some 650 m (2,130 ft) above sea level.

Satellite image showing the Iberian Peninsula

Plymouth

Portsmouth

Bay
of Biscay

A Coruña

Santander

N634

Oviedo

A66

N634

Santiago de
Compostela

N630

León

N120

N13

Vigo

Ourense

Miño

N103

N634

N611

Burgos

N620

N23

N15

Valladolid

Duero

N525

N601

Salamanca

N620

N630

N501

S   **P**

N110

MADRID

Tajo

N110

Toledo

Tajo

N502

N401

LISBON

N4

Badajoz

N430

Guadiana

Ciudad
Real

N420

N118

N502

N432

Úbeda

N433

N630

Córdoba

N432

Jaén

N120

N2

Guadalquivir

N125

Huelva

A49

Seville

NIV

A92

Grana

Faro

A4

N342

N337

N3

Málaga

Kᴇʏ

✈	International airport
⛴	Ferry service
▬	Highway/Motorway
▬	Major road
—	Main railway line
◆—	AVE high-speed railway line

Cádiz

N340

Santa Cruz de Tenerife
Las Palmas de Gran Canaria

Algeciras

GIBRALTAR

Tangier

Ceuta

Melilla

MOROCCO

THE CANARY ISLANDS

Santa Cruz de la Palma

Cádiz

Cádiz

Arrecife

Puerto de la Cruz

Santa Cruz de Tenerife

Puerto del Rosario

San Sebastian de la Gomera

Las Palmas de Gran Canaria

Valverde

Maspalomas

Biarritz

Bilbo (Bilbao)

Donostia (San Sebastián)

F R A N C E

Iruña (Pamplona)

N240

N240

ANDORRA

N20

A9

Perpignan

Huesca

N240

N330

Girona

N152

A7

A19

Ebro

Soria

Zaragoza

Lleida

NII

A2

Barcelona

N234

N232

Tarragona

A16

S P A I N

N330

M e d i t e r r a n e a n   S e a

Cuenca

N234

Maó

N320

NIII

NIII

Valencia

Palma de Mallorca

NIII

N301

Júcar

Albacete

N430

N430

N301

N330

A7

Eivissa (Ibiza)

| 0 kilometres | 100 |
| 0 miles | 50 |

Alacant (Alicante)

C3314

Segura

N340

Murcia

N332

Oran

Almería

Spain's Frontiers
*Spain has borders
with France, Portugal,
Andorra and Gibraltar. The
Strait of Gibraltar is only 13 km
(8 miles) wide between Tarifa,
the peninsula's southernmost
point, and northern
Morocco.*

**EUROPE AND
NORTH AFRICA**

NORWAY

FINLAND

SWEDEN

ESTONIA

RUSSIAN FED.

DENMARK

LATVIA

LITHUANIA

REPUBLIC OF IRELAND

UNITED KINGDOM

NETHERLANDS

RUSSIAN FED.

BELORUSSIA

BELGIUM

GERMANY

POLAND

LUXEMBOURG

CZECH REPUBLIC

UKRAINE

FRANCE

SWITZERLAND

AUSTRIA

SLOVAKIA

HUNGARY

SLOVENIA

ROMANIA

ITALY

CROATIA

BOSNIA AND HERZEGOVINA

YUGOSLAVIA

BULGARIA

PORTUGAL

SPAIN

•Madrid

ALBANIA

GREECE

MOROCCO

ALGERIA

TUNISIA

LIBYA

Putting Madrid on the Map

WITH A POPULATION of over 3 million, Madrid is the largest city in Spain. It lies in the centre of the Spanish *meseta* (high plain). The surrounding area is known as the Comunidad de Madrid, while further afield are the provinces of Guadalajara, Cuenca, Toledo, Avila and Segovia.

KEY

- ✈ International airport
- ✈ Domestic airport
- ▭ Highway/Motorway
- ▬ Major road
- ▭ Minor road
- ▬ Main railway line
- ▬ AVE high-speed railway line
- ▬ Province boundary

0 kilometres   15

0 miles   15

THE HISTORY OF MADRID

ALTHOUGH ARCHEOLOGICAL EVIDENCE *suggests that humans were attracted to the area in prehistoric times, the story of Madrid doesn't begin until 852, when the Moors built a fortress near the Manzanares river. By Spanish standards, the city is a mere adolescent – it was born 21 centuries after the Phoenicians founded Cádiz and six centuries after the Romans constructed Itálica near Seville.*

In the early 8th century, a Moorish army from North Africa landed at Gibraltar and, within a few years, conquered most of the Iberian peninsula. The Moors established an independent emirate based in Córdoba, southern Spain and, in 852, under Emir Mohamed I, they built a fortress (alcázar) to protect the northern approach to Toledo; it stood on the site of Madrid's present-day royal palace. Named Mayrit (later corrupted to Magerit, then Madrid), a small community arose around the alcázar.

Ornate Moorish warrior helmet

CHRISTIAN CONQUEST
Timidly at first, then with gathering strength, the Christians to the north rallied against the Moorish invaders, pushing southward in the so-called Reconquest. By the middle of the 11th century, the kingdom of Castile had arisen as the major Christian power, its territory extending as far south as the Cordillera central mountain range, within sight of Mayrit. In 1085, the Castilians under Alfonso VI mustered for the decisive thrust against Toledo. Mayrit stood in the path of the advancing army. According to one story, the troops mistook it for the much larger Toledo, which is why they bothered laying siege to it.

Another legend has it that the Christian attackers subdued the town after some of the more intrepid soldiers clambered up the defence walls.

Once all the excitement was over, the town of Madrid settled back into its sleepy rural existence. Many of its earliest inhabitants were monks, encouraged by the Spanish rulers to establish monasteries there and thus breathe new life into the community. Before long, Madrid had 13 churches, more than enough to serve the spiritual needs of its small population.

Among the first *Madrileños* was San Isidro Labrador, a local farmer who founded a *cofradía* (religious brotherhood). It is also said he performed miracles, but little else is known about Madrid's rustic patron saint.

In the 13th century a dispute arose over hunting rights on land owned by the Church. It was agreed that, while the Church owned the soil, *Madrileños* had rights to all that was above it, namely, game. Thus Madrid acquired its symbol – a bear (the Church's emblem) sniffing a tree.

TIMELINE

	711 Moors invade Iberian peninsula	932 Christian king Ramiro II temporarily occupies Madrid	1109 Moors unsuccessfully lay siege to Madrid	
700AD	800	900	1000	1100	1200
756 Emir Mohamed I founds emirate of Córdoba	852 Moors found Mayrit	*Bronze stag from a Moorish palace*	1085 Madrid captured by Castile	1202 Madrid granted the status of town

◁ **Tiled mural showing San Isidro Labrador, Madrid's patron saint, and another farmer tilling the soil**

Columbus setting foot in the Americas in the late 15th century

ROYAL HUNTING GROUND

Madrid's reputation as a hunting paradise attracted the attention of Castilian royals, whose visits became increasingly frequent. The city was especially favoured by Enrique IV de Trastamara who was, by all accounts, physically repellent, politically inept and morally perverted. Enrique was married to Juana of Portugal, but most people doubted that their daughter, Juana, was actually the king's; it was assumed her real father was the queen's lover, Beltrán de la Cueva, thus earning her the sobriquet, La Beltraneja (Beltrán's little one). On Enrique's death in 1474, a dynastic struggle ensued between supporters of La Beltraneja and those of Enrique's half-sister, Isabel, who later went down in history as Isabel la Católica.

Madrid's nobility threw its support behind La Beltraneja, and the forces of Isabel and her husband Fernando of Aragón laid siege, conquering Madrid with the help of supporters within the town. Although

Fernando of Aragón, the Catholic Monarch

Isabel and Fernando visited often, most of the momentous events of the age, such as the final war against the Moors and Columbus' encounter with the queen, took place elsewhere.

When Isabel died in 1504, her daughter Juana *"la Loca"* ("the Mad") was deemed unfit to rule. She and her husband the Archduke of Austria, who were living in Burgundy, returned to Spain to reassert their rights. But the archduke soon died, leaving Juana to slip further into dementia. Fernando of Aragón acted as regent until the couple's son, Charles of Ghent, acceded to the throne in 1517 as Carlos I, the first of the Spanish Habsburgs (later Holy Roman Emperor Charles V).

Carlos I (1516–56)

Carlos I ruled over a European empire that included the Low Countries, parts of Italy and Germany, and Spain's newly conquered possessions in the Americas. But he had been brought up in France, spoke no Spanish when he arrived to claim the throne and, although his reign lasted 40 years, he spent only 16 of them in Spain. The European wars and the Counter-Reformation kept him busy elsewhere. Finally, spiritually exhausted and plagued with gout, Carlos I retired to the monastery of Yuste in western Spain, where he died at the age of 58.

TIMELINE

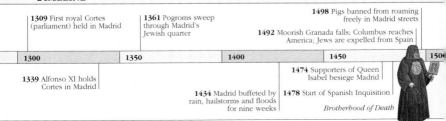

1309 First royal Cortes (parliament) held in Madrid

1339 Alfonso XI holds Cortes in Madrid

1361 Pogroms sweep through Madrid's Jewish quarter

1434 Madrid buffeted by rain, hailstorms and floods for nine weeks

1492 Moorish Granada falls; Columbus reaches America; Jews are expelled from Spain

1498 Pigs banned from roaming freely in Madrid streets

1474 Supporters of Queen Isabel besiege Madrid

1478 Start of Spanish Inquisition

Brotherhood of Death

1300   1350   1400   1450   150

A CITY IS BORN

Since the beginnings of the kingdom of Castile, its rulers travelled ceaselessly from one part of the realm to another, with the entire court tagging along. Fed up with this migrant existence, Carlos I's successor, Felipe II, established a permanent capital in Madrid in 1561. It was centrally located in the Iberian peninsula and small enough to lack the complex web of loyalties and intrigues of larger cities, such as Toledo.

Felipe V, the first Bourbon king

Artisans, cooks, poets, soldiers, thieves and hangers-on from around the peninsula flocked to the new capital. Within four decades, the population swelled from some 20,000 to 85,000.

Unlike his father, Felipe II spent most of his reign in Spain. Under him, the Inquisition became a major force, and the unsuccessful Spanish Armada was launched against England. The "Black Legend" has painted a dark picture of Felipe II, yet whatever his shortcomings, laziness and dishonesty were not among them and, during his reign, Spain's world power was virtually unchallenged.

Due to its sudden rise to prominence, Madrid's growth was haphazard. Yet under the Habsburgs the city acquired some of its most notable constructions. The best examples were built in the reigns of Felipe's successors, a period when the country enjoyed an age of cultural brilliance (the *Siglo de Oro*) just as Spain's military and political strength was declining. The Plaza Mayor *(see p44)*, the epitome of Habsburg Madrid, was built during Felipe III's reign. His successor, Felipe IV, built a stylish new palace at El Retiro. At the same time, Cervantes, Lope de Vega, Velázquez, Zurbarán and Murillo *(see pp26–7)* were active in Madrid. Money poured in from the New World and, although most was destined to finance Spain's endless foreign wars and increasing debt, enough was left to fuel an artistic boom.

THE BOURBON ZENITH

It was too good to last. The inbred Habsburg dynasty produced the gentle but dim-witted Carlos II who died without an heir in 1700, leaving the Spanish throne in dispute. France favoured Philippe of Anjou, the nephew of Louis XIV. Alarmed at the implications of a French-Spanish alliance, England, Austria and Holland supported the Archduke Charles of Austria. This dispute led to the 14-year-long War of Spanish Succession. At the end of the conflict Philippe was crowned as Felipe V – the first Bourbon king – and Spain was securely in the French orbit.

Bullfighting in Madrid's Plaza Mayor in the 17th century

1561 Felipe II establishes capital of Spain in Madrid

1600 Felipe III moves Spanish capital to Valladolid

1605 Publication of *Don Quixote* by Cervantes

1621 Felipe III dies, succeeded by Felipe IV

1701 Felipe V arrives in Madrid as first Bourbon king

1550　**1600**　**1650**　**1700**

20 Madrid ns *Comunero* ellion of stilian towns inst Carlos I

1563 Work starts on El Escorial *(see pp122–5)*

1588 Spanish Armada fails to reach Britain

1606 Madrid reinstated as capital

1632 Real Sitio del Buen Retiro palace *(see p77)* is completed

Felipe III

1734 Fire destroys Madrid's Moorish alcázar

1746 Fernando VI becomes king

The Bourbons were able administrators, availing themselves of French and Italian advisers who introduced modern improvements to Spain. Felipe V spoke little Spanish and his main concern was making Madrid look as French as possible. When the alcázar burned down in 1734, he ordered the construction of a royal palace *(see pp54–7)* modelled on Versailles, but died before it was completed. The first occupant was Carlos III, under whose rule the Bourbon dynasty, and Madrid, reached their greatest splendour. At this time the centre of the city shifted from the old Plaza Mayor to the new Paseo del Prado, and many new buildings were constructed. Such was Carlos's urbanistic zeal that he is still cited as the best "mayor" Madrid ever had.

Carlos III

The presence of foreign advisers did not sit well with *Madrileños*, however, and the Church encouraged sentiment against interloping outsiders. The most famous incident was the 1766 Esquilache affair in which the Marqués de Esquilache, adviser to the king, banned the traditional broad-brimmed hat and long cape, as they enabled weapons to be concealed. His men roamed the streets armed with scissors to trim the offending garb. The people took this as an attempt to make them conform to foreign fashions, and fierce riots ensued. The Jesuits were thought to be behind the disturbances, and the order was expelled from Spain.

On his death in 1788, Carlos was succeeded by his vacillating son, Carlos IV, who ushered in the decline of the monarchy. The real power sat with his domineering wife, María Luisa of Parma, and chief minister, Manuel Godoy.

A CITY IN ARMS

Godoy struck a deal with the France of Napoleon (who had declared himself emperor in 1804) to allow French troops to cross Spain to conquer Portugal. In the end, however, the French occupied Spain itself. *Madrileños* blamed the royals and their hated counsellor, Godoy, and riots broke out in March 1808 when the king was forced to abdicate in favour of his son, Fernando VII, though with the French occupying Madrid he ruled in name only.

On 2 May, *Madrileños* turned on the occupying troops in front of the Palacio Real. This popular uprising was met with bloody reprisals by the French the following day.

Goya's *The 3rd of May* (1814) with the French executing Spanish patriots

After the May riots Napoleon, increasingly impatient with events in Spain, installed his brother Joseph Bonaparte (José I) on the Spanish throne. Spanish sentiment against the occupying French could not be stopped, however, and the country rose up in arms. In the face of organized, well-armed French troops, Spaniards resorted to terrorist tactics, with small bands mounting surprise attacks on the enemy before vanishing into mountain hiding places.

In 1810, the army of the British Duke of Wellington landed in Portugal and started the two-year campaign to drive the French from the Iberian Peninsula.

LIBERALS VERSUS CONSERVATIVES

A century of close contact with the French left its mark on Spain. Liberal ideas found fertile soil among the Spanish enlightened classes and, while the war was at its peak, delegates in Cádiz drafted Spain's first constitution. Yet when Fernando VII was restored to the throne in 1813, he rejected the Cádiz document and ruled as an absolute monarch. This rift between reactionary and progressive sides would plague the country for the next century and a half. When an army uprising headed by the liberal Rafael de Riego in 1820 forced the king to accept the constitution, the exercise ended with Riego's execution.

After Fernando VII's death in 1833, Spanish politics became a complicated succession of *coups d'état* and uprisings. To make matters worse, the choice of his young daughter Isabel II as successor angered supporters of his brother Carlos, leading to a civil war in which 140,000 died. During Isabel's 38-year reign, Spanish politics was dominated by military brass, conservative or liberal.

Isabel II

Against this background of instability, Madrid was slowly becoming a modern European capital with a growing middle class. It was expanding relentlessly with the *Ensanche* (widening), with fashionable residential areas replacing overcrowded working-class districts.

In 1868 liberals joined forces with disgruntled military to oust Isabel II under the pretext of her corrupt and lascivious behaviour. But Spaniards still favoured a monarchy, and placed Amadeo of Savoy, son of Italy's King Victor Emmanuel, on the throne. The king received the cold shoulder from *Madrileños*, however, and abdicated after two years, at which point the Cortes (parliament) proclaimed a republic. The First Republic lasted only 11 months. In 1874, General Manuel Pavía ended it all by riding up the steps of the Cortes, declaring support for Isabel II's son, Alfonso. Under Alfonso XII (1875–85) and, later, the regency of his wife, María Cristina, who reigned on behalf of her son Alfonso XIII until 1902, Madrid enjoyed a period of prosperity and unstoppable growth, culminating with the inauguration of the Gran Vía *(see p48)* by Alfonso XIII in 1908.

THE BATTLE OF MADRID

Alfonso XIII felt it his duty to meddle in political affairs. Ministers were sacked by the dozen, and there were 33 governments between 1902 and 1923. Finally, the king resorted to General Miguel Primo de Rivera, who installed a dictatorship. It was relatively benign and had support among much of the working class. Spain underwent a flurry of public works, but Primo de Rivera was a disaster when it came to economics.

Poster for the Nationalist cause in the Civil War

Within six years the country was bankrupt. After the dictator stepped down in 1930, Republicans forced Alfonso XIII to call elections. The vote went overwhelmingly to the Republicans, and the king headed for exile after an angry Madrid crowd demanded his abdication.

During the brief Second Republic, the bourgeoisie, landowners and military were increasingly alarmed by the spread of left-wing ideas. The assassination of conservative member of parliament, José Calvo Sotelo, in July 1936 precipitated events. On 18 July news reached Madrid that a military uprising had taken several Andalusian cities, including Seville.

Madrileños flocked to the army barracks, demanding arms to defend the Republic, and within a day the working-class militia controlled the city. But, with much of the Spanish army's troops and weapons in the hands of insurgent Nationalists, the rebellion gathered

increasing territory, and by November 1936 the Nationalists had reached the outskirts of Madrid. The city was to be on the front line for the duration of the Civil War, suffering severe bombardment, until it finally fell in March 1939.

General Franco, who had manoeuvred himself into position as the uprising's *generalísimo*, was installed as dictator. Although Spain had remained nominally neutral during World War II, Franco's sympathies for Hitler and Mussolini were not forgotten, and for more than a decade the country was ostracized from the community of nations. Farms suffered a devastating drought, the black market thrived and Franco taught "autarchy" – his extreme form of isolationism and self-sufficiency. Yet the nation was starving, and millions were forced to emigrate to work in factories in France and Germany.

By the 1950s geopolitics came to the rescue. The US forgave Franco's past sins in return for support in the Cold War against the Soviet Union, in the form of US **General** military bases in Spain. **Francisco Franco** The door was open to foreign aid and investment. The first adventurous travellers soon followed.

DICTATORSHIP TO DEMOCRACY

Franco's twilight years were devoted to securing the continuity of his regime. Alfonso XIII's grandson Juan Carlos was groomed as his nominal successor, while the real power was to be wielded by the hard-line prime minister, Admiral Luis Carrero Blanco. But in 1973, the militant wing of Basque separatist group ETA assassinated Carrero Blanco.

TIMELINE

1921 Madrid Metro opens

1923 Primo de Rivera establishes dictatorship

Primo de Rivera

1929 Telefónica building *(see p49)* completed

1931 Second Republic established; Alfonso XIII goes into exile

1936 Civil War starts; Nationalists lay siege to Madrid

1939 Franco's troops enter Madrid; Civil War ends

1955 Spain joins United Nations

1953 Spain agrees to allow building of US bases on its soil; Edificio de España *(see p53)* inaugurated

| 1910 | 1920 | 1930 | 1940 | 1950 |

The Cortes being held at gunpoint in the *coup d'état* on 23 February 1981

When Franco died in November 1975, all eyes turned on his heir apparent, who was sworn in as king. Juan Carlos had been planning for Spain's reunion with the modern world while lending lip service to the Franco regime, and in a series of bold moves, he manoeuvred the country into its first post-Franco democratic elections in 1977. When die-hard supporters of the old regime seized the Cortes in 1981, the *coup* failed largely due to Juan Carlos's intervention.

The next year the government passed bloodlessly from the centrists to the social democratic PSOE, under long-serving prime minister Felipe González. The first half of his tenure coincided with a period of economic buoyancy, crowned in 1992 with the Olympic Games in Barcelona, a world fair in Seville and Madrid's stint as the "European Capital of Culture". The 1980s was a time of euphoria and cultural ferment, especially in Madrid. Under mayor Enrique Tierno Galván, the arts experienced a flurry of creativity, and the city revelled in a spirit of optimism and confidence, known as *La Movida*.

The party couldn't last forever. Creative verve can only go so far, and a series of scandals involving some people serving in high offices chipped away at the public's faith in the governing powers, ultimately costing the PSOE the 1996 elections.

Like their counterparts in other European capitals, *Madrileños* complain about traffic, never-ending public works and pollution. Yet despite this they retain a fiercely individualistic spirit, a refusal to conform to European hours and, above all, a sardonic sense of humour that sets them apart from other Spaniards. They are living in one of the world's most lively and attractive cities... and they know it.

Aerial image of present-day Madrid, a thriving metropolis

Rulers of Spain

SPAIN BECAME A NATION-STATE under Isabel and Fernando, whose marriage eventually united Castile and Aragón. With their daughter Juana's marriage, the kingdom was delivered into Habsburg hands. Carlos I and Felipe II were both capable rulers, but in 1700 Carlos II died without leaving an heir. After the War of the Spanish Succession, Spain came under the French Bourbons, who have ruled ever since – apart from an interregnum, two republics and Franco's dictatorship. The current Bourbon king, Juan Carlos I, a constitutional monarch, is respected for his support of democracy.

1665–1700 Carlos II

1479–1516 Fernando, King of Aragón

1474–1504 Isabel, Queen of Castile

1516–56 Carlos I of Spain (Holy Roman Emperor Charles V)

1598–1621 Felipe III

1400	1450	1500	1550	1600	1650
INDEPENDENT KINGDOMS			**HABSBURG DYNASTY**		
1400	1450	1500	1550	1600	1650

1469 Marriage of Isabel and Fernando leads to unification of Spain

1504–16 Juana la Loca (with Fernando as regent)

1621–65 Felipe IV

Fernando and Isabel, the Catholic Monarchs

UNIFICATION OF SPAIN

In the late 15th century the two largest kingdoms in developing Christian Spain – Castile, with its military might, and Aragón (including Barcelona and a Mediterranean empire) – were united. The marriage of Isabel of Castile and Fernando of Aragón in 1469 joined these powerful kingdoms. Together the so-called Catholic Monarchs defeated the Nasrid Kingdom of Granada, the last stronghold of the Moors *(see p14)*. With the addition of Navarra in 1512, Spain was finally unified.

1556–98 Felipe II

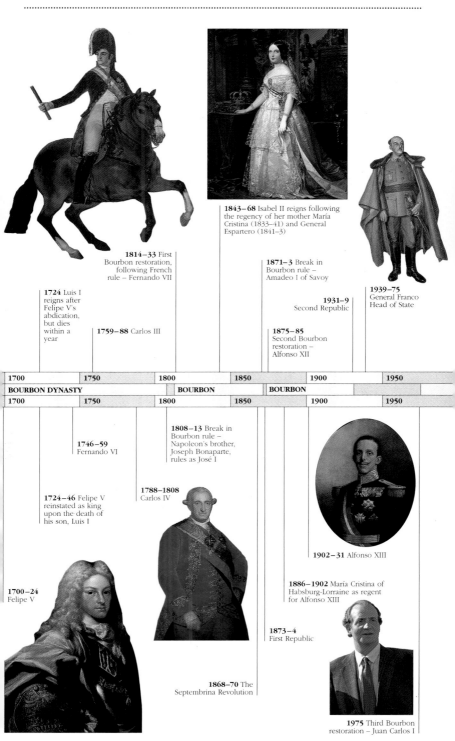

1843–68 Isabel II reigns following the regency of her mother María Cristina (1833–41) and General Espartero (1841–3)

1814–33 First Bourbon restoration, following French rule – Fernando VII

1871–3 Break in Bourbon rule – Amadeo I of Savoy

1939–75 General Franco Head of State

1724 Luis I reigns after Felipe V's abdication, but dies within a year

1759–88 Carlos III

1931–9 Second Republic

1875–85 Second Bourbon restoration – Alfonso XII

1700	1750	1800	1850	1900	1950

BOURBON DYNASTY   **BOURBON**   **BOURBON**

1700	1750	1800	1850	1900	1950

1808–13 Break in Bourbon rule – Napoleon's brother, Joseph Bonaparte, rules as José I

1746–59 Fernando VI

1724–46 Felipe V reinstated as king upon the death of his son, Luis I

1788–1808 Carlos IV

1902–31 Alfonso XIII

1886–1902 María Cristina of Habsburg-Lorraine as regent for Alfonso XIII

1700–24 Felipe V

1873–4 First Republic

1868–70 The Septembrina Revolution

1975 Third Bourbon restoration – Juan Carlos I

MADRID AT A GLANCE

OVER 100 PLACES OF interest are described in the *Madrid Area by Area* and *Beyond Madrid* sections of this book. The detailed catalogue of significant buildings and monuments traces the history of the city – beginning with the 16th- and 17th-century Habsburg Madrid ("Madrid de los Austrias"), as exemplified by the medieval Plaza de la Villa *(see p45)* and the Colegiata de San Isidro *(see p46)*. From here, it follows the development of Madrid from the Bourbon city of the 18th century with its Parque del Retiro and Plaza de Cibeles *(see p67)*, to the upmarket 19th-century Barrio de Salamanca and the modern skyscrapers in the Azca area. The list also includes recreational sights, such as Casa de Campo *(see p114)*. Pictured below are some attractions no visitor should miss.

MADRID'S TOP TOURIST ATTRACTIONS

Plaza Mayor
See p44.

Plaza de Toros de Las Ventas
See p110.

Parque del Retiro
See p77.

Museo Thyssen-Bornemisza
See pp70–73.

Museo Lázaro Galdiano
See pp100–101.

Museo Arqueológico Nacional
See pp96–7.

Centro de Arte Reina Sofía
See pp86–9.

Palacio Real
See pp54–7.

Museo del Prado
See pp80–83.

The Art Deco Capitol building along the Gran Vía

Madrid's Best: Museums and Galleries

For a city of its size, Madrid boasts an exceptional number of world-class museums and galleries. Heading the list are the Prado, with the world's largest collection of Spanish art, the Thyssen-Bornemisza, which traces the development of Western art from the 14th century, and Reina Sofía, with its outstanding display of modern art. These "big three" museums feature prominently on any visitor's itinerary. But there are many smaller, more intimate museums, too. Some, such as the Museo Lázaro Galdiano, are gems both for the sumptuous mansions housing the collections and for the untold treasures within.

Museo Municipal
Anyone with an interest in Madrid's evolution, from prehistoric to present times, will be fascinated by this museum, which features a captivating scale model of 19th-century Madrid (see p103).

Museo Cerralbo
Entering this 19th-century mansion, with its eclectic array of artifacts, paintings and sculptures, gives an uncanny sense of stepping back in time and experiencing aristocratic life in Madrid at the turn of the 20th century (see p52).

Old Madrid

Real Academia de Bellas Artes
Goya's Entierro de la Sardina is one of more than 1,000 paintings and sculptures, from the 16th–20th centuries, which can be seen at this arts academy (see p47).

Museo Thyssen-Bornemisza
Given to the nation in 1993, this vast private art collection traces Western art through the ages, with major works by Titian, Goya, Picasso and Rubens (see pp70–73).

Museo Lázaro Galdiano

The valued collection of the late José Lázaro Galdiano includes paintings, sculptures, jewellery, archeological finds and ceramics on display in his beautiful Neo-Renaissance mansion (see pp100–101).

Around La Castellana

Museo Arqueológico Nacional

This museum, situated at the back of the Biblioteca Nacional, is second only to the Prado in terms of the importance of its collection. Exhibits date from prehistoric times to the 19th century (see pp96–7).

Museo del Prado

Recognized as one of the world's greatest art galleries, the Prado is particularly notable for its collections by Velázquez and Goya (see pp80–83).

Bourbon Madrid

| 0 kilometres | 0.5 |
| 0 miles | 0.5 |

Centro de Arte Reina Sofía

Retrato de Josette, *by Spanish Cubist Juan Gris, occupies the room next door to* Guernica, *Picasso's famous depiction of the horrors of the Civil War. A former hospital, the Reina Sofía now houses an outstanding collection of 20th-century art* (see pp86–9).

Famous People of Madrid

EVER SINCE Felipe II made Madrid the capital of Spain in 1561 (see p15), the city has attracted the best artistic and literary talent in the country. Painters, writers, composers and architects in search of fame and fortune left behind their rural dwellings and migrated to Madrid, where they could take advantage of royal sponsorships and subsidies, publish their works and sell their wares to the city's ever-growing population. Thus Madrid became the cultural centre of Spain, a distinction that grew in times of political and economic stability, and flourished – as great art usually does – following times of turmoil and strife.

The prolific Golden Age dramatist, Félix Lope de Vega (1562–1635)

WRITERS

SPANISH WRITERS were the first to make their mark in Madrid, and throughout the 17th century the city acted as a magnet for the country's most famous scribes. The Barrio de los Literatos (Writers' Quarter), or Huertas district, was where Spain's greatest literary figure, Miguel de Cervantes Saavedra (1547–1616), produced his comic masterpiece, *Don Quixote*. In the local taverns he would argue with his rival, Félix Lope de Vega (1562–1635), Spain's most prolific dramatist. The Huertas area was also home to Cervantes' and Lope's 17th-century contemporaries, writer Francisco de Quevedo

y Villegas (1580–1645) and dramatist Pedro Calderón de la Barca (1600–81).

In the following centuries, this small area of Madrid continued to be the haunt of famous writers. The 18th-century Madrid native Leandro Fernández de Moratín was influenced by the French Enlightenment, as evidenced by his popular comedy *El Sí de las Niñas*. José Zorrilla y Moral (1817–93) was raised in the Huertas area, and his world-famous Romantic play, *Don Juan Tenorio* (1844), had its first showing in Madrid. In the same century, Madrid's most beloved writer, Benito Pérez Galdós (1843–1920), wrote his famous novel, *Miau* – a literary masterpiece that takes the reader on a journey through the streets and society of the Spanish capital during the city's most vibrant years. Madrid was at the centre of the "Generation of [19]27" writers that included poet and playwright Federico García Lorca (1899–1936) who, during his student years in Madrid, found inspiration as well as the theatres he needed to showcase his creations. The 20th century also produced Nobel Prize-winning novelist Camilo José Cela (born 1916), whose novel *La Colmena* depicted

José Zorrilla (1817–93)

Novelist Camilo José Cela (born 1916), painted by Alvaro Delgado

everyday life in hungry, postwar Madrid. And while 20th-century American writer Ernest Hemingway could not be mistaken for a *Madrileño*, his novels helped the world fall in love with Spain, and his antics in the city after long nights of sipping gin at the Ritz hotel (see p68) made him a local favourite. Today it is difficult to walk through Madrid's Plaza Mayor without imagining the writer swaggering down the narrow steps of the Arco de Cuchilleros on his way to a roast suckling pig dinner at El Sobrino del Botín (see p28).

PAINTERS

ALL OF SPAIN'S most famous artists had an impact, one way or another, on Madrid. But it was 17th-century artist Diego de Velázquez (1599–1660) and 18th-century painter Francisco de Goya (1746–1828) who actually formed part of the city's history. Both were Spanish court painters whose works were inspired by their surroundings in the capital. Each weekend *Madrileños* brave traffic jams to escape the grey city in search of the blue skies made famous by Velázquez, whose complete collection of works has been brought together by Madrid's Museo del Prado *(see pp80–83)*. There you can see his 1656 masterpiece, *Las Meninas*. Goya began his stint at the Spanish court in 1763 at the age of 17, and stayed on until 1826, two years before his death. He depicted life during one of the city's most violent times and was the painter of four kings – Carlos III, Carlos IV, José I (Joseph Bonaparte) and Fernando VII. While his works can be seen at several museums in Madrid, his masterpieces *The 3rd of May*, *Saturn Devouring One of his Sons* and *Naked Maja* are all displayed at the Prado.

Velázquez Bosco's Palacio de Cristal

completed in 1619. Mora learned his trade from the masterful Juan de Herrera, the designer of Felipe II's monasterial palace El Escorial *(see pp122–5)*. In the 1640s, Mora designed the Monasterio de la Encarnación *(see p53)* and the *Ayuntamiento* (town hall) in the Plaza de la Villa. A balcony was added to the town hall by Juan de Villanueva, the architect of the Prado museum. In 1781 Villanueva, along with botanist Gómez Ortega, designed the Real Jardín Botánico, or Royal Botanical Gardens *(see p84)*. In the Parque del Retiro *(see p77)* there are two beautiful palaces built by architect Velázquez Bosco in 1887: the Neo-Classical Palacio de Velázquez and the Palacio de Cristal, constructed of glass and iron. Noteworthy contemporary architects include José Rafael Moneo Valles, who redesigned the 18th-century Palacio de Villahermosa, home to the Museo Thyssen-Bornemisza *(see pp70–73)*. Also notable are Luis Gutiérrez Soto for the Ministerio del Aire in the Plaza de la Moncloa, Antonio Lamela for the Torres de Colón in the Plaza de Colón *(see p98)* and Francisco Saenz de Oiza for the Torres Blancas on Avenida de América.

Although not an architect, the Marqués de Salamanca, a flamboyant banker and speculator, had a profound effect

on the design of the upmarket Barrio de Salamanca *(see p99)*. When investors shied away from much-needed expansion plans in the 1860s, the Marqués stepped in and began work on what is today a fashionable line of housing blocks along Calle de Serrano.

POLITICIANS

SINCE MADRID IS the Spanish capital, there is a tendency here to claim or disclaim national figures as the city's own. Kings, dictators and prime ministers, while ruling from Madrid, did not always have a popular impact on the city. Felipe II *(see p15)*, for example, made Madrid the capital but then promptly left for his palace at El Escorial.

One of the best-loved political figures was the 18th-century *rey-alcalde* (king-mayor) Carlos III *(see p16)*. He took a personal interest in the city and set out to improve it with monuments, fountains, arches, street lighting and sewers. Another favourite politician was 20th-century (civilian) Socialist Mayor Enrique Tierno Galván, who became mayor in 1979, and died in 1986. He helped bring Madrid out of the grey dictatorial years by throwing his full support behind cultural events and progressive causes. He was instrumental in making Madrid's San Isidro festival *(see p34)* the popular cultural event it is today.

Las Meninas (1656) by Diego de Velázquez

ARCHITECTS

ARCHITECTURE IS AN art form of which *Madrileños* are especially proud. Some of the best architects in the world have contributed to turning the capital into the "City of a Thousand Faces". Francesco Sabatini designed the Palacio Real *(see pp54–7)*, the grand Puerta de Alcalá *(see p66)* and the 18th-century extension wing to the Palacio de El Pardo *(see p134)*. Juan Gómez de la Mora was the architect responsible for the Plaza Mayor *(see p44)*, which was

Enrique Tierno Galván, mayor of Madrid in the post-Franco era

Madrid's Best: Tabernas

IT COULD BE ASSUMED that the first business establishment in Madrid was a *taberna* (tavern). In the 14th century, the area around Plaza Mayor and Plaza de la Villa was home to over 50 *tabernas*. Two hundred years later, their number had risen to 800. But, of the classical *tabernas* that took shape in the early to mid-19th century, only about a hundred remain. Although each is unique, they share common features, such as a large clock standing guard over a carved wooden bar with a zinc counter, and wine flasks cooled by water running through a polished filter on the bar. Table tops tend to be of marble and ceramic tiles often line the façade or interior. Some popular classical *tabernas* are featured here. To find out more about traditional *tapas* see pages 30–31.

Taberna del Foro
While more modern than most, this taberna *has gone to fantastic lengths to recreate a feeling of "Old Madrid". Its bar is an authentic example of genuine* taberna *craftsmanship.*

La Bola
This small, bright red taberna *was founded nearly 200 years ago. It has a beautifully carved wooden bar and, since 1873, it has been serving some of Madrid's best* cocido (see p155).

Old Madrid

El Sobrino del Botín
Established in 1725, this is one of the city's oldest tabernas *and is considered by many to be one of Madrid's finest restaurants. It serves traditional Castilian fare, including roast suckling pig, and was, at one time, favoured by the writer Ernest Hemingway.*

0 kilometres 0.5

0 miles   0.5

Taberna Antonio Sanchez
Madrid's tabernas *take their cue from this classical, 200-year-old watering hole, where the character of the place is just as important as the service. Many later* tabernas *have emulated its decor.*

Casa Carmencita

This mid-19th-century taberna *was famous in the early 1920s as a hangout of writers, artists and politicians. Its wooden façade, elegant tiling and gas lamps add to its character.*

Casa Domingo

Almost 80 years ago this elegant taberna *was turned into a select restaurant for upmarket Madrileños. Today it serves local and international cuisine in an inviting, warm atmosphere.*

Around La Castellana

Los Gabrieles

The astonishing tile work of ceramics artist Enrique Guijo covers the walls of this museum-like taberna. *Los Gabrieles comes at the top of the list for most* taberna *-hoppers.*

Bourbon Madrid

Viva Madrid

Famous for its fine ceramic work, both inside and out, this taberna *has been adopted by the younger Madrileño crowd that gathers nightly around the lively Plaza de Santa Ana area.*

Casa del Abuelo

This diminutive taberna *more than makes up for its lack of size with its larger-than-life atmosphere. Founded in 1906, it specializes in sweet red wine and prawns cooked in four different ways.*

Choosing Tapas

MORE THAN A MORSEL of food, *tapas* are a way of life – part of a ritual which involves drink, good company and lively conversation. The custom of serving a tasty snack with each drink originated in Andalusia, but Madrid soon adopted it with gusto, and is a *tapa*-crawler's paradise. A *tapa* is any small portion of food – a brace of anchovies, a meatball, a fistful of olives, a sliver of cheese or a steaming dollop of stew. Small *tapas*, chosen by the waiter, are often served free with a drink; larger portions *(raciones)* are ordered separately.

Dry *fino* sherry

Chorizo, *a popular sausage that is flavoured with garlic and paprika, is usually eaten cold; but some kinds are fried and served hot.*

Jamón serrano, *salt-cured ham dried in mountain* (serrano) *air, can be served unadorned in chunks* (tacos) *or in thin slices* (lonchas). *This basic* tapas *dish is often accompanied by bread.*

Tortilla a la española *is the ubiquitous thick Spanish omelette, a tasty dish of onion and potato, bound together with seasoned egg. It is served in wedges or small squares.*

Queso manchego (see p166) *is sheep's cheese from La Mancha and Spain's most popular cheese. It is served with bread in a mild, semisoft form* (semicurado) *or, when left to age, a tangy mature form* (curado).

Albondigas *(meatballs) are a hearty tapa and may be served with a zesty tomato sauce.*

Olives *are common* tapas, *and come in several varieties. Gordals are fat Seville olives. Manzanillas may be pitted and stuffed with anchovies, almonds or pimientos. Some olives are marinated in herbs and oil or vinegar.*

Prawn   **Hard-boiled egg**

Olive

Gherkin

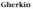

Mejillones a la marinera *is a dish of mussels cooked in a tasty sauce of sautéed onion and garlic, white wine, olive oil, lemon juice and parsley.*

Banderillas *are canapés skewered on tooth-picks. Popular ingredients include marinated fish and vegetables, egg and olives. The entire canapé should be eaten at once, to blend the flavours.*

Patatas bravas *is a piquant dish of potatoes fried in oil and coated in a spicy tomato sauce flavoured with onion, garlic, white wine, parsley and red chilli peppers. The bite-sized morsels are both delicious and filling.*

Salpicón de mariscos *is a luxurious cold salad consisting of an assortment of fresh seafood, including lobster, crab and prawn, with chopped tomatoes. The salad is coated in a zesty vinaigrette flavoured with onion and red peppers.*

Calamares fritos *are squid rings which have been dusted with flour before being deep fried in olive or vegetable oil. They are served garnished with a slice of lemon.*

Gambas a la plancha *is a simple but flavourful dish of whole grilled unpeeled prawns.*

Fritura de pescado *is a mixture of fried fish and seafood served with lemon. It includes red mullet, squid and baby hake or other available fresh fish.*

Ensalada de pimientos rojos *is a colourful cold salad of roasted red peppers and tomatoes. The juices from the roasting are combined with olive oil and vinegar to make a delicious sauce for the salad.*

Almendras fritas, *or fried salted almonds, are a common snack throughout the whole of Spain. Pistachos* (pistachios), *salted peanuts* (cacahuetes) *and sunflower seeds* (pipas) *can also be ordered to accompany a drink.*

GOOD TABERNAS FOR TAPAS AND DRINKS
(See pp28–9)

Casa Carmencita
Calle de la Libertad 16. **Map** 7 B1.
(91 521 59 66.

Casa del Abuelo
Calle de la Victoria 12. **Map** 7 A2.
(91 521 23 19.

Casa Domingo
Calle de Alcalá 99. **Map** 8 F1.
(91 576 01 37.

El Sobrino del Botín
Calle de los Cuchilleros 17.
Map 4 E3.
(91 366 42 17.

La Bola
Calle de la Bola 5. **Map** 4 D1.
(91 547 69 30.

Los Gabrieles
Calle de Echegaray 17. **Map** 7 A3.
(91 429 62 61.

Taberna Antonio Sanchez
Calle del Mesón de Paredes 13.
Map 4 F4.
(91 539 78 26.

Taberna del Foro
Calle de San Andrés 38. **Map** 2 F4.
(91 445 37 52.

Viva Madrid
Calle de Manuel Fernández y González 7. **Map** 7 A3.
(91 429 36 40.

Madrid's Best: Architecture

MADRID HAS BEEN DESCRIBED as the "city of a thousand faces", an image reflected in the diversity of its architectural styles. Among these are the rich and highly ostentatious buildings that mark the 16th-century areas of Old Madrid around the Plaza Mayor and the Plaza de la Villa. Northwest of Madrid, in El Escorial *(see pp122–5)*, the architecture of Felipe II's palace is characterized by unornamented severity of style. The 17th century brought with it the Bourbon urge to break with the previous mould, introducing new, ornate styles of Baroque architecture. In the 18th century, with the arrival of Carlos III *(see p16)*, more sedate Neo-Classical lines became fashionable. And, as the city expanded outwards, so did its love for new styles of architecture. Today Madrid's architects continue to experiment with adventurous building styles and techniques.

Modernism
The Puerta de Europa twin towers survived a financial scandal and now seem to defy gravity as they lean over Paseo de la Castellana.

Art Deco
The huge Palacio de la Música cinema on Gran Vía (see p48) *seats some 2,600 people. It is seen as a jewel of Art Deco architecture.*

Old Madrid

Habsburg
Since 1560 the red brick and granite Monasterio de las Descalzas Reales (see p52) *has been home to a society of cloistered nuns – the Royal Barefoot Sisters.*

Baroque
This art form was used mostly in the 17th century. Churriguera's 18th-century Real Academia de Bellas Artes (see p47) *begins to show signs of the new Neo-Classical trend.*

0 kilometres   0.5

0 miles   0.5

Art Nouveau
An eyecatching example of Madrid's version of this art form is the Sociedad General de Autores de España.

Bourbon
French art flourished under Bourbon rule (see p16), influencing future generations of architects. The Edificio Metrópolis (see p74) is Parisian in style.

Around La Castellana

Neo-Mudéjar
The Antiguas Escuelas Aguirre is an excellent example of this late-19th-century Moorish style that began in Madrid, characterized by its extensive use of fine brickwork, recurring balconies and row of vantage points along its bevel.

Bourbon Madrid

Neo-Classical
Designed in 1785 by Juan de Villanueva, the Museo del Prado (see pp80–83) illustrates the Neo-Classical move towards dignity and away from the excesses of Baroque architecture.

Francoesque
The Instituto de Crédito Oficial is in the Neo-Herrerismo style, invented in the Franco years and named after 16th-century architect, Juan de Herrera.

MADRID THROUGH THE YEAR

Matador with a cape playing a bull

A WIDE SELECTION of fiestas, sports competitions and cultural events crowds the calendar in Madrid. Every neighbouring district, town and village also has its own fiestas, especially during the summer, with hair-raising bull runs, music and dancing until the early hours and spectacular fireworks which rank among the best in the world. There are vibrant street processions to celebrate Christmas and Easter, and at other times the capital's roads are completely taken over by bicycles, marathon runners and even sheep. Check with the tourist information office to see if your visit coincides with any public holidays, local festivals or special fairs.

Colourful tulips in a park signalling the start of spring

SPRING

IN LATE MARCH the capital's boulevards are lined with tulips, and on the first warm day in April cafés open up their terraces. But the weather is changeable, and it may be warm one day and snow the next. May's San Isidro fiestas, which herald the start of the bullfighting season, are often marred by rain, but the countryside also looks its best at this time. Many *Madrileños* leave town for the Easter Semana Santa holiday, and the half-deserted streets resound with solemn religious processions.

MARCH

Cristo de Medinaceli *(first Fri)*, Iglesia de Medinaceli, Calle del Duque de Medinaceli. Thousands of people make three wishes before the image of Christ, one of which will hopefully come true.
Expo/Ocio, Feria del Tiempo Libre *(second week)*, Parque Ferial Juan Carlos I. This annual exhibition is dedicated to sports, leisure and hobbies.
Fiesta de San José *(19 Mar)*. Public holiday in Madrid in honour of St Joseph.

APRIL

Semana Santa *(Easter week)*. On Holy Thursday and Good Friday evening processions are held in Toledo *(see pp136–41)* and all over Madrid. On Easter Saturday there are church services and a passion play in Chinchón *(see p135)*. Easter Sunday is marked in Tiermes by the symbolic burning of a tree and an effigy of Judas at noon.
Artisans & Ceramic Fair *(Easter week)*, Plaza de las Comendadoras.
El Día de Cervantes *(23 April)*, Alcalá de Henares. Commemorates the death of Cervantes with a book fair and literary discussions.
Madrid Marathon *(last Sun)*.

MAY

Labour Day *(1 May)*. Public holiday and rally held in the Puerta del Sol *(see p44)*.
Fiestas de Mayo *(1 May)*, Ajalvir, Casarrubuelos, Fresno de Torote and Torrelaguna. Local fiestas celebrating May.
Las Mayas *(first Sun)*, around Iglesia de San Lorenzo in the Lavapiés district *(see p61)*. Each street elects a May Queen *(maya)* who sits in her best clothes surrounded by flowers in a spring fertility ritual.
La Maya *(2 May)*, Colmenar Viejo. Similar fiesta to above.
Día de la Comunidad *(2 May)*. Public holiday in Madrid with a military parade in the Puerta del Sol, a festival in Malasaña's Plaza del Dos de Mayo *(see p103)* and Móstoles.
Fiestas de San Isidro *(15 May)*. Public holiday in Madrid and the feast of the region's patron saint. For a week either side of 15 May, the city vibrates with fiestas, music and dance, including the *chotis*. Bands play nightly in the Jardines de las Vistillas, Calle de Bailén.
San Isidro Corridas *(15 May–end Jun)*. Daily bullfight fiesta at Plaza de Toros de Las Ventas *(see p110)*.
Corpus Christi *(end May)*. Public holiday with big processions in Madrid and Toledo.
Romería Alpina *(last Sun)*, Lozoya. Country procession with La Virgen de la Fuensanta.
Feria del Libro *(end May–mid-Jun)*, Parque del Retiro *(see p77)*. Book fair.

Semana Santa *(Easter Week)* observed with solemn religious processions

AVERAGE DAILY HOURS OF SUNSHINE

Hours

12 — 9 — 6 — 3 — 0

Jan Feb Mar Apr May Jun Jul Aug Sep Oct Nov Dec

Sunshine Chart
Madrid is a sunny place and, even in the depths of winter when temperatures plummet, there are usually a few hours of sunshine to brighten the skies. At the height of the Madrid summer you can expect an average of 12 hours of blistering sun a day, so come prepared with a hat and a high-factor sun cream, and avoid the midday sun.

SUMMER

MADRID'S OUTDOOR swimming pools and aqua parks open in June *(see p180)*. By August, the fierce dry heat settles in and entire families escape to the cool of the mountains, the coast or outlying villages to visit relatives. Most offices work intensively from 8am to 3pm. Many bars and restaurants close in August, but those that stay open are thronged until the early hours. With a fraction of the usual traffic on the roads, it is a pleasant month in Madrid.

Madrid's terrace bars, great for cooling down in the summer heat

JUNE

Fiesta de San Antonio de la Florida *(13 Jun)*, Ermita de San Antonio, Paseo de la Florida. *Señoritas* throw pins in a font, dip in their hands and ask St Anthony for a boyfriend. If any pins stick to their hands they will have that many boyfriends in the year ahead.

JULY

Fiestas de la Virgen del Carmen *(9–16 Jul)*. District fiestas in Chamberí.
Concierto de las Velas *(9 Jul)*, Pedraza, Segovia. Candlelit fiesta with music.

Madrileños in traditional *castizo* costume at the Fiesta de San Isidro

Fiestas de Santiago Apóstol *(25 Jul)*. Public holiday in Madrid province.
Romería Celestial *(26 Jul)*, Alameda del Valle, Lozoya. Procession climbs 3 km (1.9 miles) to La Ermita de Santa Ana. Bring your own picnic.

AUGUST

Castizo Fiestas *(6–15 Aug)*. Traditional *castizo (see p105)* fiestas in La Latina and Lavapiés. Traditional *Madrileño* fiestas of San Cayetano *(3 Aug)*, San Lorenzo *(5 Aug)* and La Virgen de la Paloma *(15 Aug)*.
Fiesta de San Lorenzo *(10 Aug)*, El Escorial *(see pp122–5)*.
Fiesta de San Roque, *(12–18 Aug)*, Chinchón. Week-long fiesta with a bullfight in the Plaza Mayor and *anís* tastings.
Asunción *(15 Aug)*. Assumption Day national holiday.
Encierros *(end Aug)*. Bull runs in San

Sebastián de los Reyes.
Fiestas de San Bartolomé *(24 Aug)*, Alcalá de Henares. Fiestas with giants, classical theatre and bullfights.
Encierros *(last week)*, Cuellar, Segovia. Spain's oldest known bull run, dating back to 1546.
El Motín de Aranjuez *(end Aug or early Sep)*, Aranjuez. Carlos IV's abdication (1808), celebrated with bullfights, outdoor concerts and fireworks.

Decorations for La Virgen de la Paloma fiesta

AVERAGE MONTHLY RAINFALL

mm												Inches
60												2.4
45												1.8
30												1.2
15												0.6
0	Jan	Feb	Mar	Apr	May	Jun	Jul	Aug	Sep	Oct	Nov	Dec	0

Rainfall Chart
Madrid has two main rainy periods – one from March to May, and the other from October to December. During the autumn, the skies tend to open in short thundery bursts, bringing the year's highest rainfall. Summers are dry and hot, and you are very unlikely to see much rain from June to September.

View of the Plaza de España *(see p53)* **in autumn**

AUTUMN

WITH THE ONSET of autumn, the first rains for months relieve the parched countryside and begin to replenish depleted reservoirs. *Madrileños* love foraging in pine forests for the wild mushrooms produced by damp nights. The hunting season begins in October, and wild *níscalos* (fungi), boar, partridge and pheasant begin to appear on restaurant menus.

Wild mushrooms

SEPTEMBER

Encierros *(first 12 days Sep)*, Torrelaguna. Exciting bull runs and local celebrations.
Procesión Marítima *(first Sun)*, Fuentidueña de Tajo. Maritime procession with illuminated barges.

Procesión de la Virgen de la Cigüeña *(6 Sep)*, Fuente de Saz de Jarama. Procession honouring the Virgin of the Stork amid burning scrub.
Romería Panorámica *(second Sun)*, San Lorenzo de El Escorial. Procession with La Virgen de la Gracia (Grace) to a picnic in La Herrería woods.
Romería de la Virgen de los Hontanares *(10 Sep)*, Riaza, Segovia. Local pilgrimage and fiesta of the Virgin of Springs.

Virgen de la Fuencisla *(27 Sep)*. Segovia fiesta.
Procesión de San Andrés *(30 Sep)*, Rascafría. Procession in honour of the local saint.
Festival de Otoño *(mid-Sep to mid-Oct)*. Madrid's annual autumn drama festival.

OCTOBER

Festival Taurino *(around 12 Oct)*, Chinchón. Bullfights.
Día de la Hispanidad *(12 Oct)*. Spanish National Day.
Virgen de Pilar *(around 12 Oct)*, Plaza Dalí, Salamanca. Various district fiestas are held.

NOVEMBER

Todos los Santos *(1 Nov)*. On All Saints' Day flowers are taken to graves of relatives for 2 November, the Day of the Dead. Bakeries sell *Huesos de Santo* (Saints' Bones).
La Almudena *(9 Nov)*. Old Madrid honours its patron saint La Virgen de la Almudena.
Romería de San Eugenio *(14 Nov)*. *Castizo* procession in open carriages to El Monte de El Pardo for picnics, collecting acorns, singing and dancing.

Celebration of Mass in Plaza Mayor to honour La Virgen de la Almudena

AVERAGE MONTHLY TEMPERATURE

Temperature Chart
*Scorching hot summers
and freezing winters
make Madrid a place of
extremes, with averages
giving scant indication
of the heights and depths
of temperature the city
can achieve. For many
people, the most com-
fortable months to visit
Madrid, in terms of
milder temperatures,
are June and October.*

WINTER

THE FIRST SNOW usually falls in
the Sierra de Guadarrama
(see p126), heralding the start
of the skiing season, and
traffic jams form on the way
up to its small resorts. Madrid,
and the higher parts of central
Spain, can become very cold.
Christmas is a special time of
celebration – an occasion for
families to reunite, share food
and attend religious services.
On New Year's Eve, crowds
gather in the Puerta del Sol.

Skiers in the Sierra de Guadarrama, north of Madrid *(see p126)*

DECEMBER

Día de la Constitución *(6
Dec)*. Constitution Day.
Inmaculada Concepción *(8
Dec)*. Immaculate Conception.
Christmas Fair *(mid-Dec–
5 Jan)*, Madrid's Plaza Mayor.
Noche Buena *(24 Dec)*.
Christmas Eve – an important
night of family celebrations.
Día de Navidad *(25 Dec)*.
Christmas Day celebration.
Belén Viviente *(last eves
Dec)*, Buitrago del Lozoya.
Nativity play on horseback.
Noche Vieja *(31 Dec)*. New
Year's Eve. Crowds in Puerta
del Sol eat a grape and make
a wish at each midnight chime.

JANUARY

Cabalgata de Reyes *(5 Jan)*.
Twelfth Night procession from
Parque del Retiro *(see p77)* to
the Plaza Mayor *(see p44)* with
floats and zoo animals.
Los Reyes Magos *(6 Jan)*.
Epiphany is celebrated with
the giving of gifts.
San Antón *(17 Jan)*, Calle de
Hortaleza 63, Madrid. Animals
blessed at Iglesia de San Antón.

Cabalgata de Cercedilla *(19
Jan)*, Cercedilla. Winter proces-
sion with horse-drawn sleighs.
Vaquillas *(20 Jan)*, Pedrezuela
and Fresnedillas. Fiesta in
which youths dress up as bulls.
San Sebastián *(20 Jan)*,
Villaviciosa de Odón. Proces-
sion, fiestas and dancing.
FITUR Tourist Fair *(end Jan)*,
Parque Ferial Juan Carlos I.

FEBRUARY

La Vaquilla Premiada *(2 Feb)*,
Colmenar Viejo. Amateur bull-
fighting contest and fiesta.
La Romería de San Blas *(3
Feb)*, Madrid and Miraflores.
Costumed celebrations.
Alcadesas de Zamarramala
(around first Sun), Segovia.
For a week village women
boss their men around.
**Semana Internacional de la
Moda** *(second week)*, Parque
Ferial Juan Carlos I. Interna-
tional fashion week.
ARCO *(mid-Feb)*, Parque Ferial
Juan Carlos I. International
contemporary art fair.
Carnaval *(run up to Lent)*.
Fancy-dress parties; parade
from Plaza de Colón *(see p98)*
to Plaza de Cibeles *(see p67)*.

Entierro de la Sardina
(Shrove Tue), Casa de Campo.
"Burial of the Sardine" parade
to mark the changeover from
Carnaval to Lent.

NATIONAL PUBLIC HOLIDAYS

Año Nuevo *(New Year's
Day)* (1 Jan)
Día de los Reyes
(Epiphany) (6 Jan)
Jueves Santo *(Maundy
Thursday)* (Mar/Apr)
Viernes Santo *(Good
Friday)* (Mar/Apr)
Día de Pascua *(Easter
Sunday)* (Mar/Apr)
Día del Trabajo *(Labour
Day)* (1 May)
Asunción *(Assumption
Day)* (15 Aug)
Día de la Hispanidad
(National Day) (12 Oct)
Todos los Santos *(All
Saints' Day)* (1 Nov)
Día de la Constitución
(Constitution Day) (6 Dec)
Inmaculada Concepción
(Immaculate Conception)
(8 Dec)
Día de Navidad
(Christmas Day) (25 Dec)

MADRID AREA
BY AREA

OLD MADRID

WHEN FELIPE II chose Madrid as his capital in 1561, it was a small Castilian town with a population of barely 20,000. In the following years, it was to grow into the nerve centre of a mighty empire. Narrow streets with houses and medieval churches began to grow up behind the old Moorish fortress *(see p13)*, which was later replaced by a Gothic palace and eventually by the present-day Bourbon palace, the Palacio Real. By the end of the century the population had more than trebled.

The 16th-century city is known as the "Madrid de los Austrias", after the Habsburg dynasty. At this time, monasteries were endowed and churches and palaces were built. In the 17th century, the Plaza Mayor was added and the Puerta del Sol became the spiritual and geographical heart of Spain.

SIGHTS AT A GLANCE

Historic Buildings
Edificio Grassy ⓫
Muralla Arabe ㉖
Palacio de Santa Cruz ❼
Palacio del Senado ⓲
Palacio Real pp54–7 ⓴
Teatro Real ㉒
Telefónica ⓬

Museums and Galleries
Museo Cerralbo ⓰
Real Academia de
  Bellas Artes ❾

Churches and Convents
Basílica Pontifica de
  San Miguel ❺
Catedral de la
  Almudena ㉔
Colegiata de San Isidro ❻
Iglesia de San Nicolás ㉓
Convento de la
  Encarnación ⓳

Monasterio de las
  Descalzas Reales ⓲
San Francisco
  el Grande ㉗

**Streets, Squares, Parks
and Districts**
Calle de Preciados ⓯
Campo del Moro ㉕
Gran Vía ❿
La Latina ㉙
Plaza de España ⓱
Plaza de la Paja ㉘
Plaza de la Villa ❹
Plaza de Oriente ㉑
Plaza de Santa Ana ❽
Plaza del Callao ⓭

Plaza Mayor ❷
Puerta del Sol ❶

Markets
El Rastro ㉚
Mercado de San Miguel ❸

GETTING THERE

Line 1 on the Metro goes to Gran Vía and Sol, while 2, 3, 5 and 10 are good for getting to the main sights. Useful buses include the 51, 52, 150 and 153 to the Puerta del Sol.

KEY

	Street-by-Street map *pp42–3*
Ⓜ	Metro station
	Main bus stop
ⓘ	Tourist information
Ⓟ	Parking

Equestrian statue of Felipe II in the centre of the Plaza Mayor *(see p44)*

Street-by-Street: Old Madrid

STRETCHING FROM THE CHARMING Plaza de
la Villa to the busy Puerta del Sol, the
compact heart of Old Madrid is steeped
in history and full of interesting sights.
Trials by the Inquisition and executions
were once held in the Plaza Mayor. This
porticoed square is Old Madrid's finest
piece of architecture, a legacy of the
Habsburgs (see p14). Other noteworthy
buildings include the Catedral de San
Isidro and the Palacio de Santa Cruz. For
a more relaxing way of enjoying Old
Madrid, sit in one of the area's numerous
cafés or browse among the colourful
stalls of the Mercado de San Miguel.

★ **Plaza Mayor**
*This beautiful 17th-
century square
competes with the
Puerta del Sol as
the focus of Old
Madrid. The arcades
at the base of the
impressive buildings
are filled with cafés
and craft shops* ❷

Mercado de San Miguel
*Housed in a 19th-century
iron structure, the market
sells a variety of fresh food* ❸

Palacio
Real

PLAZA
DE LA
VILLA

CALLE MAYOR

PLAZA
MORENAS

CALLE DE SACRAMENTO

CORDÓN

PUÑONROSTRO

CUCHILLEROS

**Town hall
(ayuntamiento)**

Casa de Cisneros

**Arco de
Cuchilleros**

★ **Plaza de la Villa**
*The 15th-century Torre de
los Lujanes is the oldest of
several historic buildings
standing on this square* ❹

0 metres	100
0 yards	100

STAR SIGHTS

★ **Plaza Mayor**

★ **Plaza de la Villa**

★ **Puerta del Sol**

**Basílica Pontífica
de San Miguel**
*This imposing 18th-
century church has
a beautiful façade
and a graceful
Baroque interior* ❺

★ **Puerta del Sol**
With its shops and cafés, the Puerta del Sol is one of the city's liveliest areas. This sign for Tío Pepe, a brand of sherry, has become synonymous with the square ❶

LOCATOR MAP
See Street Finder map 4

AROUND LA CASTELLANA

OLD MADRID

BOURBON MADRID

Iglesia de San Ginés

Sol Metro

Equestrian statue of Carlos III

Bourbon Madrid

BORDADORES

CALLE DEL ARENAL

PUERTA DEL SOL

CALLE DE ALCALÁ

CALLE MAYOR

CALLE DE POSTAS

CALLE PAZ

CALLE DE CARRETAS

BARCELONA

ESPOZ Y MINA

PLAZA MAYOR

PLAZA PROVINCIA

PLAZA DE JACINTO BENAVENTE

SALVADOR

DUQUE DE RIVAS

DE TOLEDO

CALLE DE LA COLEGIATA

Tirso de Molina Metro

Palacio de Santa Cruz
Built as the court prison in the 17th-century, this Baroque palace is now occupied by the Foreign Ministry ❼

Colegiata de San Isidro
Named after the city's 12th-century patron saint, this was Madrid's provisional cathedral until the Catedral de la Almudena was completed (see p59) ❻

KEY

– – – Suggested route

Kilometre Zero, the centre of Spain's road network, at the Puerta del Sol

Puerta del Sol ❶

Map 4 F2. Ⓜ *Sol.*

Noisy with traffic, chatter and policemen's whistles, the Puerta del Sol ("Gateway of the Sun") makes a fitting centre for Madrid. It is one of the city's most popular meeting places; huge crowds converge on this famous square on their way to the shops and sights in the old part of the city.

The square marks the site of the original eastern entrance to Madrid, once occupied by a gatehouse and castle. These disappeared long ago and in their place came a succession of churches. In the late 19th century the area was turned into a square and became the centre of café society.

Today the "square" is shaped like a half moon. Its straight southern side is occupied by an austere red-brick building, originally the city's post office, built in the 1760s under Carlos III. In 1847 it became the headquarters of the Ministry of the Interior. In 1866 the clocktower, which gives the building much of its identity, was added. During the Franco regime *(see p18)*, the police cells beneath the building were the site of many human rights abuses. In 1963, Julián Grimau, a member of the underground Communist party, allegedly fell from an upstairs window and miraculously survived, only to be executed shortly afterwards.

The building is now home to the regional government, the Comunidad de Madrid, and is the focus of many festive events. At midnight on New Year's Eve dense crowds fill the square and people swallow a grape on each stroke of the clock, a tradition supposed to bring good luck for the rest of the year. Outside the building, a symbol on the ground marks Kilometre Zero, considered the centre of Spain's huge road network.

The buildings opposite are arranged in a semicircle and contain modern shops and cafés. On the corner of Calle del Carmen is a bronze statue of the symbol of Madrid – a bear reaching for the fruit of a *madroño* (strawberry tree).

The Puerta del Sol has witnessed many important historical events. On 2 May 1808 the uprising against the occupying French forces began here, but the crowd, pitted against the well-armed French troops, was crushed *(see p16)*. In 1912 the liberal prime minister José Canalejas was assassinated in the square and, in 1931, the Second Republic *(see p18)* was proclaimed from the balcony of the Ministry of the Interior.

Plaza Mayor ❷

Map 4 E3. Ⓜ *Sol.*

The plaza mayor forms a splendid rectangular square, complete with balconies, pinnacles, dormer

Allegorical paintings on the Casa de la Panadería, Plaza Mayor

windows and steep slate roofs. The square, with its theatrical atmosphere, has a noticeably Castilian character. Much was expected to happen here and a great deal did – bullfights, executions, pageants and trials by the Inquisition *(see p15)* – all watched by crowds, often in the presence of the reigning king and queen.

The first great public scene in the Plaza Mayor was the beatification of Madrid's patron, San Isidro, in 1621. During the same year, the execution of Rodrigo Calderón, secretary to Felipe III, was held here. Although hated by the Madrid populace, Calderón bore himself with such dignity on the day of his death that the phrase "proud as Rodrigo on the scaffold" survives to this day. Perhaps the greatest occasion of all, however, was the arrival here – from Italy – of Carlos III in 1760.

Construction of the square started in 1617, and was completed in just two years, replacing slum houses on the site. Its architect, Juan Gómez de la Mora, was successor to Juan de Herrera, designer of El Escorial *(see pp122–3)*, Felipe II's austere monastery-palace. Mora echoed the style of his master, softening it slightly. The fanciest part of the arcaded construction is the **Casa de la Panadería** (bakery). Its façade, which has undergone restoration, is decorated with allegorical paintings.

The **equestrian statue** in the centre is of Felipe III, who ordered the square to be built. Begun by the Italian Giovanni de Bologna and finished by his pupil Pietro Tacca in 1616, the statue was moved here in 1848 from the Casa de Campo *(see p114).* Nowadays the square is lined with outdoor cafés and is the venue for a collectors' market on Sundays. The southern exit leads into the Calle de Toledo towards the streets where El Rastro, Madrid's famous flea-market *(see p61),* is held. A flight of steps in the southwest corner of the square takes you under the Arco de Cuchilleros to the Calle de Cuchilleros, where there are a number of *mesones,* traditional restaurants.

Colourful food stalls in the 19th-century Mercado de San Miguel

Mercado de San Miguel ❸

Plaza de San Miguel. **Map** 4 D3. Ⓜ *Sol.* ☐ *9am–2pm, 5–8pm Mon–Fri, 9am–2pm Sat.* ● *Sun & public hols.*

Although there are larger markets in Madrid, this one is the last surviving example in the capital of a marketplace constructed from iron. The unique single-level, glassed-in market was built in 1914–15. It stands on the site of the former Iglesia de San Miguel de los Octoes, which was demolished in 1810 during the reign of Joseph Bonaparte. Fresh fruit and vegetables, fish, meat and other produce are sold at individual stalls, decorated with beautiful tiles. Because of competition from modern supermarkets, several stalls are now unoccupied.

Plaza de la Villa ❹

Map 4 D3. Ⓜ *Ópera, Sol.*

This much restored and frequently remodelled square is one of Madrid's most atmospheric spots, surrounded by many historic buildings.

The oldest building is the early 15th-century **Torre de los Lujanes,** with its Gothic portal and Mudéjar-style horse-shoe arches. France's François I was allegedly imprisoned in it following his defeat at the Battle of Pavia in 1525. The **Casa de Cisneros** was built in 1537 for the nephew of Cardinal Cisneros, founder of the historic University of Alcalá *(see p131).* The façade on Calle de Sacramento is an excellent example of the Plateresque style – early Spanish Renaissance with fine detail.

Linked to this building by an enclosed bridge is the **town hall** *(ayuntamiento).* Designed in the 1640s by Juan Gómez de la Mora, architect of the Plaza Mayor, it exhibits the same combination of steep roofs with dormer windows, steeple-like towers at the corners and an austere brick-and-stone façade. Before construction was completed, more than 50 years later, the building had acquired handsome Baroque doorways. A balcony was later added by Juan de Villanueva, architect of the Prado *(see pp80–83),* so that the Royal Family could watch Corpus Christi processions passing by.

Portal of the Torre de los Lujanes

Basílica Pontífica de San Miguel ❺

Calle de San Justo 4. **Map** 4 D3. *91 548 40 11.* Ⓜ *Sol.* ⬜ *10am–2pm, 5:30–9pm Mon–Sat; 6–9pm Sun.* 🚫

STANDING ON THE SITE of an old Romanesque church dedicated to two local child-martyrs put to death by the Romans, this building is a rare example of Bourbon-inspired Baroque in the middle of old Madrid. It was built for Don Luis de Borbón y Farnesio, the youngest son of Felipe V and Archbishop of Toledo at only five years of age.

Several architects had a hand in its design and construction between 1739 and 1746. The pediment and twin bell towers topping its convex façade were, however, added later. Four allegorical statues, representing Charity, Fortitude, Faith and Hope, grace the elegant façade. There are also carvings depicting the two child-martyrs, Justo and Pastor.

Inside, there is a single nave, and the roof is supported only by the curved and crossing arches sprouting from the exterior walls. The decor is a curious mixture of old and new – the frescoes on the ceiling and the organ in the choir (above the entrance) date from the 18th century, but many of the paintings and

Statue of Charity gracing the façade of Basílica Pontífica de San Miguel

stained glass windows are contemporary. Today the church is administered by the Catholic lay organization, Opus Dei, who use it as a base for some of their activities. One of the side chapels, which is dedicated to the organization's Spanish founder, Monsignor José María Escrivá de Balaguer (1902–75), houses an eerily lifelike statue of him.

Ornate altar in the Colegiata de San Isidro

Colegiata de San Isidro ❻

Calle de Toledo 37. **Map** 4 E3. *91 369 20 37.* Ⓜ *La Latina.* ⬜ *8am–12:45pm, 6–8:30pm daily.*

THIS TWIN-TOWERED church was built in the Baroque style for the Jesuits in the mid-17th century. It was used as Madrid's unofficial cathedral until 1993 when Nuestra Señora de la Almudena *(see p59)* was finally completed and consecrated by the Pope.

After Carlos III (1759–88) expelled the influential Jesuit order from Spain in 1767 *(see p16)*, he commissioned the artist Ventura Rodríguez to redesign the church's interior. It was then re-dedicated to St Isidore, the patron saint of Madrid and, two years later, the saint's remains were brought here from the Iglesia de San Andrés. The Colegiata de San Isidro was returned to the Jesuits during the reign of Fernando VII (1814–33).

Palacio de Santa Cruz ❼

Plaza de Santa Cruz. **Map** 4 E3. *91 379 97 00.* Ⓜ *Sol.* ⬜ *By appointment in writing (Ministerio de Asuntos Exteriores, Director General del Servicio, Pl. de la Provincia No 1, Madrid 28012).*

CONSTRUCTED between 1629 and 1643, this building is one of the jewels of Habsburg architecture. Since 1901 it has been the Ministry of Foreign Affairs, but has also housed the Overseas Ministry, law courts and, originally, the Carcel de la Corte (city prison). It was here that the luckless participants in the *autos de fé* (Spanish inquisition trials), held in the nearby Plaza Mayor *(see p44)*, awaited their fate. Its more famous inmates include playwright Lope de Vega (1562–1635), imprisoned for libelling his former lover, the actress Elena Osorio. The English writer and travelling Bible salesman, George Borrow, who was accused of instigating liberal ideas, also spent three weeks here. General Rafael de Riego, who led an uprising against Fernando VII in 1820, and the famous bandit Luis Candelas spent their last hours in its cells. Candelas was a colourful Robin Hood-like character, educated in Greek and Latin, who rubbed shoulders with the aristocracy (and stole their jewels). He was executed on 6 November 1837; today one of Madrid's tourist restaurants, situated on nearby Cava de San Miguel, is named after him.

The palace underwent a restoration in 1846, following a devastating fire, and again in the aftermath of the Spanish Civil War *(see p18)*, but its original architecture remains basically intact. The style of the building is very much in keeping with the area around the Plaza Mayor, with spired towers on each of its corners and two interior courtyards. The building only became

The 17th-century Palacio de Santa Cruz – a jewel of Habsburg architecture

known as the Palacio de Santa Cruz after 1846, when it was made the headquarters of Spain's Overseas Ministry.

Plaza de Santa Ana ❽

Map 7 A3. Ⓜ Sevilla, Antón Martín.

THIS SMALL SQUARE, just four blocks southeast of the Puerta del Sol (see p44), is a popular gathering place with a lively, at times rowdy, atmosphere. Built during the reign of Napoleon Bonaparte's brother Joseph (1808–13), the square took its name from the 16th-century Convent of Santa Ana that stood here. It was demolished to make way for the square.

Scene from a play by Calderón de la Barca adorning his statue

Monuments to two of Spain's most famous writers testify to the square's strong literary connections. At one end, a statue of the poet Federico García Lorca (see p26), erected in 1998, commemorates the centenary of his birth. At the other is the older and rather more brooding marble figure of Pedro Calderón de la Barca (1600–81). Madrid-born, he was the leading playwright in the twilight years of Spain's Siglo de Oro (Golden Century) of arts. His best-known work is La Vida es Sueño (Life is a Dream). The monument, with scenes from four of Calderón's

plays adorning the pedestal, was sculpted by Juan Figueras in 1878 and faces the **Teatro Español** (see p76). Built in 1745, the theatre was originally known as the Teatro del Príncipe. It had to be restored in 1980 after a devastating fire.

The square's theatrical links go back even earlier, as the theatre stands on the spot of the Corral del Príncipe, one of Madrid's popular, 16th-century corrales de comedias (open courtyards where plays were staged). These tended to be boisterous affairs, often culminating in fights between the actors and the audience. Across from the theatre are the glassed-in balconies of Hotel Tryp **Reina Victoria** (see p147), one of Madrid's classic hostelries. Before the Tryp chain acquired it, the hotel's then-modest lodgings were used by bullfighters who could not afford luxurious city rooms. The taurine theme has been preserved.

The other two sides of Plaza de Santa Ana and adjoining streets are home to some of the city's most popular bars and restaurants. The classic **Cervecería Alemana**, built in 1904 and once frequented by author Ernest Hemingway, is always packed with customers.

Around the corner from the theatre is the **Viva Madrid** (see p29). This is a popular bar with the young, fashionable

and single, as is **Los Gabrieles** (see p29). They are both worth looking into for their extraordinary 19th-century ceramic tableaux. Tile landscapes also adorn the **Villa Rosa**, which is located on the corner of Plaza de Santa Ana and Calle de Núñez de Arce.

Real Academia de Bellas Artes ❾

Calle de Alcalá 13. **Map** 7 A2. [91 532 15 46. Ⓜ Sevilla, Sol. ⏲ 9am–7pm Tue–Fri, 9am–2:30pm Sat–Mon & public hols. 🖼 (free Sat & Sun). 🚻

DALÍ AND PICASSO are among the former students of this arts academy, housed in an 18th-century building by Churriguera. Its art gallery displays a large selection of works, including excellent drawings by Raphael and Titian. A superb collection of old masters includes paintings by Rubens and Van Dyck. Spanish artists from the 16th to the 19th centuries are particularly well represented, with several magnificent works by Ribera, Murillo, El Greco and Velázquez. One of the highlights is Zurbarán's Fray Pedro Machado, typical of the artist's paintings of monks.

An entire room is devoted to Goya, a former director of the academy. On show here are his painting of a relaxed Manuel Godoy (see p16), the Burial of the Sardine, the grim Madhouse, and a self-portrait painted in 1815.

Fray Pedro Machado by Zurbarán

Gran Vía 🔟

IN THE MID-1800s, Madrid's burgeoning middle class was pushing the city's limits outwards, destroying houses and poor districts to allow for the *Ensanche* (widening). The city fathers saw the need for a new thoroughfare – a *Gran Vía*. Departing from the haphazard growth of the past, this street was to follow a plan and be a symbol of modern Madrid. On the drawing board since 1860, with even a satirical *zarzuela (see p75)* devoted to it, the project was not approved until 1904. Inaugurated by Alfonso XIII in 1908 *(see p17)*, building was carried out in three stages, each segment bearing a different name, although they are no longer used. The first, and most elegant – Avenida Conde de Peñalver (after the Mayor) – ran from Calle de Alcalá to Red de San Luis. The second phase, to the Plaza de Callao, was completed in 1922, while the final segment, ending in the Plaza de España, was built between 1925 and 1929. The new street gave architects an opportunity to prove their skill, providing a survey of early 20th-century design trends, including some of the best examples of modern architecture in the city.

Brass detail on the Edificio Metrópolis

The Museo Chicote *cocktail bar, on the ground floor of Gran Vía No. 12, has an immaculately preserved Art Deco interior. It opened in 1932 and was patronized by Salvador Dalí, Frank Sinatra, Ava Gardner and Orson Welles.*

The rounded Art Deco *façade of this building, like many along the Gran Vía, displays a style and grandeur befitting the city's most impressive thoroughfare. Many Art Deco buildings were built as cinemas, several of which are clustered around Plaza del Callao.*

Behind La Gran Peña's *curved façade (No. 2) is a luxurious, increasingly popular men's club. In 1926, attempts to make Franco a member caused such a stir that the club was later taken over and used by the militia during the Civil War (see p18).*

Edificio la Estrella *(No. 10) is a good example of the eclectic mix of Neo-Classical design and ornamental touches evident in the first buildings to have appeared along Gran Vía.*

Today's Gran Vía *continues to be a throbbing main artery for the city of Madrid, lined with theatres and cinemas, hotels, shops and restaurants.*

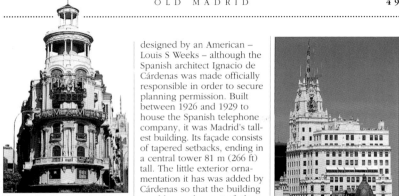

The two-tiered colonnade of the Edificio Grassy on Gran Vía

Edificio Grassy ⓫

Gran Vía 1. **Map** 7 B1. 🄲 *91 532 10 07.* Ⓜ *Banco de España, Sevilla.* 🄾 *10am–1pm, 5–8pm Mon–Sat.*

DESIGNED by Eladio Laredo on a small sliver of land between the Gran Vía and the Calle de Caballero de Gracia, the Grassy building boasts a circular end-tower similar to that of the nearby Edificio Metropolis *(see p74)*. It is crowned by a round, two-tiered colonnade. It was built in 1917, but became known as the Grassy building in the 1950s, after the jewellery shop that has occupied the ground floor since then. The prestigious jewellery firm, which was established in 1923, specializes in watches and, in the basement, is the **Museo de Reloj Grassy**, a collection of around 500 valuable timepieces, dating from the 16th to 19th centuries. Acquired by the firm over the years, they include rare clocks which belonged to European royalty.

Clock at the Grassy museum

Telefónica ⓬

Gran Vía 28. **Map** 4 F1, 7 A1. **Museum** 🄲 *91 522 66 45.* Ⓜ *Gran Vía, Callao.* 🄾 *10am–2pm, 5–8pm Tue–Fri, 10–2pm Sat, Sun & public hols.* ● *Aug.* 🚫 ♿ 📷 *(call to arrange).*

IF THE TELEFÓNICA building has an American look to it, it is because it was inspired by Manhattan's skyscrapers and designed by an American – Louis S Weeks – although the Spanish architect Ignacio de Cárdenas was made officially responsible in order to secure planning permission. Built between 1926 and 1929 to house the Spanish telephone company, it was Madrid's tallest building. Its façade consists of tapered setbacks, ending in a central tower 81 m (266 ft) tall. The little exterior ornamentation it has was added by Cárdenas so that the building would seem less out of place amid the neighbouring architecture. The clear view from the upper floors enabled the Republican defenders of the city to monitor the movements of besieging Nationalists in the Spanish Civil War *(see p18)*.

A section of the lower floors, which is entered from Calle de Fuencarral, is used for exhibitions. There are temporary exhibitions on the ground floor and a permanent one of the evolution of telecommunications on the first floor. Displays range from old phones, including the one used by Alfonso XIII to inaugurate Madrid's automatic telephone service in 1926, to a bank of switchboards complete with 19 life-sized operators and sound effects. The exhibition rooms are arranged around a gallery that overlooks the main foyer. The gallery once housed the Telefónica's formidable collection of modern art, but this is on long-term loan to the Centro de Arte Reina Sofía *(see pp86–9)*.

The Telefónica – a Manhattan-style skyscraper from the 1920s

Plaza del Callao ⓭

Plaza del Callao. **Map** 4 E1. Ⓜ *Callao.*

THIS CITY'S PASSION for films is fed by more than 60 cinemas and Plaza del Callao, the movie mecca of Madrid, has seven of them. Situated at the junction of Gran Vía and Calle de Preciados, the square was named after a naval battle off Callao, Peru, in 1866. The cinemas are the Art Deco Cine Callao, Imperial, Avenida, Rex, Capitol, Palacio de la Música (music hall) and Asociación de la Prensa de Madrid (Madrid Press Association). Films are advertised on huge, hand-painted signs. Housed in the Capitol building is the Capitol cinema, built in 1933. A superb example of Art Deco architecture, its features include a covered entrance and a vast, box-like interior, 35 m (115 ft) wide, adorned with simple lines and curves.

The Capitol cinema, a good example of Art Deco architecture

Chapel with ornate altar in the Monasterio de las Descalzas Reales

Monasterio de las Descalzas Reales ⓮

Plaza de las Descalzas 3. **Map** 4 E2.
🄲 91 542 00 59. ⓜ Sol, Callao.
🄾 10:30am–12:45pm, 4–5:45pm
Tue–Thu & Sat, 10:30am–12:45pm Fri,
11am–1:45pm Sun & public hols. 🄳

M ADRID'S MOST notable
religious building is also
a rare surviving example of
16th-century architecture in the
city. Around 1560 Felipe II's
sister Doña Juana decided to
convert the medieval palace
which stood here into a convent for nuns and women of
the royal household. Her rank,
and that of her fellow nuns,
accounts for the vast store of
art and wealth of the Descalzas
Reales (Royal Barefoot Sisters).
    The richly painted stairway
has a fresco of Felipe IV with
his family, and a fine ceiling by
Claudio Coello. It leads to a
small first-floor cloister, which
is ringed with chapels containing works of art and precious
objects of the former nuns. The
main chapel houses the tomb
of Doña Juana. The Gran Sala
de Tapices contains several
series of tapestries, one woven
in Brussels in 1627 for Felipe
II's daughter, Isabel Clara
Eugenia. There are also works
by Brueghel the Elder, Titian,
Zurbarán, Murillo and Ribera.

Calle de Preciados ⓯

Map 4 F2. ⓜ Sol, Callao.

T HIS PEDESTRIAN street leading
north from Puerta del Sol
to the busy Plaza de Callao is
now the domain of shoppers.
It was originally a humble
country path from the centre of
old Madrid to the orchards and
threshing floors of the Convent
of San Martín which, until
1810, faced the Monasterio
de las Descalzas Reales. In the
17th century two brothers,
the Preciados, purchased land
from the convent to build
their homes. They were in
charge of controlling official
weights and measures used
for trade in Madrid.
    Calle de Preciados acquired
its modern look during the
Ensanche (urban renewal) of
the mid-19th century. It is the
birthplace of Spain's most successful department store chain,
El Corte Inglés. Started by
Ramón Areces as a modest
clothes store in 1940, it now
occupies an 8-floor premises at
the southern end of the street.
At the northern end stands a
modern building occupied by
FNAC, the local branch of a

French chain which is one of
the city's best sources for
music, video and books.
Between the two superstores,
trendy boutiques share space
with old-fashioned shops.

Museo Cerralbo ⓰

Calle de Ventura Rodríguez 17.
Map 1 C5. 🄲 91 547 36 46.
ⓜ Plaza de España, Ventura
Rodríguez. 🄾 9:30am–2:30pm Tue–
Sat, 10am–2pm Sun. ⬤ Mon & public
hols. 🄳 (free Wed & Sun). 🄳 🚫

T HIS 19TH-CENTURY mansion
near the Plaza de España
is a monument to Enrique de
Aguilera y Gamboa, the 17th
Marquis of Cerralbo. A com-
pulsive collector of art and
artifacts, he bequeathed his
lifetime's collection to the
nation in 1922. They range
from Iberian pottery to 18th-
century marble busts.
    One of the star exhibits is
El Greco's *The Ecstasy of Saint
Francis of Assisi*. There are also
paintings by Ribera, Zurbarán,
Alonso Cano and Goya, which
hang in the Picture Gallery.
    The focal point of the main
floor is the ballroom, lavishly
decorated with mirrors.

Main staircase of the exuberant Museo Cerralbo

Stone obelisk with statue of Miguel de Cervantes, Plaza de España

Plaza de España ⑰

Map 1 C5. Ⓜ *Plaza de España.*

ONE OF MADRID'S busiest traffic intersections and most popular meeting places is the Plaza de España. In the 18th and 19th centuries the square was occupied by military barracks, built here because of the square's proximity to the Palacio Real *(see pp54–7)*. However, further expansion of Madrid resulted in it remaining a public space.

The square acquired its present appearance during the Franco period with the construction of the massive **Edificio de España**. Commissioned by the Metropolitana real estate developers, the 26-floor concrete structure was built between 1947 and 1953, when Spain was isolated from the western world and materials were scarce. It was seen as a triumph of "autarchy" *(see p18)*. The imposing main tower is flanked by two 17-floor wings. The eastern wing now houses the Holiday Inn Crowne Plaza hotel *(see p147)*.

Metropolitana also built the 33-floor **Torre de Madrid** on the corner of Plaza de España and Calle Princesa. Completed in 1957 and nicknamed La Jirafa (the Giraffe), for a time it was the tallest concrete structure in the world.

The most attractive part of the square is its centre, with a massive stone obelisk built in 1928. In front of it is a statue of Cervantes *(see p131)*. Below him, Don Quixote rides his horse while Sancho Panza trots alongside on his donkey.

Palacio del Senado ⑱

Plaza de la Marina Española. **Map** 3 C1. 📞 *91 538 10 00.* Ⓜ *Plaza de España, Ópera.* ⏱ *tours by prior appointment.* 🚫 ♿

THE UPPER HOUSE of the Cortes (Spanish parliament) is installed in a 16th-century monastery, adapted in 1814 for the purpose. It became the Senate headquarters when a two-chamber system was introduced 23 years later.

The monastery's courtyards were covered to create more meeting rooms. Some, such as the Salón de los Pasos Perdidos (Hall of the Lost Footsteps), contain enormous paintings depicting great moments in Spanish history. Among these are the surrender of Granada and Queen Regent María Cristina swearing to uphold the Constitution in 1897.

The library is a magnificent example of English Gothic style, dating from the turn of the 20th century. Ornate tiers of black metal bookcases contain 14,000 volumes, including a copy of Nebrija's *Gramática*, the first Spanish grammar.

Lack of space was always a problem in the Palacio del Senado, however, and in 1991 a modern granite-and-glass circular wing was added at the back of the building. The old assembly hall, installed in the former church, is used for ceremonial occasions while, for ordinary meetings, the senators convene in the new wing.

Old assembly hall of the Palacio del Senado, housed in the church of the monastery

Imposing entrance to the Convento de la Encarnación

Convento de la Encarnación ⑲

Plaza de la Encarnación 1. **Map** 3 C1. 📞 *91 547 05 10.* Ⓜ *Ópera, Santo Domingo.* ⏱ *10:30am–12:45pm, 4–5:45pm Tue–Thu & Sat, 10:30am–12:45pm Fri, 11am–1:45pm Sun & public hols.* 🎟 *(free on Wed).* ♿

SET IN A lovely tree-shaded square, this Augustinian convent was founded in 1611 for Margaret of Austria, wife of Felipe III. The architect, Juan Gómez de la Mora, also built the Plaza Mayor *(see p44)*.

The interior of the convent, which is still inhabited by nuns, has the atmosphere of old Castile, with its blue and white Talavera tiles, wooden doors, exposed beams and portraits of royal benefactors. It also contains a collection of 17th-century art, with paintings by José de Ribera and Vincente Carducho lining the walls and a polychrome wooden statue *Christ at the Column* by Gregorio Fernández.

The main attraction is the reliquary chamber, with its ceiling painted by Carducho, which is used to store the bones of saints. There is also a phial of St Pantaleon's dried blood which, according to legend, liquefies each year on 27 July, the anniversary of the saint's death. The church, rebuilt by Ventura Rodríguez after a fire in 1767, has paintings by Francisco Bayeu (Goya's brother-in-law) and frescoes by Luca Giordano.

Palacio Real ⑳

MADRID'S VAST AND LAVISH ROYAL PALACE was built to impress. The site, on a high bluff overlooking the Río Manzanares, had been occupied for centuries by a royal fortress but, after a fire in 1734, Felipe V commissioned a truly palatial replacement. Construction lasted 26 years, spanning the reign of two Bourbon monarchs, and much of the exuberant decor reflects the tastes of Carlos III and Carlos IV *(see p16)*. The palace was used by the royal family until the abdication of Alfonso XIII in 1931. The present king, Juan Carlos I, lives in the more modest Zarzuela Palace outside Madrid, but the Royal Palace is still used for state occasions.

Statue of Carlos III

★ Dining Room
This gallery was decorated in 1879. With its long table, ceiling paintings and superb tapestries, it evokes the grandeur of regal Bourbon entertaining.

★ Porcelain Room
The walls and ceiling of this room, built on the orders of Carlos III, are entirely covered in royal porcelain from the Buen Retiro factory. Most of the porcelain is green and white, and depicts cherubs and wreaths.

First floor

The Hall of Columns, once used for royal banquets, is decorated with 16th-century bronzes and Roman imperial busts.

★ Gasparini Room
Named after its Neapolitan designer, the Gasparini Room is decorated with lavish Rococo chinoiserie. The adjacent antechamber, with painted ceiling and ornate chandelier, houses Goya's portrait of Carlos IV.

STAR FEATURES
★ Dining Room
★ Porcelain Room
★ Gasparini Rooms
★ Throne Room

Plaza de la Armería
The square in front of the main entrance is named after the palace's Royal Armoury. The outstanding collection of weaponry includes the suits of armour belonging to Charles V and Felipe II.

Entrance Hall
A marble staircase by Sabatini, next to the statue of Carlos III as a Roman emperor, leads to the main floor. The painted Rococo ceiling by Giaquinto vividly depicts allegorical scenes.

Billiards room

Hall of the Halberdiers

Entrance

Royal Armoury

Plaza de la Armería

Pharmacy
This unique collection includes decorated Talavera pottery storage jars and herb drawers. The Pharmacy Museum has recipe books detailing medications prescribed for the royal family.

KEY TO FLOORPLAN

☐	Exhibition rooms
☐	Entrance rooms
☐	Carlos III rooms
☐	Chapel rooms
☐	Carlos IV rooms

Ticket office

★ **Throne Room**
The two gold and scarlet thrones here are exact reproductions of those of Charles V. The enormous mirrors were made in the royal glass factory of La Granja.

Exploring the Palacio Real

THIS SPLENDID ROYAL PALACE stands on the site of the original Moorish fortress, or alcázar, which served as a residence for visiting royals after the Christian conquest of Madrid in 1085 *(see p13)*. Following extensive modifications in 1561, it became the residence of Felipe II until the completion of El Escorial *(see pp122–5)* in 1584. The alcázar was destroyed by fire on Christmas Eve, 1734, during the reign of Felipe V. This suited Spain's first Bourbon king well – his idea of a royal palace was the Versailles of his childhood, and so he commissioned a new French-style royal palace to be erected on the spot.

Grand entrance stairway with 72 steps in Toledo marble

Stately façade of the Palacio Real, seen from the Plaza de la Armería

THE PALACE

MOST OF THE massive limestone and granite building is the work of Italian Giovanni Battista Sachetti, with later modifications by other architects. So vast was the plan that construction lasted from 1738 to 1764, by which time Felipe V was dead. His son, Carlos III, became the first royal resident. The palace remained the official home of the Spanish royal family until Alfonso XIII left for exile in 1931. The distribution of rooms and the interior decoration were altered by successive monarchs.

General Franco *(see p18)* also used the palace – known at the time as the Palacio de Oriente – for official business, and would address crowds of sympathizers from its eastern balcony overlooking the Plaza de Oriente *(see p58)*. Today it is used for state functions.

Visitors enter the palace from the **Plaza de la Armería**. The main entrance is crowned by a pediment with a clock and two bells, one of which dates from 1637 and is a survivor of the fire which destroyed the old alcázar. The interior is remarkable for its size and for the exuberant decor, carpets, tapestries and antique furnishings in many of the rooms.

ENTRANCE ROOMS

THE TOLEDO MARBLE in the main stairway, presided over by ceiling frescoes by Corrado Gialquinto, provides a regal taste of what is to follow. The first port of call is the **Salón de los Alabarderos** (Hall of the Halberdiers, or palace guards), decorated with tapestries and murals. Adjoining it is the **Salón de Columnas** (Hall of Columns), which served as the banquet hall until the new dining hall was incorporated in the 19th century. Today it is used for receptions and functions – the charter by which Spain joined the EU was signed here, on the 19th-century table supported by sphinxes. There are five tapestries of the Deeds of the Apostles, based on cartoons by Raphael and originally commissioned by the Vatican.

Finally, visitors enter the Carlos III rooms through the 18th-century Rococo **Salón del Trono** (Throne Room), whose decor has remained constant throughout generations of rulers. Completed in 1772, it has two rock crystal chandeliers, numerous candelabra and mirrors, and walls of crimson velvet with gold embroidery. The twin thrones are recent (1977), while the bronze lions that guard them date from 1651. The room is used for functions, such as the royal reception on 12 October (the Día de la Hispanidad) or the yearly reception for the diplomatic corps posted in Madrid.

Regal crimson-and-gold Throne Room with a rock crystal chandelier

CARLOS III ROOMS

LEADING OFF from the throne room are three smaller halls named after Mattia Gasparini, the original decorator. These were the king's private chambers. He would take his meals in the **Sala de Gasparini** – lonely affairs considering the queen had her own dining room. The **Antecámara de Gasparini** contains four paintings by Goya of Carlos IV and María Luisa de Parma. In the **Cámara de Gasparini** the king would be dressed, usually in the presence of courtiers. This is the only room to retain its original decor – Rococo and oriental, with a stucco ceiling and embroidered silk walls.

A small room, the **Tranvía de Carlos III**, leads into the former bedroom of Carlos III. In the Baroque **Sala de Porcelana** (Porcelain Room), 18th-century porcelain from the Buen Retiro factory covers the walls. The **Salita Amarilla** (Yellow Room), named after the tapestry covering the walls, leads to the Gala Dining Hall.

The lavish dining room, formerly the queen's private chambers

Portrait of *Carlos IV* by Goya in the Antecámara de Gasparini

DINING ROOM

THIS 400-SQ M (4,300-sq ft) banquet hall was formed in 1879 when the queen's private chambers were joined together, during the reign of Alfonso XII. It is richly adorned with gold plate decoration on the ceiling and walls, frescoes, chandeliers, Flemish tapestries, Chinese vases and embroidered curtains. The table can accommodate up to 160 diners.

The rooms leading off from the dining room house exhibits of royal household possessions. The room immediately off the dining hall is devoted to commemorative medals, and also contains the elaborate centrepiece used during banquets. Other rooms contain the silverware, china, crystal, and an extraordinary collection of musical instruments, including rare Stradivarius examples.

CHAPEL ROOMS

BUILT IN 1749–57, the chapel is still used for religious services, and also for musical soirées. While the decor is luxurious, it is the dome, with its murals by Gialquinto, that immediately catches the eye.

Next, visitors pass through the **Salón de Paso** and into María Cristina's chambers (originally Carlos IV rooms). During the reign of Alfonso XII these four small, windowless rooms served as a Neo-Gothic billiards room, oriental-style smoking room, the **Salón de Estucos** (queen's bedroom), and the **Gabinete de Maderas de Indias**, used as an office.

PHARMACY AND ARMOURY

RETURNING TO THE PLAZA de la Armería, near the ticket office is the **Botica Real** (Royal Pharmacy) founded by Felipe II in 1594. The pharmacy is a warren of rooms, with glass and ceramic jars and vials bearing the names of different potions and medicinal plants.

On the other side of the plaza is the **Armería Real** (Royal Armoury), housed in a pavilion built in 1897 after the original armoury was demolished. The armoury contains weapons and ceremonial suits of armour. On display is an elaborate suit of armour which once belonged to Carlos I, the Holy Roman Emperor Charles V. The armoury could be considered as Madrid's first museum because it has been open to the public since Felipe II started the collection. It originally contained both weapons used by the Spanish army and those taken from defeated enemy armies.

Armour of Carlos I

Equestrian statue of Felipe IV, by
Pietro Tacca, Plaza de Oriente

Plaza de Oriente ㉑

Map 3 C2. Ⓜ *Ópera.*

D URING HIS DAYS as king of
Spain, Joseph Bonaparte
(José I) carved out this stirrup-
shaped space from the jumble
of buildings to the east of the
Palacio Real *(see pp54–7)*,
providing the view of the
palace enjoyed today.

The square was once an
important meeting place for
state occasions: kings, queens
and dictators all made public
appearances on the palace
balcony facing the plaza. The
many statues of early kings
which stand here were originally intended to adorn the
roofline of the Palacio Real,
but proved to be too heavy.
The equestrian statue of
Felipe IV in the centre of the
square is by Italian sculptor
Pietro Tacca, and is based on
drawings by Velázquez.

In the southeast corner of the
plaza is the **Café de Oriente**
(see p158), with outdoor tables
for enjoying the view.

Teatro Real ㉒

Plaza de Oriente. **Map** 4 D2.
📞 91 516 06 00. Ⓜ *Ópera.*
🚫 ♿ 🎥 *10:30am–1:30pm
Tue–Sun & public hols.* ⬤ *Aug.*

M ADRID'S OPERA HOUSE stands
opposite the Palacio Real
(see pp54–7) on the Plaza de
Oriente. It is an imposing six-
sided grey building, made all
the more impressive by the
fact that there are six floors
(used as storage space) below
street level as well as the nine
floors visible above ground.

It was originally built around
1850. However, much of the
structure that exists today is
the result of a massive project
to renovate the theatre, which
took place between 1991 and
1997. The horseshoe-shaped
main theatre area, decorated
in red and gold with seating
on five levels, holds 1,630
spectators and the stage area
measures 1,430 sq m (15,400
sq ft). This, together with the
curtain and the magnificent
crystal chandelier weighing
2.5 tonnes, are among the
theatre's noteworthy features.

On the second floor, there
are four large foyers arranged
around the main hall. They
contain tapestries, paintings,
mirrors, chandeliers and
antiques. All of them are laid
with carpets produced especially for the theatre by the
Manuel Morón workshop in
Ciudad Real, south of Madrid.

The second-floor restaurant
is also worth seeing. It has a
ceiling representing Madrid's
starlit sky as it was on the night
of the theatre's
inauguration. It
is open to the
public from
Tuesday to
Sunday for tea
(at 6:30pm)
and dinner (at
9pm), but is
reserved for
theatre-goers
on nights
when
there are
perfor-
mances. The
restaurant is

Costume used in
Anne Boleyn

located in what was originally
the ballroom, where Isabel II
would often throw lively
parties. On display in glass
cabinets are costumes from the
operas *Aïda* and *Anne Boleyn*.

On the sixth floor there is a
pleasant cafeteria which has a
good view overlooking the
Plaza de Oriente and the
Palacio Real *(see pp54–7)*.

The site has always been
associated with the stage. In
1708, an Italian company built
a small theatre here, which
was demolished in 1735 to be
replaced by a more ambitious
building. However, due to the
presence of underground
streams, this theatre suffered
severe structural problems. In
1816, it was torn down to
make way for a modern opera
house instigated by Fernando
VII. Construction dragged on
in fits and starts for 32 years.
The theatre was finally inaugurated in 1850 by Isabel II on
her 20th birthday. A production

Awe-inspiring interior of Madrid's opera house, the Teatro Real of Gaetano Donizetti's *La Favorita* marked the occasion, and the theatre became a centre of Madrid culture until the late 1920s. It appeared, however, that the new building was beset with problems just like its predecessor, and needed constant repair work to keep it upright. In the Spanish Civil War *(see p18)* it was used as a weapons depot and suffered further damage from an explosion. It was finally closed in 1988.

In 1991, an ambitious project to renovate the building was also plagued with problems. The architect died of a heart attack while inspecting the works and, when the theatre finally opened in October 1997 with a performance of Falla's *The Three-Cornered Hat*, it was way over budget and five years behind schedule.

Iglesia de San Nicolás ㉓

Plaza de San Nicolás 1. **Map** 3 C2.
📞 *91 559 40 64.* Ⓜ *Ópera.*
🕐 *9am–1:30pm, 5:30–8:30pm Mon, 6:30–8:30pm Tue–Sat, 10am–2pm, 6:30–8:30pm Sun.*

THE FIRST MENTION of the church of San Nicolás is in a document written in 1202. Its striking brick tower, decorated with horseshoe arches, is the oldest surviving religious

12th-century Mudéjar-style brick tower of the Iglesia de San Nicolás

View of the Catedral de la Almudena and the Palacio Real

structure in Madrid. Thought to date from the 12th century, it is Mudéjar in style, and may originally have been the minaret of a Moorish mosque.

Catedral de la Almudena ㉔

Calle de Bailén 8–10. **Map** 3 C2.
📞 *91 542 22 00.* Ⓜ *Ópera.*
🕐 *10am–8pm Mon–Sat, 2:30–6pm Sun & public hols.* ♿

THE BUILDING OF Madrid's cathedral began in 1879, but it was not until 1993 that it was completed and subsequently inaugurated by the Pope. The slow construction, which ceased completely during the Spanish Civil War *(see p18)*, involved several architects. The cathedral's Neo-Gothic grey and white façade resembles that of the Palacio Real, which stands opposite. The crypt houses a 16th-century image of the *Virgen de la Almudena*. Further along, the Calle Mayor is the site of excavations which have unearthed remains of Moorish and medieval city walls.

Campo del Moro ㉕

Map 3 A2. Ⓜ *Príncipe Pío.*
🕐 *10:30am–8pm daily.*

THE CAMPO DEL MORO (Field of the Moor) is a pleasing park, rising steeply from the Río Manzanares to offer one of the finest views of the Palacio Real *(see pp54–7)*. The park has a varied history. In 1109, a Moorish army, led by Ali ben Yusuf, set up camp here – hence the name. The park later became a jousting ground for Christian knights.

In the late 19th century, it was used as a playground for royal children. At around the same time, it was landscaped in what is described as English style – with winding paths, grass and woodland, as well as fountains and statues.

In 1931, under the Second Republic *(see p18)*, the park was reopened to the public. Under Franco it was closed again and not reopened until 1983. The Museo de Carruajes is situated in the lower part of the park, but is closed indefinitely. It houses official royal carriages and sedan chairs.

The Muralla Arabe – archeological remains of Madrid's Moorish heritage

Muralla Arabe ㉖

Parque del Emir Mohamed I, Cuesta de la Vega. **Map** 3 C3. Ⓜ *Opera.* 🕐 *dawn – sunset.*

Other than the city's name, which comes from the Arabic *Mayrit*, a small stretch of outer defence wall is all that is left of Madrid's Moorish heritage. The Muralla Arabe (Arab Wall) stands to the south of the Catedral de Nuestra Señora de la Almudena, down the steep Cuesta de la Vega street. It is believed that one of the main gateways to the Moorish town stood near this site *(see p13)*. The wall, constructed from flintstone blocks of various shapes and sizes, rises over 3 m (10 ft) along one side of the Parque del Emir Mohamed I. The park is named after the Moorish leader who founded Madrid.

The site was discovered while excavations were being carried out in 1953. As well as Moorish ruins dating from the ninth century, there is also a segment of a 12th-century Christian wall. On the other side of the wall, and visible from Cuesta de la Vega, are examples of typically Moorish brick horseshoe arches.

Across the street, a plaque and an image of the Virgin identify this as the spot where the statue of the Virgen de la Almudena was discovered in 1085 (*almudena* is from the Arabic for "outer wall"), possibly hidden from the Moors. During the summer, outdoor concerts are occasionally held in Parque del Emir Mohamed I.

At other times, this treeless area is not well patrolled, and you should not visit the park on your own or after dark.

San Francisco el Grande ㉗

Plaza de San Francisco. **Map** 3 B4. 📞 91 365 38 00. Ⓜ *La Latina, Puerta de Toledo.* 🕐 *11am–12:30pm, 4–6:30pm Tue–Fri.* **Capilla del Cristo de los Dolores** 🕐 *11am–1pm Sat.* 📷

The site of this basilica was previously occupied by a Franciscan convent founded, according to legend, by St Francis of Assisi in 1217. When Felipe II made Madrid the capital of Spain in 1561 *(see p15)*, the convent's wealth and status grew, and it was made custodian of the "Holy Places" conquered by the crusaders.

In 1760 Carlos III ordained that the convent be replaced by a Neo-Classical basilica with a vast dome. The architect, Francesco Cabezas, designed a dome to measure over 33 m (108 ft) in diameter. However, in 1768, work had to be halted because of complications with the size. It was finally completed in 1784 by Francesco Sabatini.

The basilica was taken over by the Foreign Ministry in 1835 and used as an army barracks. A few years later it was made into a national pantheon. The Franciscan friars were forced to leave, and were only able to return to the basilica in 1926.

In 1878, a renovation project was initiated and the church decorated extravagantly. The façade is dominated by the dome and twin towers, which house 19 bells, 11 of which form the church's carillon.

The seven main doors were carved in walnut by Juan Guas, under the direction of sculptor Antonio Varela. The central image above the doors is of Christ crucified with Faith and Hope at his feet. On either side are the two thieves who were crucified with him. The panels on the doors show biblical scenes. Just inside the basilica, supported by bronze angels, are huge scallop-shaped marble bowls containing holy water. The forest of scaffolding inside the church has been in place since 1973 due to problems with the restoration of the roof and frescoes.

The main chapel contains five large paintings executed by Manuel Domínguez and Alejandro Ferrant depicting the life of St Francis. The Four Evangelists, made from wood and plaster but imitating bronze, are by Sanmartí and Molinelli.

Interior of San Francisco el Grande, a church richly endowed with the work of great artists

On each side of the basilica are three chapels, the most famous being the one just to the left of the main entrance. This chapel boasts an early painting by Goya of San Bernardino de Siena, with the painter himself appearing on the right of the picture. Work by Andrés de la Calleja and Antonio González Velázquez is also featured here. As well as the chapels, the sacristy and old cloisters can be visited.

The adjoining Capilla del Cristo de los Dolores, dating from 1162, was designed by architect Hermano Francisco Bautista. In it is the remarkable sculpture of *Cristo de los Dolores*, with bleeding holes in Christ's hands from the nails on the cross. This polychrome statue was created in 1643 by Diego Rodríguez but is, in fact, a copy of Domingo de la Rioja's original sculpture. This statue, now in Serradilla, was venerated for its association with miracles and spent some time in the alcázar, taken there by Felipe IV (*see p20*).

Plaza de la Paja ㉘

Map 4 D3. 🚇 *La Latina.*

O NCE THE FOCUS of medieval Madrid, the area around the Plaza de la Paja – literally Straw Square – is still atmospheric. Despite its location, in a less than affluent district, many interesting buildings are located around the square.

Climbing upwards from the Calle de Segovia, a glimpse left along Calle del Príncipe Anglona yields a view of the Mudéjar-style brick tower of the **Iglesia de San Pedro**, dating from the 14th century. Beyond the fountain is the **Capilla del Obispo** (Bishop's Chapel), which first belonged to the adjoining Palacio Vargas. The Baroque, cherub-covered dome of the **Iglesia de San Andrés** can be seen to the left.

Nearby is a cluster of interlinked squares, ending in the Plaza Puerta de Moros, a reminder of the Muslim community which once occupied the area. From here, a right turn leads to the domed bulk of San Francisco el Grande, an impressive landmark.

La Latina ㉙

Map 4 D4. 🚇 *La Latina, Lavapiés.*

T HE DISTRICT OF La Latina, together with the adjacent Lavapiés, is considered to be the heart of *castizo* Madrid (*see p105*). This term describes the culture of the traditional working classes of Madrid – that of the true *Madrileño*.

La Latina runs along the city's southern hillside from the Plaza Puerta de Moros through the streets where El Rastro flea market is held. To the east it merges with Lavapiés.

La Latina's steep streets are lined with tall, narrow houses, renovated to form an attractive neighbourhood. There are a number of old-fashioned bars around the Plaza de Tirso de Molina, which add to the charm of this part of Madrid. It is worth wandering through simply to savour its rich atmosphere and authenticity.

Shoppers taking a leisurely Sunday stroll around El Rastro flea market

El Rastro ㉚

Calle de la Ribera de Curtidores.
Map 4 E4. 🚇 *La Latina, Embajadores.*
⏰ 10am – 2pm Sun & public hols.

M ADRID'S CELEBRATED flea market (*see p165*), established in the Middle Ages, has its hub in the Plaza de Cascorro and sprawls downhill towards the Río Manzanares. The main street is the Calle de la Ribera de Curtidores, or "Tanners' Riverbank", once the centre of the slaughterhouse and tanning industry.

Although some people claim that El Rastro has changed a great deal since its heyday during the 19th century, there are still plenty of *Madrileños*, as well as tourists, who shop here. They come in search of a bargain from the stalls which sell a huge range of wares – anything from new furniture to second-hand clothes. The wide range of goods and the lively crowds in El Rastro make it an ideal way to spend a Sunday morning.

The Calle de Embajadores is the market's other main street. It runs down past the dusty Baroque façade of the **Iglesia de San Cayetano**, designed by José Churriguera and Pedro de Ribera. Its interior has been restored since fire destroyed it in the Civil War (*see p18*).

Further along the street is the **Real Fábrica de Tabacos** (Royal Tobacco Factory), begun as a state enterprise in 1809. Its female labour force has long had a reputation for taking an uncompromising stance in industrial disputes.

The atmospheric Plaza de la Paja, once the heart of medieval Madrid

BOURBON MADRID

To the east of Old Madrid, there once lay an idyllic district of market gardens known as the Prado – the "Meadow". In the 16th century a monastery was built on this rising ground. The Habsburgs extended it to form a palace, of which only fragments now remain; the palace gardens are now the popular Parque del Retiro *(see p77)*. The Bourbon monarchs, especially Carlos III, chose this area to expand and embellish the city in the 18th century. Around the Paseo del Prado they built grand squares with fountains, a triumphal gateway, and what was to become the Museo del Prado, one of the world's greatest art galleries. A more recent addition to the area is the Centro de Arte Reina Sofía, a collection of modern Spanish art.

SIGHTS AT A GLANCE

Historic Buildings and Monuments

Ateneo de Madrid **17**
Banco de España **5**
Bolsa de Comercio **7**
Casa de Lope de Vega **20**
Círculo de Bellas Artes **13**
Congreso de los Diputados **16**
Edificio Metrópolis **15**
Estación de Atocha **30**
Hotel Palace **11**
Hotel Ritz **9**
Ministerio de Agricultura **27**
Observatorio Astronómico **28**
Palacio de Comunicaciones **3**
Palacio de Fernán Núñez **31**
Palacio de Linares **2**
Puerta de Alcalá **1**
Real Academia de la Historia **19**
Real Academia Española **23**
Teatro Español **18**

Museums and Galleries

Centro de Arte Reina Sofía pp86–9 **32**
Museo del Ejército **24**
Museo del Prado pp80–83 **21**
Museo Nacional de Antropología **29**
Museo Nacional de Artes Decorativas **8**
Museo Naval **6**
Museo Thyssen-Bornemisza pp70–73 **12**

Churches

Iglesia de San Jerónimo el Real **22**
Iglesia de San José **14**

Streets, Squares and Parks

Parque del Retiro **25**
Plaza Cánovas del Castillo **10**
Plaza de Cibeles **4**
Real Jardín Botánico **26**

GETTING THERE

The metro is the fastest and easiest way to get to and around Bourbon Madrid. Lines 1, 2 and 4 serve all of the main sights. Useful bus routes are 2, 8, 14, 15, 27, 74 & 146 to the Plaza de Cibeles.

KEY

	Street-by-Street map *pp64–5*
Ⓜ	Metro station
🚆	Railway station
	Main bus stop
🛈	Tourist information
🅿	Parking

The Monument of Alfonxo XII in the Parque del Retiro *(see p77)*

Street-by-Street: Paseo del Prado

I N THE LATE 18TH CENTURY, before the museums, sumptuous palaces and lavish hotels of Bourbon Madrid took shape, the Paseo del Prado was laid out and soon became a fashionable spot for strolling. Today the main attractions of the wide, tree-lined Paseo are its museums and art galleries. Most notable are the Museo del Prado (just south of the Plaza Cánovas del Castillo) and the Museo Thyssen-Bornemisza, both displaying world famous collections of paintings. Among the grand monuments built under Carlos III are the Puerta de Alcalá and the Fuente de Cibeles, which stand in the middle of busy roundabouts.

★ Plaza de Cibeles
A fountain with a statue of the Greco-Roman goddess of nature, Cybele, stands in this square **4**

Banco de España Metro

Iglesia de San José
Designed by Pedro Ribera, this Baroque church was built from 1730 to 1742 **14**

Banco de España
Spain's central reserve bank is housed in this massive building with three façades at the Plaza de Cibeles **5**

Círculo de Bellas Artes
This cultural foundation, established in 1880, offers a theatre, library, artists' studios and a café overlooking Calle de Alcalá **13**

★ Museo Thyssen-Bornemisza
This excellent art collection occupies the Neo-Classical Villahermosa Palace, completed in 1806 **12**

Hotel Palace
A host of international artists, politicians and film stars have stayed at this elegant, centrally-located hotel **11**

STAR SIGHTS

★ **Museo Thyssen-Bornemisza**

★ **Puerta de Alcalá**

★ **Plaza de Cibeles**

Plaza Cánovas del Castillo
In the middle of this large square stands a sculpted fountain of the god Neptune in his chariot **10**

Museo del Prado

| 0 metres | 100 |
| 0 yards | 100 |

★ **Puerta de Alcalá**
Sculpted from granite, this former gateway into the city is especially beautiful when floodlit at night ❶

Palacio de Comunicaciones
Spain's postal service is headquartered in this ornate building, which is often likened to a wedding cake ❸

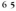

LOCATOR MAP
See Street Finder maps 7 & 8

Palacio de Linares
This grandly decorated late 19th-century palace now houses the Casa de América, an organization that promotes Latin American culture ❷

Museo Nacional de Artes Decorativas
This museum, near the Retiro, was founded in 1912 as a showcase for Spanish interior design and ceramics ❽

Museo Naval
Part of the Ministry of the Navy, this museum contains a wealth of navigational instruments, maps, models of ships and even accurate reconstructions of cabins ❻

Bolsa de Comercio
Madrid's stock exchange is housed in this attractive Neo-Classical building. Visitors can view events on the trading floor from a gallery ❼

Hotel Ritz
With its Belle Epoque interior, the Ritz is one of the most elegant hotels in all of Spain ❾

KEY

 Suggested route

View through the central arch of the Puerta de Alcalá

Puerta de Alcalá ❶

Map 8 D1. Ⓜ Retiro.

THIS CEREMONIAL GATEWAY is the grandest of the monuments erected by Carlos III *(see p21)* in his efforts to improve eastern Madrid. Designed by Francesco Sabatini, it replaced a smaller Baroque gateway which had been built by Felipe III *(see p20)* for his wife's entry into Madrid.

Construction of the gate was started in 1769 and lasted a total of nine years. It was built from granite in Neo-Classical style, with a lofty pediment and sculpted angels. It has five arches – three central and two outer rectangular ones.

Until the mid-19th century, the gateway marked the city's easternmost boundary. It now stands in the busy Plaza de la Independencia, and is best seen when floodlit at night.

Palacio de Linares ❷

Paseo de Recoletos 2. **Map** 8 D1.
Ⓒ 91 595 48 00. Ⓜ Banco de España. Ⓞ 10am–12:30pm Fri, 10am–1:30pm Sat & Sun. 🗹 🖾 🚫

IN 1873 Amadeo I *(see p21)* rewarded the Madrid banker, José de Murga, for his financial support by granting him the title of Marqués de Linares. The newly designated aristocrat quickly set about building the most luxurious, palatial residence the Spanish capital had ever known.

The rooms inside the palace are an extravaganza of ornate Rococo decor, resplendent with gold plate, inlaid wood and marble floors, glittering chandeliers, nubile nymphs and allegorical murals. The most striking rooms are on the first floor. They include the gala dining room, ballroom, the Salón China (Oriental Room), and Byzantine-style chapel. In the garden is the Pabellón Romántico, a wooden, fairy-tale-style pavilion which is also known as the Casa de Muñecas (Dolls' House).

After the Marqués died, the family fortunes declined. Many furnishings and decorations were sold, and the rest disappeared during the Spanish Civil War *(see p18)*.

By 1977 the palace was almost derelict. However, it was saved by the Spanish government's decision to restore it for Madrid's year as European Capital of Culture in 1992. The main entrance to this French Baroque palace is on Plaza de Cibeles but it is used only for rare ceremonial occasions. Public access is by a side entrance on Paseo de Recoletos. The building now houses the **Casa de América**, a cultural organization which promotes Latin-American art, literature and cinema. There is also a chic restaurant, **Paradis**, which has its like-named counterpart in the Calle del Marqués de Cubas *(see p160)*.

Mailbox at the Palacio de Comunicaciones

Palacio de Comunicaciones ❸

Plaza de Cibeles. **Map** 7 C2. Ⓜ Banco de España. **Post Office** Ⓞ 8am–9pm Mon–Fri, 8:30am–2pm Sat. **Museum** Ⓒ 91 396 26 79. Ⓞ 9am–2pm, 5–7pm Mon–Fri, 9am–1pm Sat.

OCCUPYING ONE corner of the Plaza de Cibeles, this impressive, beautiful building is the headquarters of Spain's postal service. Built between 1905 and 1917 by Antonio Palacios, its appearance – white with tall pinnacles – is often likened to a wedding cake. Its central hall is lined with counters providing services and, in the centre, are batteries of brass-and-wood lecterns where customers write their letters or fill out forms. A side door on Calle de Montalbán leads to the **Museo Postal y Telegráfico**, a little-known museum of postal and telephone communications. As well as collections of stamps, there are mailmen's uniforms, bicycles, mailboxes and old-fashioned switchboards. More curious exhibits are a stuffed carrier pigeon, a cage for mailing bees and a letter written on bread by a soldier who ran out of paper. There are also 50 letters with cryptic addresses, which had to be deciphered before the letters could be delivered. This unusual Spanish practice was banned in the 1970s.

The height of Rococo extravagance in the Palacio de Linares ballroom

Plaza de Cibeles

Map 7 C1. Ⓜ Banco de España.

IN ADDITION to being one of Madrid's best-known landmarks, the Plaza de Cibeles is also one of the most beautiful. The **Fuente de Cibeles** stands in the middle of the busy traffic island at the junction of the Paseo del Prado and the Calle de Alcalá. This fine, sculpted fountain is named after Cybele, the Greco-Roman goddess of nature, and shows her sitting in her chariot, drawn by a pair of lions. Designed in the late 18th century by José Hermosilla and Ventura Rodríguez, it is considered a symbol of Madrid.

The Fuente de Cibeles, with the Palacio de Linares in the background

Four important buildings rise around the square, the most impressive being the **Palacio de Comunicaciones**, mockingly known as "Our Lady of Communications". On the northeast side is the **Palacio de Linares**, built in 1873 about the time of the second Bourbon restoration. In the northwest corner, surrounded by attractive gardens, is the army headquarters, the **Cuartel General del Ejército de Tierra**, housed in the former Palacio de Buenavista. Commissioned by the Duchess of Alba in 1777, construction was twice delayed by fires.

Finally, occupying a whole block on the opposite corner, is the Venetian-Renaissance **Banco de España**, restored to its 19th-century magnificence.

Banco de España ❺

Paseo del Prado 2. **Map** 7 C2. 📞 *91 338 53 65.* Ⓜ *Banco de España.* ⭘ *open for guided tours only 9:30am and 11:30am Mon, Wed & Thu (write several months in advance to Servicio de Protocolo, Banco de España, Alcalá 50, Madrid 28014).* ⊘

VIEWING THIS VAST building, with façades facing Paseo del Prado, Plaza de Cibeles and Calle de Alcalá, you might wonder which is the main entrance. In fact it is the one on the Paseo del Prado, used only for ceremonial occasions nowadays. The building grew in three stages: the original bank dates from 1882–91 and occupied the corner of Cibeles, while new wings were added later. The Bank of Spain itself was founded in 1856.

The bank's vast main staircase, made of Carrara marble and overlooked by stained glass windows with mythological and allegorical themes, leads to the Patio del Reloj, a glass-roofed central courtyard with the cashiers' windows. It is a striking example of Art Deco design. The library, which is open to researchers, is located in another large hall, the interior of which is made entirely of wrought-iron filigree, painted off-white. There is also an older, smaller library with glassed-in mahogany bookshelves.

The various meeting rooms and hallways are decorated with the bank's sizeable collection of tapestries, vases, antique furniture and paintings, including a first printing of Goya's series of etchings of bullfighting, the *Tauromaquia.* In the circular Goya room are eight paintings by the Spanish master *(see p26)*, including portraits of Carlos IV and various bank governors. In *Conde de Floridablanca in the Artist's Studio,* rather than looking out at the viewer, Goya is seen gazing at his companion.

Beneath the Patio del Reloj, 30 m (98 ft) below street level and off limits to visitors, is a chamber with an island-like structure ringed by a moat. On it is the vault containing the bank's gold. Prior to sophisticated security gadgetry, this chamber would flood were there any threat of robbery.

Museo Naval ❻

Paseo del Prado 5. **Map** 7 C2. 📞 *91 379 52 99.* Ⓜ *Banco de España.* ⭘ *10:30am–1:30pm Tue–Sun.* ⬤ *Aug.* ⊘

ADDED TO THE Ministry of the Navy building in 1977, the copper-tinted-glass Naval Museum has 18 display halls charting Spain's centuries-old history of seafaring. As well as a large collection of scale models of ships throughout the ages, often dating from the same period as the ships themselves, there are figureheads, amphorae, globes, astrolabes, sextants, compasses and maps. Weapons used in Spain's conquest of the New World *(see p14)* also feature here. One of the more unusual exhibits is a map of the world dated 1500. It was drawn for Isabel and Fernando *(see p20),* and features the Americas for the first time. There is also a piece of the tree trunk upon which Hernán Cortés is said to have rested after *La Noche Triste* (The Sad Night) in 1520, when he and his men fled from Moctezuma's Aztec capital, Tenochtitlán.

Astrolabe from the Museo Naval

View from the gallery – dealers at work in the grand Bolsa de Comercio

Bolsa de Comercio ❼

Plaza de la Lealtad 1. **Map** 7 C2.
📞 *91 589 14 08.* Ⓜ *Banco de España.* ◻ *12am–Fri.* ◼ *Sat, Sun & public hols.* ∅

T HE MADRID Stock Exchange was established in 1831. It operated in 11 different, generally inadequate venues – at one time, it was housed in a convent – before moving in 1893 to the purpose-built headquarters it currently occupies. Designed by Enrique María Repullés y Vargas, the building took more than six years to construct, at a cost of around three million pesetas. Nearly one third of this went on the concave, Neo-Classical façade and main entrance, with its six giant columns topped by Corinthian capitals.

Dealers occupy the **Sala de Contratación** (trading floor). This large, vaulted space of 970 sq m (10,400 sq ft) has an ornate Neo-Baroque clock on top of a large marble plinth at its centre. Visitors can watch the proceedings from the **Salón de los Pasos Perdidos** (Hall of the Lost Steps). This gallery on the first floor is often used for exhibitions on the history of the institution.

Museo Nacional de Artes Decorativas ❽

Calle de Montalbán 12. **Map** 8 D2.
📞 *91 532 64 99.* Ⓜ *Banco de España.* ◻ *9am–3pm Tue–Fri, 10am–2pm Sat, Sun & public hols.* 📷 *(no charge Sun).* ♿

H OUSED IN AN aristocratic residence built in the 19th century and overlooking the Parque del Retiro *(see p77)*, Madrid's National Museum of Decorative Arts contains a large and interesting collection of furniture and *objets d'art*. The exhibits are mainly from Spain and date back as far as Phoenician times.

A star attraction is the 18th-century kitchen, moved here from a Valencian mansion. Its 1,500 painted tiles depict a domestic scene from the era. There are excellent ceramics from Talavera de la Reina, a town famous for them, and a collection of jewellery and ornaments from the Far East.

Hotel Ritz ❾

Plaza de la Lealtad 5. **Map** 7 C3.
📞 *91 521 28 57.* Ⓜ *Banco de España.* ∅ ♿

A FEW MINUTES' WALK from the Prado *(see pp80–83)*, this hotel is said to be Spain's most extravagant. It was commissioned in 1906 by Alfonso XIII *(see p21)*, because he was embarrassed by the lack of luxury accommodation in the city for his wedding guests.

At the start of the Civil War *(see p18)*, the hotel became a hospital, and anarchist leader Buenaventura Durruti died here of his wounds in 1936.

The opulence of the Ritz *(see p148)* is reflected in its prices. Each of the 158 rooms is beautifully decorated in a different style, with carpets made by hand at the Real Fábrica de Tapices *(see p112)*.

Plaza Cánovas del Castillo ❿

Map 7 C3. Ⓜ *Banco de España.*

T HIS BUSY ROUNDABOUT takes its name from Antonio Cánovas del Castillo, one of the leading statesmen of 19th-century Spain, who was assassinated in 1897.

Dominating the plaza is the **Fuente de Neptuno**, a fountain with a statue of Neptune in his chariot, being pulled by two horses. The statue was designed in 1780 by Ventura Rodríguez as part of a grand scheme by Carlos III *(see p20)* to beautify eastern Madrid.

The Fuente de Neptuno

The relaxed elegance of the Palace's glass-domed Rotunda Hall lounge

Hotel Palace ⓫

Plaza de las Cortes 7. **Map** 7 B3.
⌾ 91 360 80 00. Ⓜ Sevilla, Banco de España & Atocha. ⓑ

THE FORMER PALACE of the Marqués de Medinaceli was torn down to build this hotel, which opened in 1912. Alfonso XIII wanted his capital to have elegant hotels to match those in other European cities, and actively encouraged the project. Its life as an elegant hostelry was interrupted only during the Civil War, when it housed a hospital and refuge for the homeless, as well as the Soviet Embassy.

For many years, the Hotel Palace and the Ritz (opened two years earlier) were the only grand hotels in Madrid. However, while the Ritz was the exclusive reserve of its titled guests, none of whom would dare to venture from their rooms without a tie, the no less luxurious but more informal Palace was open to non-residents and was a lively meeting place for *Madrileños*. It was the first establishment in Madrid where ladies could take tea unaccompanied. It is still a favourite rendezvous and the wood-panelled **Palace Bar** and **Rotunda Hall** lounge, with its huge glass dome roof, are Madrid landmarks.

Statesmen, spies, literati and film stars have all stayed here. Past guests include Henry Kissinger, Mata Hari, Ernest Hemingway, Orson Welles, David Bowie, Richard Attenborough, Michael Jackson and Salvador Dalí, who once drew lewd pictures on the walls of his hotel room. Unfortunately, an over-zealous maid scrubbed the walls clean the next day.

The hotel underwent extensive renovation in 1997, adding a Royal Suite, solarium and fitness centre to the roof, and a wine cellar for tastings and selling to the ground floor.

Museo Thyssen-Bornemisza ⓬

See pp70–73.

La Pecera café in the Círculo de Bellas Artes

Círculo de Bellas Artes ⓭

Calle del Marqués de Casa Riera 2.
Map 7 B2. ⌾ 91 360 54 00. Ⓜ Banco de España, Sevilla. ◯ 10am–10pm. ● Mon (exhibitions); August. ◷ by prior appointment. ⊘

THE CÍRCULO DE Bellas Artes is a cultural foundation established in 1880. Since 1926, it has been housed in this six-floor building designed by Antonio Palacios, architect of the Palacio de Comunicaciones (*see p66*). The building has a vast ballroom, exhibition halls, a theatre, library and studios for use by artists and sculptors. As well as a programme of exhibitions, workshops and lectures, it hosts many cultural and social events, such as the Carnival Masquerade Ball held every February.

Although the foundation is nominally for members only, the token admission fee gives visitors access to some parts of the building, including the popular café. Known as **La Pecera** (Fishbowl) for its large picture windows, it is a great place to sip coffee and observe life on the Calle de Alcalá outside. There is also a cinema, reached by a separate entrance.

Iglesia de San José ⓮

Calle de Alcalá 43. **Map** 7 B1.
⌾ 91 522 67 84. Ⓜ Banco de España. ◯ 7am–1:30pm, 6–8pm daily (Sun from 9am).

THIS CHURCH WAS once part of a Carmelite convent founded in 1605. The convent was demolished in 1863 to build a theatre, and the church itself was rebuilt during the reign of Felipe V (*see p20*). When the Gran Vía (*see p48*) opened in 1908, the church was changed yet again. Adorning the façade, with its three arched entrances, is an attractive statue of the Virgen del Carmen. A number of the church's treasures are housed in the Prado (*see pp80–83*), but a few interesting images remain on the Neo-Classical main altar and in the Baroque side chapels. Many are by French sculptor Robert Michel, who carved Cibeles fountain's lions (*see p67*). Number 41, next door, is still referred to as the **Casa del Párroco** (parish priest's house). On 10 March 1908, Alfonso XIII symbolically struck the church with a pickaxe to signal the start of demolition work which would make way for the Gran Vía.

Museo Thyssen-Bornemisza ⑫

THIS MAGNIFICENT MUSEUM is based on the collection assembled by Baron Heinrich Thyssen-Bornemisza and his son, Hans Heinrich, the present baron. In 1992 it was installed in Madrid's 18th-century Villahermosa Palace, and was sold to the nation the following year. From its beginnings in the 1920s, the collection sought to illustrate the history of Western art, from Italian and Flemish primitives through to modern Expressionism and Pop Art. This outstanding collection, consisting of some 800 paintings, includes masterpieces by Titian, Goya, Van Gogh and Picasso, as well as works by lesser known artists. It is regarded by many as the most important privately assembled art collection in the world. There are plans to extend the museum in the near future.

★ Our Lady of the Dry Tree (*c.1450*)
This tiny painted panel is by Bruges master Petrus Christus. The letter A hanging from the tree stands for "Ave Maria".

★ Harlequin with a Mirror
The figure of the harlequin was a frequent subject of Picasso's. The careful composition in this 1923 canvas, which is thought by some to represent the artist himself, is typical of Picasso's "Classical" period.

GALLERY GUIDE
The galleries are arranged around a covered central courtyard, which rises the full height of the building. The top floor starts with early Italian art and goes through to the 17th century. The first floor continues the story with 17th-century Dutch works and ends with German Expressionism. The ground floor is dedicated to 20th-century paintings.

STAR PAINTINGS

- **★ Our Lady of the Dry Tree by Christus**

- **★ Harlequin with a Mirror by Picasso**

- **★ The Toilet of Venus by Rubens**

Hotel Room (*1931*)
Edward Hopper's painting is a study of urban isolation. The solitude is made less static by the suitcases and the train timetable on the woman's knee.

Portrait of Baron Thyssen-Bornemisza
This informal portrait of the present baron, against the background of a Watteau painting, was painted by Lucian Freud between 1981 and 1982.

★ **The Toilet of Venus**
This reflection of ideal beauty was painted by the Flemish master Rubens after 1629, showing his typically luscious use of colour and form.

VISITORS' CHECKLIST

Paseo del Prado 8. **Map** 7 C2.
91 369 01 51. Banco de
España, Sevilla. 1, 2, 5, 9,
14, 15, 20. 10am–7pm
Tue–Sun.
W www.museothyssen.org

St Jerome in the Wilderness *(c.1575)*
Titian's work shows St Jerome as a penitent, meditating on Christ's Passion. In his later career, the artist strove for poetic rather than simply narrative effects.

St Casilda *(c.1630)*
Francisco de Zurbarán, best known for his depiction of monks in white habits, also painted saints. Here, the rich pattern of St Casilda's robe stands out against the plain background.

Main entrance

KEY TO FLOORPLAN

☐ Ground floor
☐ First floor
☐ Second floor
☐ Non-exhibition space

Autumn Landscape in Oldenburg
Karl Schmidt-Rottluff was a member of the Brücke Expressionist group, founded in Dresden in 1905. He painted this north German landscape two years later.

Exploring the Museo Thyssen-Bornemisza

T HE THYSSEN-BORNEMISZA'S COLLECTION provides a sweeping overview of Western art between the 14th and
20th centuries, touching on every school and trend in
European art over the last 500 years. It is strong in
areas where the Prado is weak, such as in Italian and
Dutch primitives, 19th-century American painting,
Impressionism and Expressionism. Portraiture from
different periods is especially well represented. The
recommended itinerary through the collection follows
a chronological order, beginning on the top floor.

Young Knight in a Landscape
(1510) by Vittore Carpaccio

Christ and the Samaritan Woman
(1311) by Duccio

THE BIRTH OF THE RENAISSANCE

E ARLY ITALIAN art (room 1),
while still influenced by
medieval aesthetics and often
overwhelmingly religious in
subject matter, shows a gradual
return to naturalism. Paintings
become more three-dimen-
sional and strive to tell a story,
as in Duccio's *Christ and the
Samaritan Woman* (1311).
  The section on medieval art
(room 2) illustrates how Italian
influences combined with the
Gothic style popular in Europe,
such as Koerbecke's *Assumption of the Virgin* (c.1457).
  Room 3 shows early Dutch
art, including two jewels of the
collection, Jan van Eyck's *The
Annunciation* (c.1435–41) and
Petrus Christus' *Our Lady of
the Dry Tree* (c.1450). The stage
is set for the aesthetic revolution of the Renaissance and a
return to Classical forms, which
began in Italy in the 1400s. The
best example is Bramantino's
Resurrected Christ (room 4).
  Later, religion ceases to be
the dominant theme, as seen
in the outstanding series of
early Renaissance portraits
(room 5), including Holbein's
detailed *Henry VIII* (c.1534–6).

RENAISSANCE TO BAROQUE

T HIS SECTION encompasses
the height of the Renais-
sance, ending with Baroque
art and 18th-century Italian
painting. Outstanding examples
of high Renaissance in Italy
(room 7) include Carpaccio's
Young Knight in a Landscape
(1510) and Raphael's *Portrait
of a Young Man* (c.1515).
  Rooms 8–10 are dedicated
to German and Dutch painters
of the same period, including
Dürer, with his *Jesus among
the Doctors* (1506). Room 11
has works by Titian (*St Jerome
in the Wilderness* c.1575),
Tintoretto and El Greco.
  Room 12 begins with early
Baroque, when artists started
to break with the rigid Classical
rules of the Renaissance and
introduce elements of drama
and pathos into their work.
This new trend flourishes in
the art in rooms 13–15, with
examples from Italy, France
and Spain, where the period
corresponded with the *Siglo*

de Oro (Golden Century) of the
arts. Included here is Murillo's
*Madonna with Child with St
Rosalina of Palermo* (c.1670).
  Italy's continuing influence
on European art is recognized
in rooms 16–18, devoted to
18th-century Italian art, in
which landscapes make an
appearance. This is illustrated
by two views of the *Canal
Grande in Venice*, one by
Canaletto (before 1723) and a
later one by Francesco Guardi.

DUTCH AND FLEMISH PAINTING

T HE REMARKABLE series of
Dutch and Flemish art is a
strong point of the collection.
The first series (room 19) features 17th-century Flemish

Esau Selling His Birthright **(c.1627) by Hendrick ter Brugghen**

painting, with works by Jan Breughel the Elder and Van Dyck, though the big attraction is *The Toilet of Venus* (c.1629), one of four Rubens on display.

The growing distinction between Flemish and Dutch works can be seen by comparing the preceding works with the Dutch art in rooms 20–21. The theme here is the Italian influence on Dutch portraiture and painting, for example in *Esau Selling His Birthright* (c.1627) by Brugghen.

Some of the most interesting works are in rooms 22–26, where everyday scenes, landscapes and informal portraits reveal the unique quality of Dutch art. Excellent examples are Frans Hals's *Family Group in a Landscape* (c.1645–8) and Nicholas Maes's *The Naughty Drummer* (c.1655). Dutch still lifes from the period are well represented in room 27.

Waverly Oaks (1864) by Winslow Homer

ROCOCO TO REALISM

Rococo to Neo-Classicism is the theme of this section, indicating a rapid shift in tastes over a relatively brief period. Rococo took Europe by storm at the beginning of the 18th century. It is best represented here in room 28 by Antoine Watteau's *The Rest* (c.1709) and *Pierrot Content* (c.1712), and by François Boucher's *La Toilette* (1742). However, the increasingly exaggerated forms of Rococo were eventually rejected in favour of more restrained and elegant lines.

Meanwhile, different developments were taking shape across the ocean. Rooms 29–30 display 19th-century American painting. Landscape art fulfilled a need to express America's romantic spirit and pride in the land, as seen in the paintings of Thomas Cole. American artists were increasingly interested in depicting everyday scenes, such as idyllic fishing trips and strolls through the woods.

The coming of age of American art at the end of the century is represented by the paintings of Winslow Homer, especially *Waverly Oaks* (1864), James Whistler and John Singer Sargent.

In Europe, the 19th century saw the dawn of Romanticism (room 31), a transition best illustrated here through three works by Goya. The series also demonstrates a growing trend towards Realism, a shift that is plainly depicted in Constable's *The Lock* (1824).

MODERN MASTERS

The year 1863 was pivotal in the evolution of modern art, because artists whose work was rejected by Paris's art salon were displayed in a parallel Salon des Refusés. This show of discarded art marked the birth of Impressionism, a revolution which broke ties with academic restraints. Some of the most highly regarded exponents of the movement are represented in rooms 32–33, including Manet, Degas with *Swaying Dancer* (1877–9), Renoir and Sisley. Impressionism freed the artist and led to further developments, such as Post-Impressionism and Symbolism, which centred on the artist as an individual. Such is the case with Gauguin, whose *Mata Mua* (c.1892) is shown here, Vincent van Gogh, represented here by *Les Vessenots in*

Swaying Dancer (1877–9) by Degas

Auvers (1888), Toulouse-Lautrec with *Gaston Bonnefoy* (1891) and Cézanne with his *Portrait of a Farmer* (c.1900). A series of works in room 34, belonging to the Fauve school, demonstrates this short-lived movement based on bright colours and simplified forms.

A name that did endure was Expressionism, which started in Germany. This school drew on the artist's emotions, and sought to precipitate an emotion in the viewer. Its earliest practitioners were centred around the Dresden group, "The Bridge", founded in 1905. Among its members was Karl Schmidt-Rottluf, whose *Autumn Landscape in Oldenburg* (1907) is shown here. The collection of Expressionist art on display (rooms 35–40) numbers more than 50 works from 1888 to 1948, and is one of the museum's highlights.

Eight ground-floor rooms (41–48) deal with modern and contemporary art, divided into three themes – "Experimental Avant-Garde", "The Synthesis of Modern" and "Surrealism, Figurative Tradition and Pop Art". Among the gems here are Picasso's *Harlequin with a Mirror* (1923) and Edward Hopper's *Hotel Room* (1931).

Parisian-inspired cupola of the Edificio Metrópolis

Edificio Metrópolis ⓯

Calle de Alcalá 39. **Map** 7 B1.
Ⓜ *Sevilla.* ⬤ *to the public.*

OF UNMISTAKABLE French inspiration, this building, jutting out like a ship's prow at the corner of Calle Alcalá and the Gran Vía *(see p48)*, is a Madrid landmark. Inaugurated in 1911, it was designed by Jules and Raymond Février for the Unión y el Fenix Español insurance company.

The restrained ground level is topped by ornate colonnaded upper floors, each pair of columns serving as a pedestal for allegorical statues representing Commerce, Agriculture, Industry and Mining. The rounded corner tower is crowned by a double-layered dome of dark slate with gilded ornaments. It used to hold the symbol of the Unión y el Fenix company – a bronze statue representing the mythological Phoenix and, astride it, a human figure with upraised arm representing Ganymede. In the early 1970s, the company sold the building to its present owners, the Metrópolis insurers. In a controversial move, they decided to take the statue – by then a familiar element of the Madrid skyline – to their ostentatious new headquarters on the Paseo de la Castellana. Eventually the statue was replaced by a new one, representing Winged Victory; the original Phoenix is in the garden of the Unión y el Fenix's modern building.

Almost unnoticed on the pavement in front of the circular tower of the Edificio Metrópolis is "La Violetera", a small statue of a young woman selling violets. It recalls a character from a popular *zarzuela* (Spanish light opera), which later inspired the film, *La Violetera*, starring Sara Montiel. The violet-sellers – Madrid's answer to Eliza Doolittle of *Pygmalion* – would sell their flowers to theatre-goers on the Gran Vía after each performance. An inscription at the base of the statue bears the following simple message: "*Como ave precursora de primavera, en Madrid aparece la violetera*" ("The violet-seller appears in Madrid like a bird announcing spring").

Congreso de los Diputados ⓰

Plaza de las Cortes. **Map** 7 B2.
🄲 *91 390 60 00.* Ⓜ *Sevilla.*
◯ *10am–12:30pm Mon–Sat by appointment.* 🚫 ♿

THIS IMPOSING yet attractive building is home to the Spanish parliament, the Cortes. Built in the mid-19th century, it is characterized by Classical columns, heavy pediments and guardian bronze lions. It was here, in 1981, that Colonel Tejero of the Civil Guard held the deputies at gunpoint on national television, as he tried to spark off a military coup *(see p19)*. His failure was seen as an indication that democracy was firmly established in Spain.

Bronze lion guarding the Cortes

Ateneo de Madrid ⓱

Calle del Prado 21. **Map** 7 B2.
🄲 *91 429 17 50.* Ⓜ *Antón Martín, Sevilla.* ◯ *9am–1am Mon–Sat, 9am–10pm Sun & public hols.* 🅰

FORMALLY FOUNDED in 1835, this learned association has strongly liberal political leanings. It is similar to a gentlemen's club in atmosphere, with a grand stairway and panelled hall hung with the portraits of famous fellows. Closed down during past periods of repression and dictatorship, it is still a mainstay of liberal thought in Spain. Many leading Socialists are members of the Ateneo de Madrid, along with writers and other intellectuals.

La Tertulia – Literary Groups in Madrid

Interior of the Café Comercial

The Ateneo de Madrid was one of many homes for the unique Madrid institution of *la tertulia*. Groups of people with common interests gathered to discuss everything from politics to the arts to the finer points of bullfighting. Not a formal club, yet more than a casual conversation among friends, *tertulias* were a major source of news, ideas and gossip in the 19th century, and more than one political plot was hatched over cups of coffee. They were usually held at Madrid's historic 19th-century cafés. Those which occupied choice bits of real estate, such as the Pombo, El Oriental and the Paix, have since disappeared, but there are a few survivors. The best known are the Café Comercial on Glorieta de Bilbao and the Café Gijón *(see p94)* on Calle Recoletos.

La Zarzuela – Spanish Light Opera

THE ZARZUELA, a direct descendant of Italian light opera, started out as an amusement for kings, but was soon appropriated by the common people as Madrid's most characteristic performing art genre. The name is derived from the Palacio de La Zarzuela, current home of the Spanish royal family, outside Madrid. *Zarzuelas* were initially performed during the reign of Felipe IV, in the 17th century. With the ascendancy of the Bourbon kings *(see p15)*, who preferred traditional Italian opera, the zarzuela left the royal palaces and was taken up in the *corrales de comedias*,

Statue of "La Violetera"

the popular theatres of Madrid. It was here that it evolved into the light-hearted spectacle we know today, halfway between opera and musical comedy. Although no new *zarzuelas* have been written in decades, the genre has a tremendous following in Madrid, where there are regular performances and where record shops always have a section devoted to it. The best known title is *La Revoltosa*, a portrayal of the chemistry between the residents in a typical Madrid *corral de vecinos*, which were humble dwellings grouped around a central courtyard.

Calderón de La Barca, the famous 17th-century Spanish playwright, was one of the first great exponents of this type of opera. Others followed, most notably Tomás Breton (born 1850), who composed nearly 40 zarzuelas. His most famous is La Verbena de la Paloma.

The central theme *of zarzuelas is life in* castizo *Madrid (see p105), with its streetwise* majas *(women) and cocky* chulos *(men) dressed in traditional costumes. It combines singing, spoken dialogue and a variety of dances, such as the Madrid jig, the* chotis.

By the middle *of the 19th century, zarzuela was so popular that a theatre was specially built for performances. Today, the 1,200-seat Teatro de la Zarzuela (see p174) continues to stage* zarzuelas, *as do several others. In summer, there are also outdoor shows at La Corrala (see p113).*

A colourful *zarzuela* performance by the Compañia de Zarzuela J Tamayo

Sunlit balconies of the magnificent Teatro Español

Teatro Español 🔞

Calle del Príncipe 25. **Map** 7 A3.
🅲 91 429 62 97. Ⓜ Sol, Antón
Martín & Sevilla. 🔾 for performances
from 7pm Tue–Sun. 🔏 🔥

DOMINATING the Plaza de
Santa Ana *(see p47)* is the
Teatro Español, one of the
oldest and most beautiful
theatres in Madrid. In the late
16th century many of Spain's
finest plays by leading drama-
tists were performed in the
Corral del Príncipe which
originally stood here. Replaced
by the Teatro del Príncipe in
1745, it underwent extensive
restoration in the mid-19th
century and was renamed
Teatro Español. Engraved on
the Neo-Classical façade are
names of great Spanish drama-
tists, including that of Federico
García Lorca *(see p26)*.

Real Academia de la Historia 🔞

Calle del León 21. **Map** 7 A3: 🅲 91
429 06 11. Ⓜ Antón Martín. 🔾 for
renovation until beginning of 2001.

THIS AUSTERE BRICK building,
housing the Royal Academy
of History, was built by Juan de
Villanueva in 1788 and is aptly
located in the Barrio de los
Literatos (Writers' Quarter).
In 1898, the great intellectual
and bibliophile, Marcelino
Menéndez Pelayo, became
director of the academy until
his death in 1912. The library,
holds over 200,000 books and

several important manuscripts.
The antiques and pictures
owned by the academy will be
displayed in a new museum
scheduled to open in 2001.

Casa de Lope de Vega 🔞

Calle de Cervantes 11. **Map** 7 B3.
🅲 91 429 92 16. Ⓜ Antón Martín.
🔾 9:30am–2pm Tue–Fri, 10am–
2pm Sat. ⬤ public hols. 🔏 (free
Wed). 🔓 🚫

FELIX LOPE DE VEGA, a leading
Golden Age writer *(see
p26)*, moved into this sombre
house in 1610. Here he wrote
over two-thirds of his plays,
thought to total almost 2,000.
Meticulously restored in 1935,
using some of Lope de Vega's
own furniture, the house gives
a great feeling of Castilian life
in the early 17th century. A
dark chapel with no external
windows occupies the centre,
separated from the writer's

Félix Lope de Vega

bedroom by only a barred
window. The small garden at
the rear, complete with the
original well, is planted with
the flowers and fruit trees
mentioned by the writer in his
works. He died here in 1635.

Museo del Prado 🔞

See pp80–83.

Iglesia de San Jerónimo el Real 🔞

Calle de Moreto 4. **Map** 8 D3. 🅲 91
420 35 78. Ⓜ Banco de España,
Atocha. 🔾 Oct–Jun: 9am–1:30pm,
5–8:30pm daily (6–8:30pm Jul–Sep).
⬤ Easter Sat. 🔥

BUILT IN THE 16th century for
Isabel I *(see p20)*, but since
remodelled, San Jerónimo is
Madrid's royal church. From
the 17th century it was virtually a part of the Buen Retiro
palace which once stood here.
Originally attached to the
Hieronymite monastery, which
today stands beside it in ruins,
the church was the location
for the marriage of Alfonso XIII
(see p21) and Victoria Eugenia
von Battenberg in 1906.
The church is still a popular
venue for society weddings.
The cloisters and part of the
atrium are scheduled to form
an annex of the Prado.

Real Academia Española 🔞

Calle de Ruiz de Alarcón 17. **Map** 8 D3.
🅲 91 420 14 78. Ⓜ Banco de
España, Retiro. ⬤ closed to the public.

SPAIN'S ROYAL ACADEMY motto
is *"Limpia, brilla y da
esplendor"* ("Cleans, polishes
and shines"). It describes the
function of the organization,
which is to preserve the purity
of the Spanish language.
Founded in 1713, the academy
only moved to these Neo-
Classical headquarters in 1891.
The building's elegant façade
boasts a majestic entrance with
Doric columns and a carved
pediment. The 46 members
include scholars, writers and
journalists – the post, which
is for life, is unpaid – who

occupy seats identified by a letter of the alphabet. They meet on a regular basis to assess the acceptability of any new trends in the language.

Museo del Ejército ㉔

Calle de Méndez Núñez 1. **Map** 8 D2. 91 522 89 77. Retiro, Banco de España. 10am–2pm Tue–Sun. public hols. (Sat no charge).

The sword of El Cid, *La Tizona*, in the Museo del Ejército

SPAIN'S ARMY MUSEUM occupies one of the few remaining parts of a 17th-century palace, the Real Sitio del Buen Retiro, which was once situated here. It still has most of the original decoration, some by Velázquez *(see p26)*. Individual rooms are dedicated to military history and house a vast array of weapons, from Moorish times to the present day. The museum's grandest room, the Salón de Reinos, is named after the kingdoms which once made up Spain. These are depicted on the ceiling.

One of the highlights of the army museum is the sword of El Cid – *La Tizona* – on display in the Sala de Armas. The tunic and sword of Boabdil, the last Moorish ruler of Granada, are exhibited in the Sala Árabe.

In the Sala Colonial is a fragment of the cross that was planted in the ground by Columbus upon reaching the New World *(see p14)* and more recent events are illustrated by busts and flags from

Spain's War of Independence *(see p16)* in the Sala del Dos de Mayo. As well as rooms devoted to the Spanish Civil War and the Nationalist campaign *(see p18)*, with portraits of General Franco, there is an entire room of tin soldiers.

Parque del Retiro ㉕

Map 8 E3. 91 409 23 36. Ibiza, Retiro, Atocha. **Casa de Vacas** daily.

RETIRO PARK, in Madrid's smart Jerónimos district, was once the setting for Felipe IV's palace *(see p20)*, the Real Sitio del Buen Retiro. All that remains is the Casón del Buen Retiro *(see p83)* and the Museo del Ejército. In the 17th century

the park was the private playground of the royal family, and only became fully open to the public in 1869. Today, the Parque del Retiro is one of the most popular places in Madrid for relaxing in the open air.

A short stroll from the park's northern entrance is the lake, where rowing boats can be hired. On one side, in front of a half-moon colonnade, a statue of Alfonso XII *(see p21)* rides high on a column. On the other, portrait painters and fortune-tellers ply their trade.

To the south of the lake are the Palacio de Velázquez and the Palacio de Cristal, both built by Ricardo Velázquez Bosco. His other work includes the grandiose Ministerio de Agricultura building *(see p84)*.

The Palacio de Velázquez was intended as a pavilion to stage the National Exhibition of Mining, Metal, Ceramics, Glass and Mineral Water industries in 1884. Today it is simply used for temporary exhibitions.

Nearby, the striking iron-and-glass Palacio de Cristal was modelled on the Crystal Palace built by Sir Joseph Paxton for London's Great Exhibition in 1851. Designed to stage an exhibition of tropical plants in the Philippines Exposition of 1887, the palace has become a forum for receptions and art displays. Its reflection in the lake remains one of the best known images of Madrid.

Elsewhere in the park, the Casa de Vacas puts on free exhibitions of Madrid art.

Monument of Alfonso XII (1901) facing the boating lake in the Parque del Retiro

Museo del Prado ㉑

T HE PRADO MUSEUM contains the world's greatest assembly of Spanish painting – especially works by Velázquez and Goya – ranging from the 12th to 19th centuries. It also houses impressive foreign collections, particularly of Italian and Flemish works. The Neo-Classical building was designed in 1785 by Juan de Villanueva on the orders of Carlos III. It opened as a museum in 1819 to display the royal collection of paintings, sculpture and decorative arts. The Casón del Buen Retiro, the Prado's annexe, is currently undergoing a major renovation and should re-open to the public in summer 2001.

★ **Velázquez Collection**
The Triumph of Bacchus *(1629)*, *Velázquez's first portrayal of a mythological subject, shows the god of wine (Bacchus) with a group of drunkards.*

The Three Graces *(c.1635)*
This was one of the last paintings by the Flemish master Rubens, and was part of the artist's personal collection. The three women dancing in a ring – the Graces – are the daughters of Zeus, and represent Love, Joy and Revelry.

The Adoration of the Shepherds *(1612–14)*
This dramatic work shows the elongated figures and swirling garments typical of El Greco's style. It was painted during his late Mannerist period for his own funerary chapel.

STAR EXHIBITS
- ★ **Velázquez Collection**
- ★ **Goya Collection**

The Garden of Delights *(c.1505)*
Hieronymus Bosch (El Bosco in Spanish), one of Felipe II's favourite artists, is especially well repre-sented in the Prado. This enigmatic painting de-picts paradise and hell.

Main entrance

Second floor

GALLERY GUIDE

The best way to enter the Prado is through the Puerta de Goya, on Calle Felipe IV, which leads on to the first floor. The works are arranged in schools, with the oldest works displayed on the lowest floors. The second floor, recently opened to the public, includes collections of works by Goya and Velázquez.

VISITORS' CHECKLIST

Paseo del Prado. **Map** 5 C2.
91 420 28 36. Atocha,
Banco de España. 6, 10, 14,
19, 27, 34, 37, 45. 9am–
7pm Tue–Sat, 9am–2pm Sun &
public hols. 1 Jan, Good Fri,
1 May, 25 Dec. (free Sat pm &
Sun). **Casón del Buen**
Retiro: Calle de Alfonso XII 28.
91 420 26 28. until 2001.
www.museoprado.mcu.es

First floor

★ Goya Collection

In The Clothed Maja *and* The Naked Maja *(both c.1800), Goya tackled the taboo subject of nudity, for which he was later accused of obscenity.*

Ground floor

The Martyrdom of St Philip *(c.1639)*
José de Ribera moved from his native Valencia to Naples as a young man. There he was influenced by Caravaggio's dramatic use of light and shadow, known as chiaroscuro, as seen in this work.

KEY TO FLOORPLAN

☐	Spanish painting
☐	Flemish and Dutch painting
☐	Italian painting
☐	French painting
☐	German painting
☐	Sculpture
☐	Temporary exhibitions
☐	Non-exhibition space

The Annunciation
Fra Angelico's work of c.1425–28 is a high point of Italy's Early Renaissance, as illustrated by the detailed architectural setting and deep perspective of the interior.

Exploring the Prado's Collection

THE IMPORTANCE OF THE PRADO is founded on its royal collections. The wealth of foreign art, including many of Europe's finest works, reflects the historical power of the Spanish crown. The Low Countries and parts of Italy were under Spanish domination for centuries. The 18th century was an era of French influence, following the Bourbon accession to the Spanish throne. The Prado is worthy of repeated visits, but if you go only once, see the Spanish works of the 17th century.

St Dominic of Silos Enthroned as Abbot (1474–7) by Bermejo

SPANISH PAINTING

RIGHT UP TO THE 19th century, Spanish painting focused on religious and royal themes. Although the limited subject matter was in some ways a restriction, it also offered a sharp focus that seems to have suited Spanish painters.

Spain's early medieval art is represented somewhat sketchily in the Prado, but there are some examples, such as the anonymous mural paintings from the Holy Cross hermitage in Madero in Madueruelo, which show a Romanesque heaviness of line and forceful characterization.

Spanish Gothic art can be seen in the Prado in the works of Bartolomé Bermejo and Fernando Gallego. The sense of realism in their paintings was borrowed from Flemish masters of the time.

Renaissance features began to emerge in the works of painters such as Pedro de Berruguete, whose *Auto-da-fé* is both chilling and lively. *St Catherine*, by Fernando Yáñez de la Almedina, shows the influence of Leonardo da Vinci, for whom Yáñez probably worked while training in Italy.

What is often considered as a truly Spanish style – with its highly-wrought emotion and deepening sombreness – first started to emerge in the 16th century in the paintings of Mannerists. This is evident in Pedro Machuca's fierce *Descent from the Cross* and in the Madonnas of Luis de Morales, "the Divine". The elongation of the human figure in Morales' work is carried to a greater extreme by Domenikos Theotocopoulos, who is better known as El Greco *(see p139)*. Although many of his masterpieces remain in his adopted

Saturn Devouring One of his Sons (1820–23) by Francisco de Goya

town of Toledo, the Prado has an impressive collection, including *The Nobleman with his Hand on his Chest*.

The Golden Age of the 17th century was a productive time for Spanish art. José de Ribera, who lived in (Spanish) Naples, followed Caravaggio in combining realism of character with the techniques of *chiaroscuro* (use of light and dark) and tenebrism (large areas of dark colours, with a shaft of light). Another master who used this method was Francisco Ribalta, whose *Christ Embracing St Bernard* is here. Zurbarán, known for still lifes and portraits of saints and monks, is also represented in the Prado.

This period, however, is best represented by the work of Diego Velázquez. As Spain's leading court painter from his late twenties until his death, he produced scenes of heightened realism, royal portraits, and religious and mythological paintings. Examples of all of these are displayed in the Prado. Perhaps his greatest work is *Las Meninas (see p27)*.

Another great Spanish painter, Goya, revived Spanish art in the 18th century. He first specialized in cartoons for tapestries, then became a court painter. His work went on to embrace the horrors of war, as seen here in *The 3rd of May (see p16)*, and culminated in a sombre series known as *The Black Paintings*.

Still Life with Four Vessels (c.1658–64) by Francisco de Zurbarán

CASÓN DEL BUEN RETIRO

On the hill behind the Prado is its annexe, the Casón del Buen Retiro, once part of the Palacio del Buen Retiro *(see p77)*. Its exhibits have included late 19th-century and early 20th-century works, as well as Neo-Classical and Romantic art, and paintings on historical themes. However, the Casón del Buen Retiro is currently closed for refurbishment and is not due to reopen until the middle of 2001.

Children at the Beach (1910) by Joaquín Sorolla

FLEMISH AND DUTCH PAINTING

SPAIN'S LONG CONNECTION with the Low Countries led naturally to an intense admiration for the so-called Flemish primitives. Many exceptional works of art now hang in the Prado. *St Barbara*, by Robert Campin, has a quirky intimacy, and Rogier van der Weyden's *The Deposition* is an unquestioned masterpiece. Most notable of all, however, are Hieronymus Bosch's weird and eloquent inventions, which were collected by Felipe II. The Prado has some of his major paintings, including the *Temptation of St Anthony* and *The Haywain*. Works from the 16th century include the magnificent *Triumph of Death* by Brueghel the Elder. There are nearly 100 canvases by the 17th-century Flemish painter Peter Paul Rubens, of which the greatest is *The Adoration of the Magi*. The two most notable Dutch paintings on display are by Rembrandt: *Artemisia*, and a fine self-portrait.

David Victorious over Goliath (c.1600) by Caravaggio

ITALIAN PAINTING

THE PRADO IS THE ENVY of many museums, not least for its vast collection of Italian paintings. Botticelli's dramatic wooden panels telling *The Story of Nastagio degli Onesti*, a vision of a knight forever condemned to hunt down and kill his own beloved, are a sinister high point. Raphael contributes the superb *Christ Falls on the Way to Calvary* and the sentimental *The Holy Family of the Lamb*.

Christ Washing the Disciples' Feet, by Tintoretto, is a profound masterpiece. Venetian masters Veronese and Titian are also very well represented. Titian served as court painter to Charles V, and few works express the drama of Habsburg rule so deeply as his sombre painting *The Emperor Charles V at Mühlberg*. Also on display are works by Giordano, Caravaggio and Tiepolo, the master of Italian Rococo.

FRENCH PAINTING

MARRIAGES BETWEEN French and Spanish royalty in the 17th century, culminating in the Bourbon accession to the throne in the 18th century, brought French art to Spain. The Prado has eight works attributed to Poussin, among them his serene *Parnassus* and *Landscape with St Jerome*. The magnificent *Landscape with the Embarkation of St Paula Romana at Ostia* is the best work here by Claude Lorrain. Among the 18th-century artists featured are Antoine Watteau and Jean Ranc. *Felipe V* is the work of the royal portraitist Louis-Michel van Loo.

GERMAN PAINTING

ALTHOUGH GERMAN ART is not especially well represented in the Prado, there are several paintings by Albrecht Dürer, such as his lively *Self-Portrait*, painted at the age of 26. Lucas Cranach also figures. Works by the late 18th-century painter Anton Raffael Mengs include portraits of Carlos III.

The Deposition (c.1430) by Rogier van der Weyden

Real Jardín Botánico ㉖

Plaza de Murillo 2. **Map** 8 D4.
☎ *91 420 30 17.* Ⓜ *Atocha.*
◯ *10am–dusk daily.* 🈂️ ⑁

SOUTH OF THE Prado *(see pp80–3)*, and a suitable place to rest after visiting the gallery, are the Royal Botanic Gardens. The inspiration of Carlos III *(see p21)*, they were designed in 1781 by Gómez Ortega and Juan de Villanueva, architect of the Prado.

Interest in the plants of the Philippines and South America was taking hold in Spain around this time, and the neatly laid out beds offer an enormous variety of flora, ranging from trees and shrubs to medicinal plants and herbs.

Statue of Bourbon King, Carlos III, in the Real Jardín Botánico

Ministerio de Agricultura ㉗

Paseo de la Infanta Isabel 1.
Map 8 D5. ☎ *91 347 53 48.*
Ⓜ *Atocha.* ◯ *by appointment.*

THIS MAGNIFICENT, imposing building was originally the home of the Ministry of Development, whose remit was to promote economic, industrial and scientific growth in Spain in the late 19th century. Today the enormous edifice houses the Ministry of Agriculture, and as such is frequently the target of protests by Spanish farmers and olive oil producers.

The elaborate but daunting face of Spain's Ministerio de Agricultura

The building itself is adorned with sculptures, friezes and painted tiles and brings together elements of both Neo-Classical and Romantic styles. It was constructed between 1884 and 1886 by Ricardo Velázquez Bosco, architect of the Palacio de Velázquez in the Parque del Retiro *(see p77)*. The artist Ignacio Zuloaga was later involved in its design.

Gigantic Corinthian columns line the exterior walls, with areas of coloured bricks and decorative glazed tiles en-hancing the spaces between them. The pediment above the columns is decorated with the Spanish coat of arms. Crowning the building are allegorical sculptures created by Agustín Querol. The three central figures represent Glory personified bestowing laurels on Science and Art. On either side are statues of Pegasus. These were originally made of marble, but were replaced by bronze replicas when the stone deteriorated.

Observatorio Astronómico ㉘

Calle de Alfonso XII 3. **Map** 8 E5.
☎ *91 527 01 07.* Ⓜ *Atocha.*
◯ *9am–2pm Mon–Fri.* ◉ *public hols.* ⑁ *by prior appointment.*

WHEN THIS BUILDING opened in 1790, it was one of only four observatories in Europe, the others being in London, Paris and Berlin. It was designed by Juan de la Villanueva along Neo-Classical lines. The vertical slit window was used for telescopes, and the colonnaded roof cupola for weather observation.

There is one room open to the public where some 18th- and 19th-century telescopes, as well as a modern Foucault pendulum, are on display. You can apply in writing to view the larger telescopes and a collection of English clocks, or to peer through a telescope made in 1790 by Sir Frederick William Herschel, the astrono-mer who discovered Uranus. These visits only take place once a month at night and are dependent on the weather.

Colonnaded roof cupola of the Observatorio Astronómico

Museo Nacional de Antropología ㉙

Calle de Alfonso XII 68. **Map** 8 D5.
☎ *91 530 64 18.* Ⓜ *Atocha.*
◯ *10am–7:30pm Tue–Sat; 10am–2pm Sun.* ◉ *public hols.* 🈂️ *(free Sat & Sun).* ⑁ *book 15 days in advance.*

PREVIOUSLY KNOWN AS the Museo Nacional de Etnolo-gía, this three-floor museum, which is built around a grand open hall, was inaugurated by Alfonso XII *(see p21)* in 1875.

Through the displays, the anthropology and ethnology of geographical groups of people are studied. The ground floor houses an important collection from the Philippines. Originally shown in 1887 in the Palacio de Velázquez *(see p77)*, the centrepiece is a 10 m- (33 ft-) long dug-out canoe made from a single tree trunk. There are also some gruesome exhibits, such as deformed skulls from Peru and the Philippines, the mummy of a Guanche from Tenerife and the skeleton of Don Agustín Luengo y Capilla, a late 19th-century giant from Extremadura. He was 2.35 m (7 ft 4 in) tall and died aged 26.

The first floor is dedicated to Africa. As well as clothing, weapons, jewellery, ceramics and utensils, there is a reproduction of a Bubi ritual hut from Equatorial Guinea, in which tribal members met with the *boeloelo* (witch doctor).

Occupying the second floor is the American section, which houses exhibits on the lifestyles of indigenous native groups.

Estación de Atocha ③⓪

Plaza del Emperador Carlos V. **Map** 8 D5. 91 506 68 46. Atocha RENFE. 5:30am–midnight daily.

MADRID'S FIRST rail service, from Atocha to Aranjuez, was inaugurated in 1851 by Isabel II *(see p21)*. Forty years later, the original station at Atocha was replaced by the present one, which acquired a modern extension in the 1980s.

The older part of the station was one of the first large-scale constructions in Madrid to be built from glass and wrought iron. Nowadays, it houses an

Entrance of Madrid's Estación de Atocha, busy with travellers

extraordinary indoor palm garden for travellers to enjoy. Adjoining it is the modern AVE terminus, providing high-speed train links from Madrid to Córdoba and Seville *(see p196)*.

Palacio de Fernán Núñez ③①

Calle de Santa Isabel 44. **Map** 7 B4. 91 527 18 12. Atocha. by appointment.

ALSO KNOWN AS the Palacio de Cervellón, this building has a plain façade that gives scant indication of the riches within. Built for the Duke and Duchess of Fernán Núñez in 1847, the palace served as the

family home until 1936. It was requisitioned by the Republican militia at the start of the Civil War *(see p18)*; the lower part served as a bomb shelter while the upper floor was occupied by a Socialist Youth organization. Amazingly, when the palace was returned to the Duke's family, they found that none of its treasures had been damaged or stolen.

In 1941, the palace was sold and became the headquarters of the Spanish State Railway. It now houses the Foundation of Spanish Railways, which organizes exhibitions here.

That the palace was built in two phases is clear. The large, restrained rooms in the first section contrast sharply with the Rococo flourishes of the second. The older section has some interesting carpets from the Real Fábrica de Tapices *(see p112)*, as well as antique furniture, clocks and copies of paintings by Goya *(see p26)*. Attention, however, is inevitably drawn to the lavish gold-plated ornamentation of the later section, especially the ballroom with its mirrors, chandeliers and cherubs playing musical instruments. Rooms in this part are often used for official receptions.

Near the palace is the cloistered Convento Santa Isabel with its octagonal dome. It was founded in 1595 by Felipe II.

The sumptuously decorated ballroom of the Palacio de Fernán Núñez

Centro de Arte Reina Sofía ㉜

THE HIGHLIGHT of this museum of 20th-century art is, without doubt, Picasso's *Guernica*. However, there are also other major works by influential artists, including Miró and Picasso. The collection is housed in the former premises of Madrid's General Hospital, which was built in the late 18th century. Two exterior glass elevators were added in 1990 when the building was given National Museum status. Although the interior is now a computer-controlled environment, it retains much of the atmosphere of the original building.

Portrait II *(1938)*
Joan Miró's huge, enigmatic work shows elements of Surrealism, despite being painted more than ten years after the end of his true Surrealist period.

★ **Woman in Blue** *(1901)*
Picasso disowned this work after it won only an honourable mention in a national competition. Decades later it was located and acquired by the Spanish state.

Guernica

Landscape at Cadaqués
Salvador Dalí was born in Figueres in Catalonia. He became a frequent visitor to the town of Cadaqués, on the Costa Brava, where he painted this landscape in the summer of 1923.

Second floor

Accident
Alfonso Ponce de León's disturbing work, painted in 1936, prefigured his death in a car crash later that same year.

STAR EXHIBITS

★ **Woman in Blue**
  by Picasso

★ **La Tertulia del Café**
  de Pombo by Solana

★ **Guernica by Picasso**

AROUND LA CASTELLANA

THE AXIS of modern Madrid is the tree-lined Paseo de la Castellana, a long, grand boulevard. A journey along it gives a glimpse of Madrid as Spain's commercial and administrative capital. The main north-south artery, it was first developed in the 19th century by the city's aristocracy with a string of summer palaces from Plaza de Colón northwards. The Museo Lázaro Galdiano, one of Madrid's best art museums, is housed in the former mansion of the financier José Lázaro Galdiano. To

Façade detail, Iglesia de Santa Bárbara

the east, La Castellana skirts the Barrio de Salamanca, an upmarket district of stylish boutiques and apartment blocks named after the 19th-century aristocrat who built it. To the southwest are Chueca and Malasaña, neighbourhoods offering a more authentic *Madrileño* atmosphere.

The southern section of the boulevard is called Paseo de Recoletos. Nearby are the Museo Arqueológico Nacional, founded by Isabel II in 1867, and Café Gijón, an intellectuals' café founded in the early 20th century.

SIGHTS AT A GLANCE

Museums and Galleries
Fundación Juan March ⑪
Museo Arqueológico
  Nacional pp96–7 ⑧
Museo de Cera ⑥
Museo de Escultura
  al Aire Libre ⑭
Museo Lázaro Galdiano
  pp100–101 ⑫
Museo Municipal ⑯
Museo Romántico ⑮
Museo Sorolla ⑬

Churches
Iglesia de Santa Bárbara ④

Streets, Squares, Parks and Districts
Calle de Serrano ⑨
Calle del Almirante ②
Malasaña ⑰
Plaza de Chueca ③
Plaza de Colón ⑦
Salamanca ⑩

Historic Buildings
Café Gijón ①
Cuartel del Conde Duque ⑱
Palacio de Liria ⑲
Tribunal Supremo ⑤

GETTING THERE
The metro is the easiest way to get to and around this area. Lines 1, 4, 5, 6, 8, 9 and 10 serve the main sights. Useful buses include routes 27, which runs the length of La Castellana, and 5, 7, 12, 13, 40, 45 and 150. The Airport bus terminal lies beneath Plaza de Colón.

KEY

▨ Street-by-Street map
  pp92–3

Ⓜ Metro station

🚌 Main bus stop

🅿 Parking

0 metres   250

0 yards   250

◁ **One of four enormous concrete sculptures at the Plaza de Colón**

Street by Street: Paseo de Recoletos

PLAZA DE COLÓN is bordered by the fashionable designer shopping streets Calle de Serrano and Calle de Goya, the Museo Arqueológico Nacional, the Biblioteca Nacional (National Library) and Paseo de Recoletos, which is home to the classic Café Gijón. Between Calle del Almirante, another popular fashion street, and Calle de Génova is the Tribunal Supremo and the Iglesia de Santa Bárbara. Towards the Gran Vía are the narrow streets of Chueca with some interesting old taverns and eclectic bistros.

Iglesia de Santa Bárbara
Both Bárbara de Braganza and her husband, Fernando VI (see p21), are entombed in this fine Baroque church ④

Tribunal Supremo
Spain's supreme court of law is located in the former convent and school of the adjoining Iglesia de Santa Bárbara ⑤

Calle de Barquillo
contains the best shops in the city for stereo equipment, mobile phones and other electronic goods.

0 metres   100
0 yards   100

STAR SIGHTS

★ **Museo Arqueológico Nacional**

★ **Plaza de Colón**

Plaza de Chueca
The immaculate, exquisitely decorated Bodega de Angel Sierra bar in the Plaza de Chueca has hardly changed since it was built in 1897 ③

Calle del Almirante
Originally a street of basket shops, Calle del Almirante now boasts several of the city's own-label fashion shops ②

Museo de Cera
*Madrid's wax museum
has likenesses of many
historical figures* 6

LOCATOR MAP
See Street Finder map 6.

CALLE DE GENOVA

CALLE DE GOYA

PLAZA DE COLÓN

BRAGANZA

PASEO DE RECOLETOS

CALLE RECOLETOS

CALLE DE SERRANO

★ **Plaza de Colón**
*This large square is a
monument to Christopher
Columbus (Colón)* 7

El Espejo is the most beautifully decorated Belle Epoque
bar and restaurant in the city.

★ **Museo Arqueológico
Nacional**
*On display in this palatial
museum are around 100,000
exhibits showing the rich and
varied history of Spain* 8

Calle de Serrano
*Madrid's smartest shopping street
is home to top Spanish designers* 9

Café Gijón
*For over a century, intellectuals
have held discussion groups
or tertulias (see p74) in this
wood-panelled café* 1

KEY

– – – Suggested route

Café Gijón ❶

Paseo de Recoletos 21. **Map** 5 C5.
📞 91 521 54 25. Ⓜ *Banco de
España.* 🕐 *8am–1:30am Sun–Fri,
8am–2am Sat & public hols.* ♿

MADRID'S CAFÉ LIFE was one
of the most attractive
features of the city from the
turn of the 20th century, right
up to the outbreak of the Civil
War. Many intellectuals' cafés
once thrived *(see p74)*, but
the Gijón is one of the few
that survives. It still attracts
a lively crowd of *literati*.
Although it is better known
for its atmosphere than its
appearance, the café has a
striking interior with cream-
painted wrought-iron columns
and black and white table tops.

Interior of the literary Café Gijón

Calle del Almirante ❷

Map 5 C5. Ⓜ *Banco de España,
Colón & Chueca.*

RUNNING BETWEEN the Paseo
de Recoletos and Calle
Barquillo, this street is famous
for its dozen own-label fashion
shops. For most of the 20th
century it was known as "Calle
de Cesterías" (basketwork
street). Now the only cane
shop left is that of Antonio
del Pozo, founded in 1891.
In earlier days there were
five cane shops, where baskets,
chairs and other woven wares
were sold. There were also
several taverns where neigh-
bours gathered to pass the
time. Such was the fame of
the street that the wives of
both Winston Churchill and
the Shah of Persia visited the
del Pozo cane shop.

During the transition to democracy following Franco's death
in 1975, Calle del Almirante
gained a certain notoriety.
Fewer police patrolled the
area, and street crime rose.
Two gay bars opened in the
street and male prostitutes
touted openly for business.
During this time Jesús del
Pozo – Antonio's brother and
a fashion designer – opened
the first boutique selling
clothes of his own design
next to the family cane shop.
However, it was not until the
1980s, with the cultural movement of *La Movida (see p104)*,
that the area became fashionable and other clothes shops
opened, along with a number
of chic furnishings and decor
outlets. Now the street is
referred to as "Calle de la
Moda" (fashion street), and
is a favourite haunt of the
wealthy and business people
from neighbouring offices.
Jesús del Pozo has become
famous, and his showrooms
on the first floor at No. 9 Calle
del Almirante sell outfits for
society weddings and events.
However, the street also retains
other original shops and
cafés. Manolo Huerta's family
have run the *panadería*
(bakery) since 1910 and the
Cafetería Almirante, which
serves *bocatas* (sandwiches) for
those in a hurry, has been run
by Juan Encinas since 1972.
At No. 23 is the fascinating
Regalos Originales, a must-
see for browsers of antiques
and old curiosity shops.

View along the fashionable Calle del Almirante

Newsstand in the Plaza de Chueca

Plaza de Chueca ❸

Map 5 B5. Ⓜ *Chueca.*

THE PLAZA DE CHUECA is
situated between Calle
Augusto Figueroa and Calle
Gravina. The square was
originally called Plaza de San
Gregorio after a statue of the
saint that stood in Calle San
Gregorio, at the main gate
to the manor house of the
Marqueses of Minaya. In 1943
the square was renamed after
Federico Chueca (1846–1908),
a composer of *zarzuelas (see
p75)*. His works include *Agua,
Azucarillos and Aguardiente*
and *La Gran Vía*.
Lining the plaza are small
shops, bars and apartment
buildings. On one side of the
square is the Bodega de Angel
Sierra *(see p92)*, a *taberna* full
of character that was founded
in 1897. On the
outside there are
Andalusian-style
tiles advertising
vermouth, beers
and wines, while
inside there is a
bar adorned with
finely polished
faucets (taps).
The neighbour-
hood around the
plaza is an intricate
maze of little streets.
Also called Chueca,
by night it is the
main focus of
Madrid's gay com-
munity, with a
good selection of
modish bars and
chic restaurants.

Iglesia de Santa Bárbara ❻

Calle General Castaños 2. **Map** 5 C5.
Ⓜ *Alonso Martínez, Colón.*
◯ *9am–1pm, 5–9pm Mon–Fri,
10am–1pm, 5–9pm public hols.*

No EXPENSE WAS SPARED on this fine Baroque church, which was built, along with an adjoining convent (now the Tribunal Supremo), for Bárbara de Braganza, wife of Fernando VI. To run the convent, which was to include a school for daughters of the nobility, Bárbara chose Las Salesas Reales – an order of nuns founded in 1610 by St Francis de Sales and St Jane Frances de Chantal in Annecy, France. The church is sometimes referred to as Las Salesas Reales.

François Carlier (1707–60), whose father worked on the gardens of La Granja de San Ildefonso *(see p127)*, was appointed architect. The first stone was laid in 1750 and, in 1757, the huge edifice was finished by builder Francisco de Moradillo. He added towers on the roof to Carlier's plans.

The main door is reached through pleasant gardens, added in 1930. The central medallion on the façade, by Doménico Olivieri, shows *The Visitation* of the pregnant Virgin to her cousin Elizabeth. The angels on either side hold the Cross and the two tablets of the Ten Commandments.

The extravagant interior decoration was assigned to Doménico Olivieri. To the right of the entrance is a painting of St Francis de Sales and St Jane de Chantal by Corrado Giaquinto. Opposite is *La Sagrada Família* (The Holy Family), painted by Francesco Cignaroni.

To the right of the central aisle is the tomb of Fernando VI, adorned with tiers of angels crafted by Francisco Gutiérrez to a Neo-Classical design by Francesco Sabatini. Above the nearby altar is a painting of Francisco Javier and Santa Bárbara. It is by Francesca de Mora, as is *La Visitación* above the high altar. The high altar is decorated with sculptures of San Fernando and Santa Bárbara. To the left is the

Elaborately decorated interior of the Iglesia de Santa Bárbara

19th-century tomb of General O'Donnell, a former prime minister, by sculptor Jerónimo Suñol. Alongside it is the *Surrender of Seville* by the French artist Charles Joseph Flipart. The tomb of Bárbara de Braganza is to the right of the altar in a separate chapel.

Tribunal Supremo ❺

Plaza de la Villa de Paris. **Map** 5 C5.
◖ *91 397 12 62.* Ⓜ *Alonso Martínez, Colón.* ◯ *by appointment in writing (Gabinete Técnico, Plaza de la Villa de Paris, Madrid 28004).*

Built by François Carlier in the 1750s as a convent and school for the adjoining Iglesia de Santa Bárbara, this stately Baroque building was run by the French order of nuns called Las Salesas Reales. It was built on the orders of Bárbara de Braganza, wife of Fernando VI. After her death, the nuns were allowed to remain in the convent until 1870, when the building was expropriated by the secular government to become the Palace of Justice. The building fell into disrepair, which was made worse by fires in 1907 and 1915. Fortunately,

the Iglesia de Santa Bárbara was unaffected. Later restoration work was undertaken by Joaquin Rojí in 1991–5. In the 1990s, the building became the country's supreme court.

In front of the palace is the Plaza de la Villa de Paris, a large French-style square. In the middle of it are statues of Fernando VI and Bárbara de Braganza. Across the square is the modern Audiencia Nacional (National Court). The surrounding roads are often lined with official cars, police officers and reporters.

Statue of Bárbara de Braganza in the Plaza de la Villa de Paris

Museo Arqueológico Nacional ❽

WITH HUNDREDS OF EXHIBITS, ranging from prehistoric times to the 19th century, this palatial museum is one of Madrid's best. It was founded by Isabel II in 1867 and contains many items uncovered during excavations all over Spain, as well as pieces from Egypt, ancient Greece and the Etruscan civilization. Highlights include items from the ancient civilization of El Argar in Andalusia, 7th-century gold votive crowns from Toledo province, Roman mosaics and Islamic pottery. Steps outside the museum's entrance lead underground to an exact replica of the Altamira cave in Cantabria, northern Spain. The walls are covered with copies of superb early Paleolithic paintings.

A bison, one of the wall paintings in the replica of the Altamira cave

Basement

★ Visigothic Crown
This 6th-century gold crown with pearls, sapphires and garnets was found at Guarrazar, Toledo. Letters spelling "RECCESVINTHVS REX OFFERET" hang from it, indicating it was a church offering from Visigoth King Recesvinto.

Moorish Arch
Constructed from plaster, this 11th-century arch was more decorative than functional. It formed part of the Palacio de Aljafería in Zaragoza (north central Spain).

STAR SIGHTS

★ **Dama de Baça**

★ **Roman Mosaic**

★ **Visigothic Crown**

Medieval religious paintings and icons

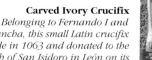

Carved Ivory Crucifix
Belonging to Fernando I and Queen Sancha, this small Latin crucifix was made in 1063 and donated to the church of San Isidoro in León on its dedication. At the back is a recess for a relic of the True Cross.

Ceremonial Sword
*This exceptional lami-
nated, gold-handled
sword from the Bronze
Age Argar culture (19th–
14th century BC) was
discovered in
Guadalajara
(see p131).*

VISITORS' CHECKLIST

Calle de Serrano 13. **Map** 6 D5.
91 577 79 12. Serrano,
Retiro. 1, 19, 51, 74.
9:30am–8:30pm Tue–Sat,
9:30am–2:30pm Sun. public
hols, 15 May, 9 Nov, 24–5 & 31
Dec. (free Sat pm & Sun).
W www.man.es

Celtic-style Gold Bowls
*These late Bronze Age bowls
(13th–12th century BC)
have beaten patterns. They
were found in Axtroki in
the Basque country, where
they had been hidden, probably by a sun-worshipping cult.*

Ground
floor

★ Roman Mosaic
*From a Roman villa in Albacete, this
3rd-century mosaic shows the
monogram of the family who lived
there, surrounded by allegories of the
months. This section represents April.*

★ Dama de Baça
*This ancient stone
statue (4th century BC)
is from Granada. Covered
in polychrome stuccowork,
it has a niche at the back
for the ashes of the dead.*

Main
entrance

Replica of the
Altamira cave

KEY

☐ Paleolithic to Iron Age

☐ Iberian, Phoenician and Punic
exhibits

☐ Ancient Rome

☐ Ancient Africa and Middle East

☐ Ancient Greece and Etruria

☐ Visigothic, Romanesque and
Mudéjar exhibits

☐ Non-exhibition space

GALLERY GUIDE

*The museum is arranged
chronologically, beginning in the
basement with prehistory and the earliest colonizers.
The ground floor is largely devoted to the period between
Roman and Mudéjar Spain, but also includes exhibits of
Iberian, Phoenician, Punic and medieval artifacts. The
building's façade is currently being remodelled, but all the
rooms are still open. Outside the museum, in the garden by
the front gate, is the entrance to the replica Altamira cave.*

Museo de Cera ⑥

Paseo de Recoletos 41. **Map** 6 D5.
📞 91 308 08 25. Ⓜ *Colón.*
🕐 10am–2:30pm, 4:30–8:30 pm
*Mon–Fri, 10am–8:30pm Sat–Sun &
public hols.* 🅿 ♿

MADRID'S WAX MUSEUM, off
Plaza de Colón, houses
some 450 wax dummies of
well known Spanish and international figures, mostly set
in scenes. One in particular
shows a wax likeness of
Miguel de Cervantes, author
of *Don Quixote*, sitting at his
desk writing, with windmills
behind him. Another imitates
Goya's famous painting, *The
3rd of May*, depicting French
reprisals for the rebellions of 2
May 1808 in Madrid *(see p16)*.
Also shown is Christopher
Columbus' return from the
New World. Other scenes
show navigators and scientists,
the Last Supper and the history of the Spanish colonies.

More recent figures include
cowboys from the Wild West,
pop stars, Hollywood actors,
athletes and the Pope. There
is also a café scene where
visitors to the museum are
encouraged to try to identify
Spanish intellectuals, past and
present. Those with children
should bear in mind that
some of the scenes are quite
ghoulish. Particularly gruesome
is a bullfighting scene with a
horn piercing a matador's eye.

Upstairs is *Multivision*, a cinema where 27 projectors are
used simultaneously to show
a 60-minute history of Spain.

**Wax figure of Miguel de Cervantes
in the Museo de Cera**

**Modern monument to Christopher
Columbus, Plaza de Colón**

Plaza de Colón ⑦

Map 6 D5. Ⓜ *Serrano, Colón.*

THIS LARGE SQUARE, one of
Madrid's focal points, is
dedicated to Christopher
Columbus (Colón in Spanish).
It is overlooked by 1970s'
high-rise buildings, which
replaced the 19th-century
mansions that once stood
here. On the south side is
a palace housing the
National Library and
Archeological Museum
(see pp96–7). On the
north side, on the corner
of La Castellana, the Post-
Modernist skyscraper of
the Heron Corporation
towers over the square.

The real feature of the
square, however, is the
pair of monuments dedi-
cated to the discoverer of
the Americas. The oldest,
and prettiest, is a Neo-
Gothic spire built in 1885,
with Columbus at its top,
pointing west. Carved
reliefs on the plinth
give highlights of his
discoveries. Across
the square is the
second, more modern
monument – a cluster
of four large concrete
shapes inscribed with
quotations relating to
Columbus' historic
journey to America.

Constantly busy with the
flow of traffic, the plaza may
seem an unlikely venue for
cultural events. Beneath it,

**Statue of
Columbus, Plaza
de Colón**

however, is an extensive complex, the Centro Cultural de
la Villa de Madrid, which
includes the city's municipal
art centre, exhibition halls,
lecture rooms, a theatre and
a café. The terminal for the
bus which runs to and from
the airport *(see p192)* is also
located underground.

Museo Arqueológico Nacional ⑧

See pages 96–7.

Calle de Serrano ⑨

Map 8 D1. Ⓜ *Serrano.*

NAMED AFTER a 19th-century
politician, Madrid's smartest shopping street runs north
from the triumphal Plaza de
la Independencia to the Plaza
del Ecuador, in the well-heeled
district of Salamanca. The street
is lined with shops *(see p164)*
– many specializing in
luxury items – housed in
old-fashioned mansion-
blocks. Several of Spain's
top designers, including
Adolfo Domínguez and
Roberto Verino, have bou-
tiques towards the northern
end of the street, near the
ABC Serrano mall *(see p165)*
and the Museo Lázaro
Galdiano *(see pp100–101)*.
Branches of the Italian shops
Versace and Armani can be
found on Calle de José
Ortega y Gasset. Lower
down Calle de Serrano,
towards Serrano metro
station, is a branch of the
British chain store Marks
& Spencer, which has
become popular with
the Spanish and with
tourists. Their sand-
wiches, flown out
fresh from England
every day, are partic-
ularly popular with
Madrid's aspiring
middle classes. On
the Calle de Claudio
Coello, which runs
parallel with Serrano, there
are several lavish antique
shops, in keeping with the
area's up-market atmosphere.

Statue of Salamanca's founder, the Marqués de Salamanca

Salamanca ⑩

Map 6 E3. Ⓜ Velázquez, Serrano, Núñez de Balboa, Lista, Príncipe de Vergara, Goya, Diego de León.

Madrid's SALAMANCA district (Barrio de Salamanca) was developed in 1862–3 as an area for the bourgeoisie, and takes its name from its founder, José "Pepito" Salamanca, Marqués de Salamanca (1811–83). He was a lawyer who, by the age of 23, had already been elected as a deputy to the Cortes (Spanish parliament). The Marqués had a great flair for politics and business, and made his vast fortune from salt, railways and the building of Salamanca. He was also the founder of Banco de Isabel II, which was the forerunner of Banco de España (see p67).

The Marqués inaugurated his magnificent palace at Paseo de Recoletos 10, (now the Banco Hipotecario) in 1858, and by 1862 began developing his land behind it. The streets were planned to run north-south or east-west, and the area was to comprise apartment blocks, churches, schools, hospitals and theatres. He also built the first tramways in Madrid, connecting the Barrio de Salamanca with the centre of Madrid. A statue of the Marqués stands at the confluence of Ortega y Gasset and Príncipe de Vergara.

To this day the barrio consists mainly of six- to eight-floor apartment blocks, and is home to many well-to-do families. This is an area where just a hint of cool weather brings out the mink coats. Some of Madrid's best shops and markets can be found here, as well as a number of discreet restaurants. The pijos (rich spoilt children) gather at the cervecerías and bars around Calle de Goya and Calle de Alcalá.

The oldest church of the barrio, San Andrés de los Flamencos (Calle de Claudio Coello 99), built in 1884, now houses the Fundación Carlos de Amberes, a cultural centre maintaining links between Spain, Holland and Belgium. Behind the altar is a painting of St Andrew by Rubens. The unofficial parish church of Salamanca is the Iglesia de la Concepción (Calle de Goya 26), built between 1902 and 1914, with a notable white iron spire topped by a statue of the Virgin. At Calle de Hermosilla 45 is the charming Protestant Church of St George (1926).

The best preserved of the area's Neo-Classical palaces is Palacio de Amboage (1918) by Joaquín Roji on the corner of Velázquez and Juan Bravo. It is now the Italian Embassy, and features a lovely garden.

Modern and fascinating is the architecture inside Teatriz, an avant-garde restaurant at Calle de Hermosilla 15, designed by Philippe Starck. Diners sit in the auditorium of a former theatre and cinema, while on the stage is a back-lit onyx bar and steel stools, all reflected in a gigantic mirror.

Sculpture by Chillida, Fundación Juan March

Fundación Juan March ⑪

Calle de Castelló 77. 📞 91 435 42 40. Ⓜ Núñez de Balboa. 🕐 10am–2pm, 5:30–9pm Mon–Sat, 10am–2pm Sun & public hols. ♿

Established in 1955 with an endowment from financier Juan March, this cultural and scientific foundation is best known for its art exhibitions and concerts. The marble-and-glass headquarters, in Madrid's Barrio de Salamanca, opened in 1975. The foundation has published over 380 books and collections. It also owns the Museo de Arte Abstracto in Cuenca and a gallery of modern Spanish art in Palma, Majorca. The ground floor houses a shop, as well as the main exhibition area. Works by Kandinsky, Picasso and Matisse have been shown here, alongside a permanent collection made up of over 1,300 contemporary Spanish artworks. There is a 400-seat auditorium in the basement where free concerts are held. The second-floor library has a collection of contemporary Spanish music, with listening desks. There is also a library on contemporary Spanish theatre and entertainment.

Hidden away from the public are the Juan March Institute for Study and Investigation – one of the world's top forums in the field of biology – and the Centre for Advanced Study in the Social Sciences.

Sculpture by Barrocol, by the main entrance to the Fundación Juan March

Museo Lázaro Galdiano ⑫

THIS NEO-RENAISSANCE mansion houses nearly 5,000 items from the private collection of financier José Lázaro Galdiano (1862–1947). The exhibits, ranging from the 7th century BC to the 20th century, include archeological finds, religious artifacts, Limoges enamels, Old Masters, medieval ivory, armour, jewellery and silver. In 1903 Galdiano married Argentine heiress Paula Florido and they built the mansion to celebrate – and to show off the growing collection. By the time Galdiano died, some 15,000 items were brought together in Madrid. The splendid house has hardly changed since it was bequeathed to the nation in 1948.

The grand Central Hall with its richly decorated doorways

Second floor

First floor

Ground floor

★ **The Witches' Sabbath** *(1798)*
This painting by Francisco de Goya is based on a legend from Aragón, the artist's birthplace. It shows two sisters who poisoned their children in order to attract the devil, represented here by a huge billy goat.

Doña Inés de Zúñiga
This painting of the Countess of Monterrey was executed by Juan Carreño de Miranda in the late 17th century. She is dressed for her wedding in a wide Spanish farthingale.

GALLERY GUIDE

The ground floor houses archeological artifacts, Limoges enamels, 15th- and 16th-century religious items, jewellery and Italian Renaissance art. The old foyer is lined with suits of armour. The first floor contains Spanish paintings, silverware and furniture. Highlights of the second floor, which is given over to paintings, include works by Goya, Hieronymus Bosch and El Greco.

KEY TO FLOORPLAN

- ☐ Ground floor
- ☐ First floor
- ☐ Second floor
- ☐ Non-exhibition space

★ **Jarra Púnica**
One of the oldest and most interesting archeological items displayed in the museum is this Phoenician bronze jug, which has a fine feline head as its spout. It was made in the mid-7th century BC, in the Punic era.

Main entrance

St John the Baptist
Surrounded by the lamb of spiritual life and other allegorical animals and birds, Hieronymus Bosch's contemplative St John the Baptist (c.1485–1510) reclines in an almost pastoral landscape punctuated by grotesque plants.

VISITORS' CHECKLIST

Calle Serrano 122. **Map** 6 E1.
91 561 60 84. Rubén Darío.
9, 12, 16, 19, 51. 10am–
2pm Tue–Sun (Jun, Jul & Sep: also
7–11pm Thu). 20, 21 Apr, 2
May, Aug, 12 & 31 Oct, 24 & 31
Dec & public hols. (free Wed).
W www.flg.es

Marquetry Writing Desk
This elaborate, 16th-century German desk was designed to hold writing materials and was among many exported to Spain by cabinetmakers in Augsburg and Nuremberg. Felipe II is known to have bought desks similar to this.

Portrait of a Lady
Joshua Reynolds painted this portrait in the late 18th century. Other British artists represented in the museum include Constable, Romney and Hoppner.

★ Crosier Head
This beautiful gilded and enamelled object was made in Limoges in the 13th century for the top of a bishop's staff (crosier). It is decorated with stylized plants to evoke the tree of life and a figure, believed to be St Matthew, holding a book.

STAR EXHIBITS

★ **Jarra Púnica**

★ **Crosier Head**

★ **The Witches' Sabbath**

Former studio of Impressionist Joaquín Sorolla in the Museo Sorolla

Museo Sorolla ⓲

Paseo del General Martínez Campos 37.
Map 5 C1. ☎ 91 310 15 84. Ⓜ
Rubén Dario, Gregorio Marañon.
◯ 10am–3pm Tue–Sat, 10am–
2pm Sun. 🖼 (free Sun).

THE STUDIO-MANSION of
Valencian Impressionist
painter Joaquín Sorolla is
now a museum dis-
playing his paintings,
left virtually as it was
when he died in 1923.

Although Sorolla is
perhaps best known
for his brilliantly lit
Mediterranean beach
scenes, the changing
styles of his paintings
are well represented here,
with examples of his gentle
portraiture and a series of
works depicting people from
different parts of Spain. Also
on display are various objects
amassed during the artist's
lifetime, including Spanish
tiles and ceramics. The house,
built in 1910, is surrounded
by an Andalusian-style garden,
designed by Sorolla himself.

Museo de Escultura al Aire Libre ⓴

Paseo de la Castellana. **Map** 6 E2.
Ⓜ *Rubén Dario.*

IN THE EARLY 1970s J Antonio
Fernández Ordóñez and
Julio Martínez Calzón, the
architects of the Calle Juan
Bravo bridge, filled the space
underneath it with abstract
sculptures by 20th-century
Spanish artists. The space on
the east side of Paseo de la

Castellana is dominated by
Sirena Varada, or *Stranded
Mermaid* (1972–3), a concrete
sculpture hanging from four
rods by Eduardo Chillida,
the noted Basque sculptor.
Alberto Sánchez's *Toros
Ibéricos* is another dramatic
installation, and there is a
penguin by Joan Miró.
Other sculptors repre-
sented here are Andrés
Alfaro, Julio González,
Rafael Leoz, Mariel
Martí, José María
Subirachs, Francisco
Sobrino, Martín Chirino
and Eusebio Sempere.
On the west side are
two bronzes by Pablo
Serrano. Visitors should
take care when crossing the
busy Paseo de la Castellana.

Toros Ibéricos, **Alberto Sánchez**

Museo Romántico ⓯

Calle de San Mateo 13. **Map** 5 A4.
☎ 91 448 10 71. Ⓜ *Tribunal,
Alonso Martínez.* ◯ 9am–3pm
Tue–Sat, 10am–2pm Sun and public
hols. ⬤ Aug. 🖼 (free Sun). ♿
🎞 11:30am & 12pm Sun (in Spanish).

THIS SMALL NEO-CLASSICAL
mansion was designed by
Manuel Martín in 1776 for the
Marqués de Matallana. By
1924 it had been turned into
a museum by the Marqués de
la Vega-Inclán, the founder
of Spain's fine network of
state-owned parador hotels
(see p145), who was an avid
art lover and collector. The
Marqués donated his hoard of
19th-century paintings, books
and some furniture to form
the nucleus of a museum.

Three years later the museum
was acquired by the state, and
reorganized to look like the
home of a wealthy mid-19th-
century family, evoking the
artistic, literary and musical
epoch of the Romantic period.

The exhibits are housed in
20 rooms on the first floor of
the building. As well as a vast
array of 19th-century objects,
such as musical instruments,
photographs, dolls and ornaments, there are many portraits
by leading artists. They include
General Prim by Esquivel,
José de Madrazo's *Fernando
VII* and *María Cristina* by
Salvador Gutiérrez. Several
works by Leonardo Alenza
include the disturbing *Satire
of a Romantic Suicide*.

In the ballroom is a Pleyel
piano that belonged to Isabel
II *(see p21)*. The ceiling is by
González, and the carpet
comes from the Real Fábrica
de Tapices (see p112).

The museum contains a fine
collection of works by the
costumbristas – artists who
painted scenes of everyday
life in Andalusia and Madrid.
Many of their works depict
local festivals and traditions.

Some earlier works are also
displayed, including a painting of *St Gregory the Great* by
Goya *(see p26)*, which can be
seen above the altar in the
intimate chapel.

The Mariano José de Larra
Room is dedicated to this
great satirical journalist and
writer. Among his personal
effects is the duelling pistol he
used to kill himself, after
being rejected by his lover.

**Goya's *St Gregory the Great* in the
chapel of the Museo Romántico**

Baroque façade of the Museo
Municipal, by Pedro de Ribera

Museo Municipal ⑯

Calle de Fuencarral 78. **Map** 5 A4.
📞 *91 588 86 72.* 🚇 *Tribunal.*
🕐 *9:30am–8pm Tue–Fri, 10am–2pm
Sat & Sun.* ⬤ *public hols.* 🎫 *(free
Wed & Sun).* 🎟 *by prior arrangement.*

THE MUNICIPAL MUSEUM is
worth visiting just for its
majestic Baroque doorway by
Pedro de Ribera, arguably the
finest in Madrid. Housed in the
former hospice of St Ferdinand,
the museum was inaugurated
in 1929. The basement is devoted to the city's archeology,
while upstairs is a series of
bird's-eye views and maps
showing how radically Madrid
has been transformed over
the years. Among them is Pedro
Texeiro's map made in 1656,
thought to be the oldest of the
city. There is also a meticulous
model of Madrid, made in
1830 by León Gil de Palacio.

Modern exhibits include a
reconstruction of the collage-
filled study of Ramón Gómez
de la Serna, a key figure in the
famous literary gatherings in
the Café de Pombo *(see p87)*.
In the garden is the Baroque
Fuente de la Fama (Fountain
of Fame), also by Ribera.

Malasaña ⑰

Map 2 E4. 🚇 *Tribunal, Bilbao, San
Bernardo.*

OFFICIALLY CALLED *Barrio de
Maravillas*, or District of
Miracles, after a 17th-century
church that once stood here,
this area is more widely known
as Malasaña. Thin streets slope
down from Carranza and Fuencarral to its bohemian hub, the
Plaza del Dos de Mayo.

In 1808, *Madrileños* made an
heroic last stand here against
Napoleon's occupying troops
at the gate of Monteleón barracks. The arch in the square
is all that is left of the barracks.
In front of it is a memorial by
Antonio Solá to artillery officers Daoiz and Velarde, who
defended the barracks.

In the 1940s and '50s the
area deteriorated, but residents
fiercely fended off demolition
threats. It acquired its bohemian atmosphere in the 1960s,
when hippies were lured into
the district by cheap rents.
Later it became the centre of
La Movida (see p104), the
frenzied nightlife that began
after the death of Franco.

Today Malasaña's streets
combine the best of both
worlds. Artists and writers
have once again moved
into the area, along with
antiques sellers and yup-
pies. The charming streets
have been cobbled, and
boast pretty fountains and
plenty of trees. At night,
however, the streets are
still thronged with people
looking for a wild time.

Malasaña is rich in sites
of historical and cultural
interest. **Plaza de San
Ildefonso**, one of many
squares remodelled by
José I (Joseph Bonaparte)
(see p17), has an attractive
central fountain with ser-
pents entwined around
conch shells. Near the
Neo-Classical **Iglesia de
San Ildefonso**, built in
1827, is the **Vaquería**, a

dairy shop opened in 1911 and
hardly changed since. Outside
decorative cows frame the
door, while inside there are
ageing oil paintings of the
seasons in Art Deco style.

In Calle de la Puebla, the
17th-century **Iglesia de San
Antonio de los Alemanes** is
remarkable for its elliptical
interior, swathed in frescoes
by Juan Carreño, Francisco de
Ricci and Luca Giordano.

Close by is the 17th-century
Iglesia de San Placido with
a cupola painted by Francisco
Rizi and the work of Claudio
Coello adorning the altars.

The **Iglesia de San Martín**,
in Calle de San Roque, was
built in 1648. The painting
above the altar depicts St
Martin of Tours giving half his
cloak to a naked beggar.

The main altar of Iglesia de San Placido
in Malasaña painted by Claudio Coello

MANUELA MALASAÑA

The daughter of Juan Manuel
Malasaña, a craftsman and hero
of the 1808 uprising *(see p16)*,
Manuela Malasaña died at the
age of 16 in the struggle against
Napoleon. She was a seam-
stress who, according to local
legend, was caught carrying a
pair of scissors by the French
and was subsequently shot
for possession of a concealed
weapon. In 1961 Calle de
Manuela Malasaña, which lies
between Fuencarral and San
Bernardo where the Monteleón
artillery park had been, was
named after this local heroine.

Ribera's sculptured door at the Cuartel del Conde Duque

Cuartel del Conde Duque ⓲

Calle del Conde Duque 9–11. **Map 2** D4. ⓘ *91 588 58 24.* Ⓜ *Noviciado, San Bernardo.* ⓞ *10am–2pm, 5:30–9pm Tue–Sat, 10:30am–2:30pm Sun.* ⓖ *by prior arrangement.*

THIS ENORMOUS rectangular complex is named after Gaspar de Guzmán (1587–1645), Conde Duque de Olivares. As a minister and a favourite of Felipe IV *(see p20)*, the count had a palace on this site. After his death, the palace was neglected and, with the passage of time, fell into ruin. Subsequently, the plot came to be divided into two distinct sections. On one section, the Palacio de Liria was built for the Duke of Alba. On the other, the barracks for Los Guardias de Corps were constructed between the years 1717 and 1730 by Pedro de Ribera, who adorned them with a Baroque façade.

The three-floor barracks were in use for over a century but, in 1869, they suffered a major fire and eventually fell into a state of total dilapidation. A hundred years later, in 1969, Madrid's city hall made the decision to restore the old army barracks. The building now houses a police station, council offices, a municipal library and a cultural centre with two exhibition halls. The cultural centre is a venue for major concerts, usually using marquees in one of the three interior patios. Jazz and flamenco festivals are often staged in the main patio. The entrance to the cultural centre is the uppermost door, opposite Calle de Montserrat. The main door of the Cuartel del Conde Duque is a Baroque masterpiece carved in stone by Pedro de Ribera.

Palacio de Liria ⓳

Calle de la Princesa 20. **Map 1** C4. ⓘ *91 547 53 02.* Ⓜ *Ventura Rodríguez.* ⓞ *by appointment.*

THE LAVISH BUT much restored Palacio de Liria was completed by Ventura Rodríguez in 1780. Once the residence of the Alba family, and still

LA MOVIDA

With Franco's death in 1975 came a new period of personal and artistic liberty. For the young, this was translated into the freedom to stay out late, drinking and sometimes sampling drugs. The phenomenon was known as *la movida*, "the action", and it was at its most intense in Madrid. Although analysts at the time saw it as having serious intellectual content, *la movida* has had few lasting cultural results, except for the emergence of satirical film director Pedro Almodóvar.

Poster for Almodóvar's *Women on the Verge of a Nervous Breakdown*

owned by the Duchess, it may be visited by prior appointment only. The sumptuous palace rooms are home to the Albas' outstanding collection of art and Flemish tapestries. The walls are adorned with paintings by many famous masters, among them Titian, Rubens and Rembrandt.

Spanish art itself is particularly well represented, and the Albas' collection includes a number of major works by Goya *(see p26)*. One such significant canvas is his 1795 portrait of the Duchess of Alba. Also featured are several interesting works by El Greco *(see p139)*, Zurbarán and Velázquez *(see p26)*.

Room adorned with paintings by Goya in the Palacio de Liria

Castizos of Madrid

THE TRUE WORKING-CLASS *Madrileños,* whose families have lived in the neighbourhoods of Old Madrid, Chamberí and Cuatro Caminos for many generations, are known as *castizos.* Around 1850, in their revolt against the bourgeoisie, who were basking in the Romantic and patriotic cultural revolution that followed the defeat of the French earlier in the 19th century, the *castizos* decided to reclaim their proud heritage. The Madrid equivalent of London's Cockneys, *los castizos Madrileños* not only revived their district fiestas, one of the world's best neighbourhood-bonding traditions, but also reinvented costumes to go with them and formed numerous associations that still thrive today. At any of the traditional Madrid fiestas or *romerías* (processions) you will see the *castizos,* or *majos* (dandies) as they are known, with their *manolas,* or partners, attired in what is now their smart, traditional uniform.

Religious celebration – festivities on vehicle floats

Typical manola *costume* *consists of a flowery headscarf with at least one carnation in the front, an* alfombra *(literally translated as carpet), which is actually a huge embroidered shawl, or* mantón de Manila, *worn over the shoulders, and a* falda vestida *(long dress), sometimes with an apron.*

Carnation on the headscarf

Alfombra – shawl with a long fringe

Colourful dress (falda vestida)

Black-and-white *parpusa* (hat)

White *barbosa* (shirt)

Black *alares* (trousers)

Men's clothes are *referred to in* castizo argot*: black or black-and-white check* parpusa *(cap), a white* barbosa *(shirt), a black* chupín *(waistcoat), a black or black-and-white check* chupa *(jacket), a* safo *(white handkerchief), a* peluco *(pocket watch), a red carnation in the buttonhole, black or black-and-white check* alares *(trousers),* picantes *(socks) and shining* calcos *(shoes).*

In May, *the* castizos *are out in force during the Dos de Mayo fiesta. On 15 May is the Fiesta de San Isidro, with a* romería *from the Puerta de Toledo down to the Río Manzanares. The next major fiestas are on 13 June at San Antonio de la Florida; and 15 August, with the Fiesta de la Virgen de Paloma, a castizo favourite. Castizo processions include the Romería de San Blas on 3 February, and the Romería de San Eugenio on 14 November.*

FURTHER AFIELD

S EVERAL OF MADRID's best sights, including interesting but little-known museums, lie outside the city centre. The Museo de la Ciudad gives an overview of the development of the city, with models of buildings and districts, while the Museo de América displays artifacts from Spain's former colonies. There is a wealth of historic buildings outside the city centre, ranging from the Egyptian Templo de Debod to the Puerta de Toledo, a triumphal arch

Mosaic by Miró on the Palacio de Congresos y Exposiciones in Azca

begun in 1813 on the orders of José I (Joseph Bonaparte), to the old-style apartment building of La Corrala. There are a number of other attractions surrounding the centre of Madrid. To the north lies the modern commercial district of Azca, with skyscrapers, office blocks and upmarket shops. If you need to escape from the bustle of the city for a while, west of Old Madrid, across the Río Manzanares, is Madrid's vast, green recreation ground, the Casa de Campo.

SIGHTS AT A GLANCE

Historic Buildings
Arco de la Victoria ❷
Estación de Príncipe Pío ⑰
La Corrala ⑪
Puente de Segovia and
  Río Manzanares ⑬
Puerta de Toledo ⑫
Real Fábrica de Tapices ❾
Sala del Canal de Isabel II ❸
Templo de Debod ⑯

Churches and Convents
Ermita de San Antonio de la
  Florida ⑮

Museums and Galleries
Museo Casa de la Moneda ❽
Museo de América ❶
Museo de Ciencias Naturales ❺
Museo de la Ciudad ❻
Museo Nacional Ferroviario ⑩

Squares, Parks & Districts
Azca ❹
Casa de Campo ⑭
Plaza de Toros de Las
  Ventas ❼

| 0 kilometres | | 2 |
| 0 miles | | 1 |

KEY

    Main sightseeing area

    Parks and open spaces

🚉 Railway station

═ Highway/Motorway

▬ Major road

═ Minor road

SIGHTS OUTSIDE THE CITY CENTRE

Old and new – the Mirador del Faro alongside the Museo de América

Museo de América ❶

Avenida de los Reyes Católicos 6.
[91 549 26 41. **⦿** Moncloa.
◯ 10am–3pm Tue–Sat, 10am–
2:30pm Sun & public hols.
▨ (free on Sun). **♿**

A UNIQUE COLLECTION of artifacts relating to Spain's
colonization of the Americas
is housed in this fine museum.
Many of the exhibits, which
range from prehistoric to more
recent times, were brought to
Europe by the early explorers
of the New World *(see p14)*.

The collection is arranged
on the first and second floors,
and individual rooms are given
cultural themes such as society,
religion and communication.
Documentation is given about
the Atlantic voyages made
by the first explorers, as well
as some artifacts they found.

For many visitors, the highlight of the museum is the rare
Mayan *Códice Tro-cortesiano*
(AD 1250–1500) from Mexico.
This is a type of parchment
illustrated with hieroglyphics
of scenes from everyday life.

Also worth seeing are the
Treasure of the Quimbayas, a
collection of pre-Columbian
gold and silver objects from
around AD 500–1000, and the
collection of contemporary
folk art from some of Spain's
former American colonies.

Arco de la Victoria ❷

Avenida de la Victoria. **Map** 1 A1.
⦿ Argüelles.

E RECTED IN 1956, this white
arch was designed to celebrate the Nationalist victory in
the 1936–9 Spanish Civil War
(see p18). General Franco
would have passed by it each
time he came to Madrid from
his home in the Palacio de El
Pardo *(see p134)*. Topped by
a green sculpture of a chariot
with horses, the arch stands
39 m (128 ft) tall – one of the
city's highest commemorative
puertas (gateways). The architects, Pascual Bravo and
Modesto López Otero, built a
room high up inside the arch.
It contains a 25-sq m (270-sq
ft) model of the neighbouring
university and the plans for
the arch itself. However, it is
not open to the public.

Nearby is the **Faro de
Moncloa** observation tower.
Opened in 1992, it measures
92 m (300 ft). The tower offers
excellent views of Madrid and
the Guadarrama mountains.

The imposing Arco de la Victoria

Sala del Canal de Isabel II ❸

Calle de Santa Engracia 125. **[** 91
445 10 00. **⦿** Ríos Rosas. **◯** 11am–
2pm, 5–8:30pm Tue–Sat, 10am–2pm
Sun & public hols. **●** 1 Jan & 25
Dec. **♿**

T HIS RENOVATED WATER tower
is used to great effect as a
venue for photographic exhibitions but, on the whole, most
visitors come to marvel at its

**Sala del Canal de Isabel II, a water
tower turned exhibition centre**

complex construction. In the
late 19th century the water
supply for Madrid was based
on a project patronized by
Isabel II *(see p21)* in 1851 and
known as Canal de Isabel II,
the name given to Madrid's
water company. The first dam
was built in the Lozoya Valley,
about 80 km (50 miles) north
of Madrid in the Guadarrama
mountains, and a duct carried
the water south to a reservoir.

More reservoirs were built to
cope with the capital's ever-
increasing needs but, in 1903,
the development of the high-
lying suburbs of Chamberí
and Cuatro Caminos dictated
the need for a water tower to
supply new pipes by gravity.
Martín y Montalvo was the
engineer enlisted to carry out
the task. He designed a
polygonal tower of brick and
iron, 36 m (118 ft) high, sur-
mounted by a 1,500-sq m
(16,145-sq ft) tank resting on
an iron ring. Work started in
1908, and by 1911 the water
tower was finished at a cost
of nearly 350,000 pesetas. It
was in service until 1952.

The regional government of
Madrid decided to restore the
tower in 1985, taking out the
water works but retaining the
huge tank. Access to the exhibition floors within the tower
has been made possible by
hydraulically driven elevators
(lifts) and steel staircases.

Bordering the tower are the
busy Calle de Santa Engracia
and the gardens and turf that
form a roof over one of the
major underground reservoirs
of the Canal de Isabel II.

Azca ❹

⚫ *Nuevos Ministerios, Santiago Bernabeú.*

IN 1969, WORK BEGAN on the development of this mini-Manhattan along the west side of the Paseo de la Castellana. It stretches from the **Nuevos Ministerios** complex in the south to the **Palacio de Congresos y Exposiciones** in the north. The idea was to create a modern commercial area away from the congested city centre. Today, some 30,000 people work here.

By day Azca is a mecca for shoppers. A branch of the department store El Corte Inglés *(see p164)* runs alongside Nuevos Ministerios metro and railway station, and there is a Moda Centro Comercial mall served by Lima metro. Across from the Plaza de Lima is the **Estadio Santiago Bernabeu**, the home of Real Madrid Football Club. It was built in 1950, but has since had a few facelifts, especially for the 1982 World Cup Finals.

Major companies operate in the tower blocks, alongside hotels, apartments, cinemas, restaurants and bars. The elderly are drawn by bingo halls, while the young throng the discos at the weekends.

In the centre of Azca is the multi-level pedestrian **Plaza Pablo Ruiz Picasso** with trees, benches, fountains and walkways. If driving, do not try to negotiate the maze of roads underneath the complex unless you are very sure about where you intend to park or emerge.

Azca is dominated by the sleek, aluminium-clad **Torre Picasso**, Madrid's tallest office building. Completed in 1989, it has 46 floors, bronzed windows and a heliport. It was designed by Minoru Yamasaki, architect of the twin towers of New York's World Trade Centre. The 18 elevators can carry 60,000 people a day.

The **Torre Europa** on Plaza de Lima is another notable building. Designed by Miguel Oriol e Ybarra and completed in 1982, its exterior concrete supports incorporate a clock. As well as 28 floors of offices, it has three commercial floors below street level.

The rust-coloured **Banco Bilbao Vizcaya** on Azca's south corner was designed by Francisco Javier Sáenz de Oiza. Built in 1980, it stands over the underground rail line between Chamartín and Atocha.

Museo de Ciencias Naturales ❺

Paseo de la Castellana 80. 📞 *91 411 13 28.* ⚫ *Gregorio Marañón, Nuevos Ministerios.* ⬜ *10am–6pm Tue –Fri, 10am–8pm Sat, 10am– 2:30pm Sun & public hols.* ⬤ *1 Jan, 1 May, 25 Dec.* 🎟 📷 *by prior arrangement.* ♿

THIS MUSEUM, built in 1897, contains 16,400 minerals, 220 meteorites, 30,000 birds and mammals and many more items in its archives. The entrance on the left leads to the Rhythm of Nature section.

Inside the modern Origins of Life section of Madrid's Museo de Ciencias Naturales

This is an ecological display of numerous examples of wildlife, from exotic birds to rare animals, insects and butterflies. Lions, tigers and deer stare out from the walls, while the shelves are heavy with bottled lizards, fish and snakes. An interactive computer display room provides valuable insight into the sounds and habitats of animals and birds.

A recent addition to this part of the museum is a cross-section of the Atapuerca site near Burgos, north of Madrid, where Europe's earliest human remains (some 780,000 years old) were discovered in 1997. There is also a huge African elephant. Shot by the Duke of Alba in the Sudan in 1916, the elephant's skin was sent back to Spain and reassembled.

The right entrance to the museum, by the gift shop, leads to a modern two-floor section, with displays on the origins of the earth and of life. The star of the show is the 1.8-million-year-old skeleton of *Megatherium americanum*, a bear-like creature from the late Cenozoic period found in Argentina in 1788. Nearby is a Glyptodon (giant armadillo), also from Argentina, and a life-size reproduction of a Diplodocus dinosaur skeleton found in the United States.

The Industrial Engineers' School is also housed in the museum building and behind are the headquarters of Spain's state scientific institute, CSIC. Opposite the entrances to the museum is a pleasant terrace bar which looks out over a small park with a fountain and a statue of Isabel I *(see p20)*. Beyond the park is the Paseo de la Castellana.

The Torre Europa rising above the commercial centre of Azca

Interior of the Museo de la Ciudad arranged around a central atrium

Museo de la Ciudad ❻

Calle del Príncipe de Vergara 140.
📞 *91 588 65 99.* Ⓜ *Cruz del Rayo.*
🕐 *10am–2pm, 4–6pm (5–7pm Jul–Aug) Tue–Fri, 10am–2pm Sat & Sun.* ⬤ *public hols.* ♿

THIS MODERN MUSEUM in the northeast of Madrid shows how the city has evolved since the earliest settlement, using detailed panoramic models.

The museum consists of five floors built around an octagonal atrium. Here stands a copy of the Mariblanca statue in the Puerta del Sol (see p44). Right of the entrance is a bookshop. The ground and first floors house temporary exhibitions.

The displays on the second floor concern Madrid's utility companies. A subject that fascinates the many school-children who visit the museum is how Madrid gets its water from the mountains. Also on this floor is a huge model of the city, from Barajas Airport to Cuatro Ventas airfield.

The third floor deals with the history of Madrid from prehistory to Bourbon times. As well as books, charts and maps, there are models of Old Madrid, some monuments and the Palacio Real (see pp54–7).

The fourth floor is devoted to the 19th and 20th centuries, and has a superb model of the new part of the city from Plaza de Colón (see p98) to Torre Europa (see p109). Nearby there is also an impressive model of Plaza de Toros de Las Ventas, Madrid's bullring.

Plaza de Toros de Las Ventas ❼

Calle de Alcalá 237. 📞 *91 356 22 00.* Ⓜ *Ventas.* 🕐 *for bullfights and concerts only.* **Museo Taurino** 📞 *91 725 18 57.* 🕐 *Mar–Sep: 9:30am–2:30pm Tue–Fri & Sun; Oct–Feb: 9:30am–2:30pm Mon–Fri.* ♿

WHATEVER YOUR opinion of bullfighting, Las Ventas is undoubtedly one of the most beautiful bullrings in Spain. Built in 1929 in Neo-Mudéjar style, it replaced the city's original bullring, which stood near the Puerta de Alcalá (see p66). Its horseshoe arches around the outer galleries and elaborate tilework decoration make it an attractive venue for the *corridas* (bullfights), held from May to October. The statues outside the bullring are monuments to two renowned Spanish bullfighters, Antonio Bienvenida and José Cubero.

Adjoining the bullring is the **Museo Taurino**. This contains a varied collection of bull-fighting memorabilia, including portraits and sculptures of famous matadors, as well as the heads of several bulls killed during fights at Las Ventas. Visitors can examine bullfighters' capes and *banderillas* – sharp darts used to wound the bull. The gory highlight of the exhibition, for some people, is the blood-drenched *traje de luces* worn by Manolete during his fateful bullfight at Linares in Andalusia in 1947. Also on display is a costume which belonged to Juanita Cruz, a

female bullfighter of the 1930s who was forced, in the face of prejudice, to leave Spain. In September and October the bullring is used as a venue for a season of rock concerts.

Museo Casa de la Moneda ❽

Calle del Doctor Esquerdo 36. 📞 *91 566 65 44.* 🕐 *Sep–Jul: 10am–2:30pm, 5–7:30pm Tue–Fri, 10am–2pm Sat & Sun.* ⬤ *Aug & public hols.* 🌐 *www.fnmt.es/museo*

THE SPANISH MINT and stamp factory is located in a vast granite building, and visitors pass through metal detectors on entering and leaving. The museum, in the north side of the building, traces the history of currency, from early trading in salt, shells and bracelets up to the Euro – the monetary unit of the European Union.

Coins feature prominently, with maps and photographs complementing displays of Greek and Roman coins. The earliest coins have images of mythical gods; the picture of Cybele, mother of the gods, on a Roman coin from 78 BC is similar to the sculpture in the Plaza de Cibeles (see p67).

As well as later Roman coins endowed with more symbolic images, there are Visigothic and Moorish coins. Early Moorish coins are inscribed in Latin and later ones in Arabic.

There are also engravings for currency notes, stamps, medals and official documents.

Plaza de Toros de Las Ventas, Madrid's beautiful Neo-Mudéjar bullring

The Art of Bullfighting

BULLFIGHTING IS A sacrificial ritual in which men (and a few women) pit themselves against an animal bred for the ring. In this "authentic religious drama", as poet Federico García Lorca *(see p26)* described it, the spectator experiences the same intensity of fear and exaltation as the matador. There are three stages, or *tercios*, in the *corrida* (bullfight). The first two are aimed at progressively weakening the bull. In

Poster for a bullfight

the third, the matador moves in for the kill. Despite opposition on the grounds of cruelty, bullfighting is still very popular. For many Spaniards, talk of banning bullfighting is an assault on the essence of their being. For them, the *toreo*, the art of bullfighting, is a noble part of their heritage. However, fights today are often debased by practices designed to disadvantage the bull, in particular shaving its horns to make them blunt.

*The **toro bravo (fighting bull)**, bred for courage and aggression, enjoys a full life prior to its time in the ring. Bulls must be at least four years old before they can fight.*

Manolete is regarded by most followers of bullfighting as one of Spain's greatest ever matadors. He was finally gored to death by the bull Islero at Linares, Jaén, in 1947.

The matador wears a *traje de luces* (suit of lights), a colourful silk outfit embroidered with gold sequins.

Joselito was a leading matador, famous for his purist style. He displayed superb skill with the capa (red cape) and the muleta (matador's stick). Now retired, he still hopes to return to the ruedos (bullring).

Banderillas, barbed darts, are thrust into the bull's back muscles to weaken them.

THE BULLRING

The *corrida* audience is seated in the *tendidos* (stalls) or in the *palcos* (balcony), where the *presidencia* (president's box) is situated. Opposite are the *puerta de cuadrillas*, through which the matador and team arrive, and the *arrastre de toros* (exit for bulls). Before entering the ring, the matadors wait in a *callejón* (corridor) behind *barreras* and *burladeros* (barriers). Horses are kept in the *patio de caballos* and the bulls in the *corrales*.

Plan of a typical bullring

KEY

- Tendidos
- Palcos
- Presidencia
- Puerta de cuadrillas
- Arrastre de toros
- Callejón
- Barreras
- Burladeros
- Patio de caballos
- Corrales

Real Fábrica de Tapices ❾

Calle de Fuenterrabia 2. **Map** 8 F5.
91 434 05 51. Ⓜ *Menéndez Pelayo.*
◯ *9am–12:30pm Mon–Fri.* **Museum**
◯ *Mon–Fri 10am–2pm.*

Founded by Felipe V in 1721, the Royal Tapestry Factory alone survives from the factories opened by the Bourbons in the 18th century. In 1889 the factory was moved to this building, just south of the Parque del Retiro *(see p77)*.

Visitors can see the making by hand of the carpets and tapestries, a process which has changed little since the factory was built. Goya *(see p26)* and his brother-in-law Francisco Bayeu drew cartoons on which the tapestries for the royal family were based. Some of the cartoons are on display here, in the newly opened museum; others are in the Prado *(see pp80–83)*. Several tapestries can be seen at the Palacio de El Pardo *(see p134)* and at El Escorial *(see pp122–5)*. Today one of the factory's main tasks is making and repairing the beautiful carpets decorating the Hotel Ritz *(see p68)*.

Museo Nacional Ferroviario ❿

Paseo de las Delicias 61. *91 506 83 33.* Ⓜ *Delicias.* ◯ *10am–3pm Tue–Sun.* (free on Sat). book in advance. W www.ffe.es/delicias

Although railways had existed in the country since 1848, it was only in 1880 that Madrid's first proper railway terminus opened – the station of Delicias. This was the main station for Portugal, and it remained in use until 1971.

In 1984 the station re-opened as a railway museum. The majority of exhibits, in the form of trains, are located in the main terminus on tracks next to the original platforms. There are more than 30 locomotives –

1950s' Talgo locomotive at the railway museum

Cafeteria of the Museo Nacional Ferroviario, set in a 1930s' dining car

steam, diesel and electric – as well as rolling stock. Explanatory plaques give details and describe the routes of the locomotives. You can explore some of the carriages, including a 1930s' dining car that now serves as the site's cafeteria.

One of the most interesting engines is "La Pucheta", a steam locomotive built in 1884 by Sharp Stewart in Britain. Its water supply was on top of the boiler, in a container that resembles a bowler hat.

A 1931 electric locomotive, built in Spain, earned itself the nickname "The Lioness" because of its enormous weight – more than 150 tonnes. This was the heaviest engine ever used by the Spanish state railways (RENFE), as well as the longest of its kind in Spain, measuring approximately 25 m (82 ft).

Also of special interest is a 1950s' Talgo. These Spanish-designed express trains revolutionized railway transport in the country, and this model was in service until 1971. The train was light, with a very low centre of gravity, reduced height, and an articulated system, all of which enabled it to travel much faster than conventional carriages.

The 1928 wooden-sided carriage, the ZZ-307 Coche Salon, was the most luxurious the West Railway Company had to offer. Peering through the windows, you can still see an elegantly laid table in the dining room, the sleeping compartments and a tiny galley.

One of the popular sights on show is the Mikado, a steam locomotive built in 1960, which has been cut away to reveal the mysteries of steam propulsion. This engine was in service until 1975, when the use of regular steam-hauled services came to an end in Spain.

To one side of the station are four large halls that house detailed model train layouts, scale models of train stations and railway memorabilia, including signals, lights, telegraphs and photographs.

La Corrala **⓫**

Calle de Mesón de Paredes, between Calle Tribulete & Calle del Sombrerete. **Map** 4 F5. ⓦ *Lavapiés*. ◗ *to the public.*

A *zarzuela* performance, using La Corrala as a backdrop

CORRALAS ARE timber-framed apartment blocks, or tenements, built during the 19th century mainly in poorer parts of the city, especially in the neighbourhood of Lavapiés. The buildings were arranged around an interior courtyard; balconies overlooked the courtyard and provided access to individual apartments.

La Corrala exemplifies this type of housing. Construction began in 1872, but some of the building permits were not in order, which may explain why only half of the building seems to exist. The courtyard, rather than being completely surrounded by the building, opens out on to a plaza. Its exposure means that there are good views of the building, and of the ubiquitous laundry hanging from the balconies.

In 1977, La Corrala was declared a monument of historic interest, and two years later it underwent complete restoration. On summer nights, La Corrala is now used as a backdrop to outdoor *zarzuela,* or light opera *(see p75),* which is staged in the plaza.

In the near vicinity are several other corralas. One can be seen on the corner of Calle de Miguel Servet with Calle del Espino, one at Calle de Provisiones 12 and another at Calle de la Esperanza 11.

Puerta de Toledo **⓬**

Glorieta de Puerta de Toledo. **Map** 4 D5. ⓦ *Puerta de Toledo.*

THE CONSTRUCTION of this triumphal arch began in 1813 on the orders of French-born Joseph Bonaparte, José I *(see p17).* It was intended to commemorate his accession to the Spanish throne after the 1808 rout of Madrid. But in 1814, after a short-lived reign, José I fled Spain and was replaced by Fernando VII *(see p17).* By the time the arch was completed in 1827, by the architect Antonio López Aguado, it had to be dedicated to Fernando VII.

The Puerta de Toledo is one of Madrid's two remaining city gates, and is topped by a group of sculptures that represent a personification of Spain. On either side of these are the allegorical figures of Genius and the Arts. All were carved in their entirety from Colmenar stone by Ramón Barba and Valeriano Salvatierra, and are flanked on each side by sculptures based on military themes.

The majestic form of the Puerta de Toledo, one of Madrid's two remaining triumphal arches

Puente de Segovia and Río Manzanares ⑬

Calle de Segovia. ⬗ *Puerta del Angel.*

PUENTE DE SEGOVIA, a grand granite bridge over the Río Manzanares, was commissioned by Felipe II *(see p20)* not long after he had decided to establish his court in Madrid. The bridge was to be a main entry point to Madrid and he chose Juan de Herrera, his favourite architect, to build it. Construction began in 1582. The bridge, with its nine arches topped with decorative bosses, was rebuilt in 1682.

Further downstream is the magnificent pedestrian bridge, **Puente de Toledo**, built between 1718 and 1732 for Felipe V *(see p21)*. The architect was Pedro de Ribera.

The Manzanares, which is more of a stream than a river, never deserved such splendid bridges. It was the butt of many jokes; a German ambassador by the name of Rhebiner once said the river was the best in Europe because it had the advantage of being "navigable by horse and carriage". Alexandre Dumas (1802–70), author of *The Three Musketeers*, wrote of the Manzanares during his visit to Madrid that "however hard I looked for it, I could not find it".

The river now has several dams, and the introduced fish and ducks have been able to survive, showing that the water is fairly clean. Rising in the Sierra de Guadarrama and eventually joining the River Tagus, the river forms a link between Spain's capital and Lisbon, the capital of Portugal.

Casa de Campo ⑭

Avenida de Portugal. 📞 *91 463 63 34.* ⬗ *Batán, Lago, Príncipe Pío.*

THIS FORMER ROYAL hunting ground of pine forests and scrubland extends over 1,740 ha (4,300 acres) of western Madrid. Its range of amenities and proximity to the centre make it a popular recreation area for *Madrileños*. Among its attractions are tennis courts, swimming pools, a boating lake, funfair – the **Parque de Atracciones** with over 50 rides – and the **Zoo-Aquarium**. In summer the park also stages concerts.

One way to visit the park and take in the city's sights is to ride the **Teleférico** (cable car), which connects the Parque del Oeste with the Casa de Campo.

Tiger from the zoo at Casa de Campo

🦌 **Zoo-Aquarium**
📞 *91 512 37 70.* ⬗ *Batán.* ⏰ *10am–dusk daily.* 🎫 ♿
🎡 **Parque de Atracciones**
📞 *91 463 29 00.* ⬗ *Batán.* ⏰ *Oct–Apr: from noon Sat & Sun; May–Sep from noon daily. Closing times vary from month to month, check locally.* 🎫
🚡 **Teleférico**
Paseo del Pintor Rosales. 📞 *91 541 74 50.* ⬗ *Argüelles.* ⏰ *Oct–Mar: noon–dusk Sat, Sun & public hols; Apr–Sep: 11am–dusk daily.* 🎫 ♿

Ermita de San Antonio de la Florida ⑮

Glorieta San Antonio de la Florida 5. 📞 *91 542 07 22.* ⬗ *Príncipe Pío.* ⏰ *10am–2pm, 4–8pm Tue–Fri, 10am–2pm Sat & Sun.* ⬤ *public hols.* 🎫 *(free Wed & Sun).* 🚫 ♿

GOYA ENTHUSIASTS should not miss an opportunity to visit this remarkable Neo-Classical church, built during the reign of Carlos IV *(see p21)*. Standing on the site of two previous churches, the present building is dedicated to St Anthony and is named after the pastureland of La Florida, on which the original church was built.

It took Goya *(see p26)* just four months in 1798 to paint the cupola with an immense fresco. It depicts St Anthony raising a murdered man from the dead so that he can prove innocent the saint's falsely accused father. Ordinary characters from late 18th-century

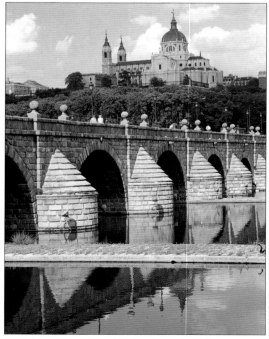

The buttressed arches of Puente de Segovia over the Río Manzanares

Egyptian temple of Debod, with two of its original gateways

Madrid are also featured in the painting. They include lurking low-life types and lively *majas* – shrewd but elegant women of the people. The fresco is considered to be one of Goya's finest works. The artist, who died in 1828, lies buried under the dome of this church.

Templo de Debod ⓰

Paseo del Pintor Rosales. **Map** 1 B5. 91 409 61 65. Plaza de España, Ventura Rodríguez. 10am–2pm Sat & Sun; Apr–Sep: 10am–2pm, 6–8pm Tue–Fri; Oct–Mar: 10am–2pm, 4– 6pm Tue–Fri. public hols.

THE AUTHENTIC Egyptian temple of Debod was built in the 2nd century BC. It was given to Spain in 1968 by the Egyptian government as a tribute to Spanish engineers involved in rescuing ancient monuments from the flood-waters of the Aswan Dam on the River Nile. The temple is carved with shallow reliefs depicting Amen, a Theban god with a ram's head, symboli-zing life and fertility, to whom the temple is dedicated.

Situated on high ground above the Río Manzanares, and surrounded by the pleasantly landscaped gardens of the **Parque del Oeste**, the temple stands in a line with two of its original three gateways. From this point in the park there are sweeping views over Casa de Campo park, stretching as far as the Guadarrama mountains in the distance. The Parque del Oeste is the site of the former Montaña barracks. In 1936, they were stormed by the people of Madrid in their hunger for weaponry. It was a desperate bid on their part to arm themselves against General Franco's encroaching army at the start of the Spanish Civil War *(see p18)*. It is also a place where many lost their lives to Napoleon in 1808.

Nearby is the **Paseo del Pintor Rosales**, popular for its pavement (sidewalk) cafés.

Estación de Príncipe Pío ⓱

Paseo de la Florida 2. **Map** 3 A1. 90 224 02 02. Príncipe Pío.

ALSO KNOWN AS Estación del Norte, this railway station was opened in 1880 to supply train services between Madrid and the north of Spain. Built by French engineers Biarez, Grasset and Mercier, iron from French and Belgian foundries was its main component.

In 1915, the station's look was enhanced by Mudéjar-style pavilions designed by Demetrio Ribes. The entrance façade was added by architect Luis Martínez Ribes in 1926. Speculators hope to turn this part of the station, currently in ruins, into a shopping centre.

The main part of the station, which has been remodelled, is a major transport interchange for trains, the metro and buses. Above the train platforms is a splendid lattice-work canopy. Looking out along the railway lines, it is possible to see the distant Sierra de Guadarrama.

The elegant main entrance to the Estación de Príncipe Pío

BEYOND MADRID

BEYOND MADRID

S PAIN'S VAST CENTRAL PLATEAU *consists mainly of wheat fields and awe-some expanses of sienna and ochre plains which exude an empty beauty. Yet it also has mountains, gorges, forests and lakes filled with wildlife, while the towns and cities are permeated with history, reflected in some stunning architecture – Toledo's Gothic cathedral, Segovia's alcazar and the 15th-century castle at Manzanares el Real.*

It is surprising how quickly one can escape past Madrid's dormitory towns and industrial estates to the real countryside. There is plenty of superb scenery and good walking country in the sierras to the north – a refuge for city dwellers who go there to ski in winter or sail and wind-surf during the torrid summers. The Sierra Norte offers a paradise for bird-watchers, especially around the Moorish town of Buitrago del Lozoya.

In the western foothills of these mountains stands El Escorial, the royal monastery-palace built by Felipe II, from which he ruled his empire. Close by is the Valle de los Caídos, the war monument erected by Franco. The smaller royal palace of El Pardo is on the outskirts of Madrid, and south of the city is the 18th-century Aranjuez summer palace, set in lush parkland.

Historic towns include Alcalá de Henares – the birthplace of Cervantes, Sigüenza, with its impressive castle-parador, and Chinchón, where local garlic, wine and anis are sold beneath the creaking wooden balconies of its medieval plaza. Segovia, from where Felipe II's predecessors ruled Castile, is packed at weekends as visitors sample the famous roast lamb and suckling-pig and stop to admire its aqueduct – the largest Roman structure in Spain.

Toledo, which was the capital of Visigothic Spain, is an outstanding museum city. Its rich architectural and artistic heritage derives from a coalescence of Muslim, Christian and Jewish cultures with medieval and Renaissance ideas.

The picturesque Monasterio de El Parral in Segovia

◁ **Celebration of Mass in the church of the Monasterio de Santa María de El Paular**

Beyond Madrid Pictorial Map

Sᴛʀᴇᴛᴄʜɪɴɢ ᴀʟᴏɴɢ ᴛʜᴇ northern horizon of the province of Madrid are the peaks of the Sierra de Guadarrama. Reaching to 2,430 m (7,972 ft), they are often capped with snow until June. There are many hiking and even skiing opportunities in these mountains. Below, in the pine-scented southern folds of the Guadarrama, basks the monolithic monastery of El Escorial.

To the south lies the *meseta*, Spain's vast central plateau. Thanks to the mountains, rivers flow towards the arid plains, creating fertile valleys where olives grow. The historic towns of Castile nestle amid the rocky promontories. The River Jarama joins the Tagus *(Tajo)* near the 18th-century Royal Summer Palace and gardens in Aranjuez. Downstream it curls around ancient Toledo.

The 15th-century Casa de los Picos *(see p128)* in Segovia

Vast, fertile plain of the Spanish *meseta*

Sɪɢʜᴛs ᴀᴛ ᴀ Gʟᴀɴᴄᴇ

Alcalá de Henares ⓬
Buitrago del Lozoya ❽
Chinchón ⓯
El Escorial pp122–5 ❶
Guadalajara ⓫
Illescas ⓱
La Granja de San Ildefonso ❻
Manzanares el Real ❸
Monasterio de Santa María de El Paular ❺
Museo del Aire ⓮
Palacio de El Pardo ⓭
Palacio Real de Aranjuez ⓰
Santa Cruz del Valle de los Caídos ❷
Segovia see pp128–9 ❼
Sierra Centro de Guadarrama ❹
Sierra Norte ❾
Sigüenza ❿
Toledo see pp136–41 ⓲

Exterior of Casa-Museo de El Greco *(see p139)* in Toledo

SEGOVIA ❼

LA GRANJA DE SAN ILDEFONSO ❻
REVENGA
MONASTE. DE SANTA MA DE EL PAU.
N603
SIERRA CENTRO DE ❹ GUADARRAMA
NAVACER.
MANZAN. EL R
GUADARRAMA
SANTA CRUZ ❷ DEL VALLE DE LOS CAÍDOS ❶
EL ESCORIAL

MÓSTOLES

Rio Guadarrama

ILLE.

TOLEDO ⓲

GETTING AROUND

The best way to explore sites beyond Madrid is with a car and a good map reader – signposts can be confusing. Six toll-free divided highways (dual carriageways), the NI to NVI, and one toll highway (motorway), the N401 to Toledo, fan out from the city, linked by the M30 and M40 ring roads that enable you to avoid Madrid's traffic. If possible, do not travel at peak weekend times. Tour buses serve the major sites. Scheduled bus services can to be limited and slow. Railways serve the historic cities.

SIERRA NORTE **9**

MAJAELRAYO

PRADENA
DEL RINCÓN

Embalse
de Alcorlo

10

SIGÜENZA

Embalse
de Belena

8 BUITRAGO
DEL LOZOYA

TAMAJÓN

UADRÓN
ZOYA

Embalse
de El Atazar

Río Jarama

PUEBLA DE
BELENA

Río Henares

JADRAQUE

NII

UCEDA

SOTO DEL REAL
alse de
illana

TORRELAGUNA

TORRE DEL
BURGO

NII

COLMENAR
VIEJO

NI

11

KEY

	Highway (motorway)
	Major road
	Minor road
	Scenic route
	River
☼	Viewpoint

mbalse de
l Pardo

EL PARDO

13

GUADALAJARA

AZUQUECA DE
HENARES

PALACIO DE EL PARDO

MAJADAHONDA

12 ALCALÁ DE
HENARES

MADRID

SEE ALSO

• **Where to Stay** pp150–51

• **Restaurants, Cafés and Bars** p163

MUSEO DEL AIRE

NIII

NIV

CLEMPOZUELOS

15 CHINCHÓN

16
PALACIO REAL DE ARANJUEZ

Tajo

N400

0 km   10

0 miles   10

The tranquil Montes de Toledo

El Escorial ❶

Fresco by Luca Giordano

Felipe II's imposing grey palace of San Lorenzo de El Escorial stands out against the foothills of the Sierra de Guadarrama to the northwest of Madrid. It was built between 1563 and 1584 in honour of St Lawrence, and its unornamented severity set a new architectural style which became one of the most influential in Spain. The interior was conceived as a mausoleum and contemplative retreat rather than a splendid residence. Its artistic wealth, which includes some of the most important works of art of the royal Habsburg collections, is concentrated in the museums, chapterhouses, church, royal pantheon and library. In contrast, the Royal Apartments are remarkably austere.

★ Royal Pantheon
The funerary urns of Spanish monarchs line the marble mausoleum.

Tourist entrance

Bourbon Palace

Architectural Museum

Sala de Batallas (closed)

Basilica
The highlight of this huge, partially decorated church is the lavish altarpiece. The main chapel houses statues of Felipe II and Carlos I (Holy Roman Emperor Charles V) at prayer.

The Alfonso XII College
was founded by monks in 1875 as a boarding school.

Patio de los Reyes

Main entrance

★ Library
This impressive library held Felipe II's personal collection. At its peak it boasted 40,000 volumes and an exceptional number of precious manuscripts. The long Print Room has beautiful 16th-century ceiling frescoes by Tibaldi.

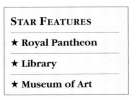

STAR FEATURES

★ Royal Pantheon

★ Library

★ Museum of Art

The Royal Apartments, on the second floor of the palace, consist of Felipe II's modestly decorated living quarters. His bedroom opens directly on to the high altar of the basilica.

★ **Museum of Art**
Flemish, Italian and Spanish paintings hang in the museum, which is located on the first floor. One highlight is The Calvary, *by 15th-century Flemish artist Rogier van der Weyden.*

In the Patio de los Evangelistas is a temple by Herrera. This courtyard is closed to the public.

VISITORS' CHECKLIST

Paseo de Juan de Borbón y Batemberg. **(** 91 890 59 02. **◘** *from Atocha or Chamartín.* **◙** *661, 664 from Moncloa.* **○** *10am–6pm Tue–Sun (till 5pm Oct–Mar).* **●** *public hols.* **▨ ✝** *9:30am daily; 7pm, 8pm Sat & Sun.* **✦ ◩** **w** *www.patrimonionacional.es*

Chapterhouses
On display here is Carlos I's portable altar. The allegorical ceiling frescoes are Grotesque in style.

Felipe II commissioned the monastery in 1558. Since 1885, it has been run by Augustinian monks. It is closed to the public.

The Glory of the Spanish Monarchy by Luca Giordano
This beautiful fresco, above the main staircase, depicts Carlos I and Felipe II, and scenes of the building of the monastery.

The Building of El Escorial
When chief architect Juan Bautista de Toledo died in 1567 he was replaced by Juan de Herrera, royal inspector of monuments. The plain architectural style of El Escorial is called desornamentado, *literally, "unadorned".*

Exploring El Escorial

FELIPE II BUILT this palace as the final resting place of his revered father, Carlos I of Spain – Holy Roman Emperor Charles V – whom he succeeded in 1556. The gigantic building, with thousands of windows, was sited on the slopes of the Guadarrama and offered a stunning view that stretched away to the Spanish Empire. Felipe II, as King of Naples, Sicily, Milan, the Netherlands, Spain and the New World, used the finest talent available in the realm to decorate the austere monastery. The official tour goes through the Royal Apartments and Royal Pantheon in 45 minutes, leaving you to explore the rest by yourself.

Infanta Isabel Clara by Bartolomé González in the Royal Apartments

ROYAL APARTMENTS

THE PALACIO de los Austrias, or Royal Apartments, are built around and adjoining the basilica. From her bed, the Infanta Isabel Clara (Felipe II's daughter) could see the high altar and the officiating priest. On the right wall are paintings of her and her sister Catalina by Bartolomé González (1564–1627); between them is a portrait of Felipe II by Sánchez Coello (1531–88).

The **Sala de Retratos** is full of portraits, beginning above the fireplace with *Carlos I* by Juan Pantoja de la Cruz (1553–1608) – a copy of the original painting by Titian lost in a fire in 1604. Moving anti-clockwise, the next portrait is of *Felipe II* by Antonio Moro (1519–76), then *Felipe III* by Pantoja de la Cruz, young *Felipe IV* by Bartolomé González and young *Carlos II* by Juan Carreño de

Miranda (1614–85). In a corner of the room, in a glass case, is the folding chair that Felipe II, afflicted by gout, used during the last years of his life.

At both ends of the **Salas de los Paseos** are magnificent German marquetry doors. Blue Talavera tiles cover the lower part of the walls, while the upper parts are decorated with 16th-century maps and paintings of famous Spanish military victories. Inlaid in the floor of this room and the next-door dining room are solar adjusters made in 1755 for setting clocks.

In the king's chamber, the bed stands where Felipe II died in September 1598, with a view of the basilica's high altar. In his study is the last portrait of the king from Pantoja's studio.

PANTHEONS

DIRECTLY beneath the high altar of the basilica is the **Royal Pantheon**, where almost all Spanish monarchs since Carlos I are laid to rest. This pantheon, with Spanish

Altar in the Royal Pantheon, where most of the Spanish monarchs are laid to rest

black marble, red jasper and Italian gilt bronze decorations, was finished in 1654. Kings lie on the left of the altar and queens on the right. The most recent addition to the pantheon is the mother of Juan Carlos I.

Of the eight other pantheons, one of the most notable is that of **Juan de Austria**, Felipe II's half-brother, who became a hero after defeating the Turks at the Battle of Lepanto. Also worth seeing is **La Tarta**, a white marble polygonal tomb that resembles a cake, where royal children are buried.

CHAPTERHOUSES

THE SALAS CAPITULARES, or Chapterhouses, in the monastery's southeast corner, contain wooden benches for the monastery's 100 monks. These four light and spacious rooms with their fine vaulted ceilings are decorated with numerous paintings.

Enamelled and gold-plated retable in the Chapterhouses

Among the highlights are some by Titian (1490–1576), who painted many scenes for El Escorial. Here can be seen his *St Jerome at Prayer* and *The Last Supper*, the latter unfortunately trimmed to fit its place. Diego Veláz-quez (1599–1660) is also represented here, with *Joseph's Tunic* (1630), painted while the artist was in Italy.

A collection of paintings by Hieronymus Bosch (1450–1516), known as "El Bosco", is found here. A version of *The Haywain* – the original hangs in the Prado (*see p80*) – was executed by the Bosch school. This painting is said to originate from the Flemish proverb, "The world is like a hay-cart and everybody takes what he can". Felipe II kept it in his bedroom, along with Bosch's *The Garden of Earthly Delights*, also in the Prado. A copy of one panel is displayed here.

Nearby is the beautiful enamelled and gold-plated wooden retable of Carlos I, Holy Emperor Charles V. The king took this portable altar with him on military campaigns.

The Martyrdom of St Maurice and the Theban Legion by El Greco

THE MUSEUMS

WITHIN EL ESCORIAL are several small museums. The north façade entrance leads to St Maurice's Hall, home of *The Martyrdom of St Maurice and the Theban Legion* by El Greco (1541– 1614). Nearby stairs lead down to the small **Architectural Museum**, which contains plans, models and engravings of the palace.

Upstairs, the **Museum of Art** covers mostly 16th- and 17th-century works. The first room is dedicated to Italian masters, while the next two contain Flemish art. Michel Coxcie (1499–1592), known as the "Flemish Rafael", is featured here. Most notable is *The Martyrdom of St Philip* triptych.

The long fourth room is dominated by the superb *Calvary* by Rogier van der Weyden (c.1400–64), and copies of the Flemish master's *Virgin* and *St John* by Juan Fernández Navarrate (c.1538– 79), on either side.

In the fifth room is *St Jerome Doing Penance* by José de Ribera (1591–1652). In the last room are 16th- and 17th-century Spanish and Italian paintings.

THE LIBRARY

ESTABLISHED BY Felipe II, this was the first public library in Spain, and boasts a vaulted ceiling and a marble floor. In 1619 the king issued a decree that a copy of each new publication in his empire should be sent to him. At its zenith, it contained some 40,000 books and manuscripts, mainly from the 15th and 16th centuries.

The long **Print Room** has a marble floor and glorious vaulted ceiling. The ceiling frescoes by Pellegrino Tibaldi (1527–96) depict Philosophy, Grammar, Rhetoric, Dialectics, Music, Geometry, Astrology and Theology. The Doric wooden shelving was designed by Juan de Herrera (1530–97).

On each of the four main pillars hang portraits of the members of the royal House of Austria – Carlos I, Felipe II, Felipe III and Carlos II. On display are coins and Felipe II's pine Ptolemaic sphere (1582), which placed the earth in the centre of the universe.

THE BASILICA

HISTORICALLY, ONLY the aristocracy were permitted to enter the basilica, while the townspeople were confined to the vestibule at the entrance. The Monks's Choir above is still closed to the public.

The basilica contains 45 altars. Among its highlights are the exquisite statue of *Christ Crucified* (1562) in Carrara marble by Benvenuto Cellini. It is found in the chapel to the left of the entrance, with steps leading up to it. Either side of the altar, above the doors leading to the royal bedrooms in the Palacio de los Austrias, are fine gilded bronze cenotaphs of Carlos I and Felipe II worshipping with their families.

The enormous altarpiece was designed by Juan de Herrera with coloured marble, jasper, gilt-bronze sculptures and paintings. The central tabernacle, backlit by a window, took Italian silversmith Jacoppo da Trezzo (1515–89) seven years to craft. The paintings are by Federico Zuccaro (1542– 1609) and Pellegrino Tibaldi, who also executed the fresco above. The wood for the cross (also used for Felipe II's coffin) came from a Spanish ship, the *Cinco Llagas* (Five Wounds).

PALACE OF THE BOURBONS

IN CONTRAST TO the simple rooms of the Palacio de los Austrias (Felipe II's royal apartments), the Bourbon apartments are sumptuously furnished. They were created by Carlos IV (reigned 1788– 1808), and are hung with framed tapestries, some by Goya, from the Real Fábrica de Tapices (*see p112*).

A china cabinet displays the dinner service which was part of the trousseau of Victoria Eugenia (Queen Victoria's grand-daughter), when she married Alfonso XIII in 1906.

Dining room in the sumptuous Palacio de los Borbones (Palace of the Bourbons)

Gigantic cross at Valle de los Caídos, a symbol of Franco's dictatorship

Santa Cruz del Valle de los Caídos ❷

Madrid. North of El Escorial on M600.
C 91 890 56 11. **R** from El Escorial.
O Tue–Sun. **O** some public hols. 🎟

G ENERAL FRANCO had the
Holy Cross of the Valley
of the Fallen built as a memorial to those who died in the
Spanish Civil War (see p18).
The vast cross is located some
13 km (8 miles) north of El
Escorial (see pp122–5), and
dominates the surrounding
countryside; it can be seen for
miles in every direction. Some
Spaniards find it too chilling a
symbol of the dictatorship to
be enjoyable, while for others
its sheer size is rewarding.
  The cross is 150 m (490 ft)
high and rises above a basilica
carved 250 m (820 ft) deep
into the rock by Republican
prisoners of war. A number of
them are said to have died in
the 16-year project.

Next to the basilica's high
altar is the plain white tomb-
stone of Franco and, opposite,
that of José Antonio Primo de
Rivera, founder of the Falange
Española party. Another 40,000
coffins of soldiers from both
sides in the Civil War lie here
out of sight, including those
of two unidentified victims.
  An elevator (lift) takes visitors
up to the arms of the cross,
from where there are magnificent views over the pine trees.

Manzanares el Real ❸

Madrid. 🏘 4,000. 🚌 🛈 Plaza del
Pueblo 1 (91 853 00 09). 🛒 Tue &
Fri. 🎉 Fiesta de Verano (early Aug),
Cristo de la Nave (14 Sep).

F ROM A DISTANCE, the skyline
of Manzanares el Real is
dominated by its restored 15th-
century castle. Although the
castle is equipped with some
traditional military features,
such as double machicolations
and turrets, it was used mainly
as a residential palace by the
Dukes of Infantado. Below the
castle is a 16th-century church,
a Renaissance portico and fine
capitals. Behind the town, bordering the foothills of the Sierra
de Guadarrama, is **La Pedriza**,
a mass of granite screes and
ravines, very popular with
climbers. It now forms part of
an attractive nature reserve.

ENVIRONS: Colmenar Viejo,
12 km (7.5 miles) to the southeast of Manzanares, has a
superb Gothic-Mudéjar church.

Sierra Centro de Guadarrama ❹

Madrid. 🚉 Puerto de Navacerrada,
Cercedilla. 🚌 Navacerrada, Cercedilla.
🛈 Navacerrada (91 856 00 06).

T HE CENTRAL SECTION of the
Sierra de Guadarrama was
linked to Madrid by train in
the 1920s. The pine-covered
granite slopes are now dotted
with holiday chalets. Villages
such as **Navacerrada** and
Cercedilla have grown into
popular resorts for skiing,
mountain biking, rock climbing, horse riding and walking.

Breathtaking Navacerrada pass in the Sierra de Guadarrama

The **Valle de Fuenfría**, a nature reserve of wild forests, is best reached via Cercedilla. It has a well-preserved stretch of Roman road, as well as picnic spots and marked walks.

Altarpiece in the Monasterio de Santa María de El Paular

Monasterio de Santa María de El Paular ❺

Southwest of Rascafría on M604.
📞 91 869 14 25. 🚌 Rascafría. ⏰ noon–5pm Mon–Sat, 1–6pm Sun. ✉

CASTILE'S FIRST Carthusian monastery was founded in 1390 on the site of a medieval royal hunting lodge. Although Santa María de El Paular was built in the Gothic style, many Plateresque and Renaissance features were added later.

In 1836, when government minister Mendizábal ordered all church property to be given over to the state, the monastery was abandoned and fell into disrepair. It was not until the 1950s that the state decided to restore it. Today the complex, in a beautiful, tranquil setting, comprises a private hotel *(see p151)*, a working Benedictine monastery and a church.

The church's delicate alabaster altarpiece dates from the 15th century and is thought to be the work of Flemish craftsmen. Its panels are decorated with scenes from the life of Jesus Christ. The sumptuous Baroque *camarín* (chamber), behind the altar, dates from 1718 and was designed by Francisco de Hurtado.

Every Sunday, the monks sing an hour-long Gregorian chant in the church. It is worth asking them to show you the cloister's Mudéjar brick vaulting and double sundial. They will normally be happy to do this if they are not busy.

The monastery constitutes an excellent starting point from which to explore the attractive country towns of **Rascafría** and **Lozoya** in the surrounding Lozoya valley. To the southwest lies the **Lagunas de Peñalara** nature reserve.

La Granja de San Ildefonso ❻

Segovia. 📞 921 47 00 19. 🚌 from Madrid or Segovia. ⏰ Tue–Sun (the fountains start at 5:30pm on irregular days – check beforehand). ✉ ✉

THIS SUMPTUOUS ROYAL pleasure palace is set against the striking backdrop of the Sierra de Guadarrama mountains. It stands on the site of a hunting lodge built by Enrique IV during the 15th century.

In 1720, Felipe V embarked on a project to recreate his grandfather Louis XIV's court at Versailles. A succession of artists and architects contributed to the rich furnishings and the splendid gardens.

Many rooms were damaged in a fire in 1918. Although they were sumptuously restored, the interior never quite re-gained its original splendour.

There are countless salons decorated with *objets d'art* and Classical frescoes. From the ceilings hang huge, glittering chandeliers. The church is fittingly adorned in lavish high Baroque style, and the Royal Mausoleum contains the tomb of Felipe V and his queen.

In the gardens, stately chestnut trees, clipped hedges and statues frame a complex series of pools. There are also some spectacular water fountains.

Serenely beautiful royal gardens at La Granja de San Ildefonso, inspired by the palace of Versailles

Segovia ❼

Tower of San Esteban

SEGOVIA IS THE MOST SPECTACULARLY SITED city in Spain. The old town is set high on a rocky spur and is surrounded by the Río Eresma and Río Clamores. From afar it looks like a ship, the medieval alcázar on its sharp crag forming the prow, the pinnacles of the Gothic cathedral rising up like masts, and the aqueduct trailing behind like a rudder. The view of the old town from the valley below at sunset is magical.

A relatively short journey from Madrid by car, bus or train, Segovia is readily accessible to visitors to the capital and well worth a look. Easy to negotiate on foot, there is plenty to see and do for a day trip or an overnight stay. Weekends, particularly in summer, are the busiest time in Segovia.

The imposing Gothic cathedral of Segovia

Exploring Segovia

Segovia is dotted with many notable churches, including the 11th-century Romanesque **San Juan de los Caballeros**, with an outstanding sculptured portico; 13th-century **San Esteban** with a striking five-storey tower; and 11th-century **San Martín** with its beautiful arcades, capitals and gilded altarpiece. The **Iglesia de San Millán**, a Romanesque jewel in the newer part of town, has a Mozarabic tower and richly decorated interior with a 14th-century Gothic crucifix. The **Iglesia de la Vera Cruz**, outside the old town, is a 12-sided crusader's church (1208).

🔒 Cathedral

Plaza Mayor. **☎** 921 46 22 05. ◯ Oct–Mar 9:30am–5:45pm; Apr–Sep 9:30am–7pm daily.
Dating from 1525, this massive Gothic structure replaced the old cathedral, which was destroyed in 1511. The old cloister, however, survived and was rebuilt on the new site. Architect Juan Gil de Hontañón devised the austere but elegant design. The pinnacles, flying buttresses, tower and dome form an impressive silhouette.

The interior is light and elegantly vaulted, with stained-glass windows. It has a high altar designed by Sabatini in 1768. More than 20 beautiful chapels, most enclosed by graceful iron-work grilles, line the nave and apse. The most interesting is the Chapel of the Pietà, which took its name from the beautiful sculpture by Juan de Juni. The cloister, whose pointed arches are divided by slender mullions and perforated tracery, is accessed through an outstanding Gothic arch by Juan Guas in the Chapel of Christ's Solace. The cloister leads to the chapterhouse museum, which houses 17th-century Brussels tapestries, paintings, sculptures, silver, furniture, books and coins.

🏛 Museo de Segovia

Casa del Sol, Calle Socorro 11. **☎** 921 46 06 13. ◯ till 2001 for renovation.
This archaeological museum contains 15,000-year-old Stone Age engravings as well as tools, arms, pottery and metalwork through the centuries. There are Roman coins and inscriptions, wall fragments from Arab houses and, in the centre, an interesting collection of belt buckles.

Also worth seeing are two huge Celtic stone bulls which were excavated in the Calle Mayor. It is thought they may have been divine protectors of people or livestock. In the nearby province of Avila, such icons are linked with burials.

▦ Casa de los Picos

Just inside the city walls is the Casa de los Picos, a mansion whose 15th-century façade is adorned with diamond-shaped stones. The building houses an art gallery and school.

🔂 Aqueduct

In use until the late 19th century, this aqueduct was built at the end of the 1st century AD by the Romans, who turned ancient Segobriga into an important military base. With this feat of engineering, water from the Río Frío flowed into the city, filtered through a series of tanks along the way.

The Roman aqueduct running through the old town

The Alcázar, like a fairy-tale castle rising above the cliff

♠ Alcázar

Plaza de la Reina Victoria Eugenia. 📞
921 46 07 59. ⏱ *10am–6pm daily.*
● *1 Jan, 25 Dec.* 💶 *(free Tue).* 📷 ♿
Although there has been a
fortress on this site since the
Middle Ages, the present castle
is mostly a fanciful reconstruction following a fire in 1862.
It contains a series of rooms,
decorated with armour, paintings and furniture, to create a
medieval atmosphere. There
is also a weaponry museum.

The virtually impregnable
castle had its heyday in the
Middle Ages. The rectangular
Juan II tower was completed
during the reign of Enrique IV
in the 15th century and named
after his father. It is worth
climbing the narrow stairs to
the top to experience breathtaking views of Segovia and
the Guadarrama mountains.

In 1764 Carlos III founded the
Royal School of Artillery here.
Two of its pupils, Doaiz and
Velarde, became heroes in the
1808 uprising of *Madrileños*
against the French *(see p16).*

🏛 Palacio Episcopal

Plaza de San Esteban. 📞 *921 46 09*
63. ⏱ *Jul–Sep: Tue–Sat; Oct–Jun:*
Fri & Sat. 💶 ♿
Built for the Salcedos family,
this 16th-century building was
later acquired by Bishop
Murillo, whose coat of arms
is above the door. Its museum
contains paintings, sculptures
and gold and silver objects.

♠ Monasterio de El Parral

Just north of the city walls,
Segovia's largest monastery
has three floors, four cloisters
and a fine Plateresque altarpiece. It contains the superb

Plateresque tombs of its
benefactor, the Marqués de
Villena, and his wife, María.

♠ Convento de los Carmelitas

Alameda de la Fuencisla. 📞 *921 43*
13 49. ⏱ *10am–1:30pm, 4–8pm*
Tue–Sun.
In a secluded Eresma valley,
St John of the Cross founded
this convent in the 16th century
and was Prior from 1588–91.
The mystical poet was also
co-founder, with Santa Teresa,
of a barefooted *(descalzos)*
order of Carmelites which ran
to the strictest of disciplines.

The tree-lined Plaza Mayor

SEGOVIA CITY CENTRE

Alcázar ⑨
Aqueduct ②
Casa de los Picos ③
Cathedral ⑦
Iglesia de San Esteban ⑥

Iglesia de San Juan
  de los Caballeros ①
Iglesia de San Martín ④
Museo de Segovia ⑧
Palacio Episcopal ⑤

KEY

🅿   Parking

ℹ   Tourist information

🕆   Church

⛪   Convent or monastery

0 metres   250
0 yards   250

Buitrago del Lozoya, standing next to the river

Buitrago del Lozoya ❽

Madrid. 🏠 *1,500.* 🚉 ℹ️ *Calle Tahona 11 (91 868 00 56).* 🚌 *Sat.* 🎉 *La Asunción y San Roque (15 Aug).*

Picturesquely sited above a meander in the Río Lozoya is the walled town of Buitrago del Lozoya. Founded by the Romans, it was fortified by the Arabs, and became a bustling market town in medieval times. The Gothic-Mudéjar castle, built in the 14th century, is in ruins, although the gatehouse, arches and stretches of the original Arab wall have survived. Today, the castle is used as a venue for bullfights and hosts a festival of ancient theatre and music in the summer.

The old quarter, within the town's walls, retains its charming atmosphere. The church of **Santa María del Castillo**, dating from the 15th century, has a Mudéjar tower and ceilings moved here from the old hospital. The **town hall**, or *ayuntamiento*, in the newer part of the town preserves a 16th-century processional cross. In the basement is the small **Museo Picasso**. The prints, drawings and ceramics on display were collected by the artist's friend and barber, Eugenio Arias, an inhabitant of the town.

🏛 **Museo Picasso**
Plaza de Picasso 1. 📞 *91 868 00 56.* ⭕ *Tue.*

Sierra Norte ❾

Madrid. 🚉 *Montejo.* ℹ️ *Calle Real 64, Montejo (91 869 70 58).*

The black slate hamlets of the Sierra Norte, which was once known as the Sierra Pobre (Poor Sierra), are located in the most attractively rural part of the Comunidad de Madrid (Madrid province). At **Montejo de la Sierra**, the largest village in the area, an information centre organizes riding, the rental of traditional houses and visits to the nearby nature reserve of the **Hayedo de Montejo de la Sierra**. This is one of the southernmost beech woods in Europe and a relic of a previous era, when climatic conditions here were more suitable for the beech. From Montejo, you can drive on to picturesque hamlets such as **La Hiruela** or **Puebla de la Sierra**, both of which are set in lovely walking country.

The drier southern hills slope down to the **Embalse de Puentes Viejas**, a reservoir where summer chalets cluster around artificial beaches. On the eastern edge of the Sierra Norte lies **Patones**, which supposedly escaped invasion by the Moors and Napoleon due to its isolated location.

Sigüenza ❿

Guadalajara. 🏠 *4,800.* 🚉 ℹ️ *Ermita del Humilladero (949 34 70 07).* 🚌 *Sat.* 🎉 *San Juan (24 Jun), San Roque (15 Aug).*

Dominating the hillside town of Sigüenza is its impressive castle-parador *(see p151).* The **cathedral**, in the old town, was begun in the 12th century. It is Romanesque

Semi-recumbent figure of El Doncel on his tomb in Sigüenza cathedral

in style, with later additions, such as the Gothic-Platerèsque cloisters. In one of the chapels is the Tomb of *El Doncel* (the young nobleman). It was built for Martín Vázquez de Arce, Isabel of Castile's *(see p20)* pageboy, who was killed in a battle against the Moors in Granada in 1486. The sacristy has a beautiful ceiling carved with flowers and cherubs, by Alonso de Covarrubias.

Intricate diamond stonework on the façade of the Palacio de los Duques del Infantado

Guadalajara ⓫

Guadalajara. 👥 *66,000.* 🚊 🚌
ℹ️ *Plaza de los Caídos 6 (949 21 16 26).* 🗓 *Tue, Sat.* 🎎 *Virgen de la Antigua (Sep).*

ALTHOUGH GUADALAJARA'S history is largely lost in the modern industrial city, traces of its past splendour survive.

It was founded as the Roman settlement of Arriaca, and then replaced by the Moorish settlement of Wad-al-Hajarah. In 1085 it was taken by Alfonso VI in the Christian Reconquest *(see p13)*, and rose to prominence in the 14th century.

The **Palacio de los Duques del Infantado**, built from the 14th to the 17th century by the powerful Mendoza dynasty, is an outstanding example of Gothic-Mudéjar architecture. The main façade and the two-storey patio are adorned with delicate carvings. Following Civil War bombing, the palace was restored. It now houses the Museo Provincial – the local art museum.

Among the town's churches is the **Iglesia de Santiago**, which has a Gothic-Platerèsque chapel by Alonso de Covarrubias. In the 15th-century **Iglesia de San Francisco** is the family mausoleum of the Mendoza family, while the cathedral is built on the site of a mosque. The **Iglesia de Santa María**, which was built in the 13th century, has typical Mudéjar horseshoe arches and a bell tower.

Lupiana, 11 km (7 miles) east, is home to the Monasterio de San Bartolomé, which was founded in the 14th century.

🏛 Palacio de los Duques del Infantado
Avenida del Infantado del Ejército.
📞 *949 21 33 01.* ⭕ *daily.* 🎫

Façade of Colegio de San Ildefonso in Alcalá de Henares

Alcalá de Henares ⓬

Madrid. 👥 *167,000.* 🚊 🚌 ℹ️
Callejón Santa María (91 889 26 94).
🗓 *Mon & Wed.* 🎎 *Feria de Alcalá (late Aug).*

AT THE HEART of a modern industrial town is one of Spain's most renowned university quarters. Founded in 1499 by Cardinal Cisneros, Alcalá's **university** became one of the foremost places of learning in 16th-century Europe, famous for its language teaching. The university was transferred to Madrid in 1836. Although most of the original 40 colleges have since been destroyed and replaced with new buildings, the most historic one, the much-restored Renaissance **Colegio de San Ildefonso**, survives. It has a Platerèsque façade (1543) by Rodrigo Gil de Hontañón. Former students include Golden Age playwright Lope de Vega *(see p26)*. In 1517 the university produced Europe's first polyglot bible, which had parallel texts in Latin, Greek, Hebrew and Chaldean.

Alcalá's other sights are the cathedral and the **Casa-Museo de Cervantes**, birthplace of the Golden Age author. It is now an intriguing museum. Alcalá was also the birthplace of Catherine of Aragón, the first wife of England's Henry VIII and the daughter of the Catholic Monarchs *(see p20)*.

🏛 Casa-Museo de Cervantes
Calle Mayor. 📞 *91 889 96 54.*
⭕ *Tue–Sun.* ⬤ *public hols.*

MIGUEL DE CERVANTES

Miguel de Cervantes Saavedra, Spain's greatest literary figure *(see p26)*, was born in Alcalá de Henares in 1547. After fighting in the naval Battle of Lepanto (1571), he was held captive by the Turks for more than five years. In 1605, when he was almost 60 years old, the first of two parts of his comic masterpiece *Don Quixote* was published to popular acclaim. Cervantes continued writing novels and plays until his death in Madrid on 23 April 1616, the same day that Shakespeare died.

Lavish, finely woven 18th-century tapestry inside the Palacio de El Pardo

Palacio de El Pardo **⑬**

El Pardo, northwest of Madrid on N605.
⦿ 91 376 15 00. **⊟** from Moncloa.
◯ 10:30am–6pm Mon–Sat (till 5pm Oct–Apr), 9:30am–1:30pm Sun and public hols. **⦿**

THIS ROYAL HUNTING lodge and palace, set in parkland just outside Madrid's city limits, lists King Juan Carlos I and General Franco among its former residents. A tour takes visitors around the palace's original Habsburg wing and identical 18th-century extension by Francesco Sabatini.

The Bourbon interior is decorated with frescoes, tapestries and gilt mouldings, many of which were woven at the Real Fábrica de Tapices *(see p112)* to designs by Goya. Today the palace is used to entertain visiting heads-of-state and other royal guests. Surrounding the palace and the elegant 18th-century village of El Pardo is an enormous oak forest. The area is popular for picnicking.

Museo del Aire **⑭**

Carretera de Extremadura, km 10.5.
⦿ 91 509 16 90. **⊟** from Estación del Príncipe Pío (Norte) any bus towards Alcorcón or Móstoles. **◯** 10am–2pm Tue–Sun. **●** 1 Jan, Easter Thu & Good Fri, 10 & 25 Dec. **⦿** (free Wed). **⦿**

AMONG THE MANY magnificent flying machines on display at the museum of Spanish aviation, the star exhibit is the Breguet-XIX *Jesús de Gran Poder*, which made the first Spanish transatlantic flight in 1929. Others include the 1911 Vilanova-Acedo, one of the first planes made in Spain, and the Henkel 111 German warplane, the only one ever made. Also on display is *La Cierva* – half-plane, half-helicopter.

Some of the planes are linked with famous people. For example, in 1936 General Franco flew from the Canary Islands to Tetuán to start the Spanish Civil War in the De Havilland *Dragon Rapide*; Juan Carlos I flew a Bell 47G solo; Prince Felipe made his first solo flight in a T-Mentor; and in the Trener Master, Tomás Castaños won the 1964 World Aerobatic Championships.

Prototypes of various Spanish aircraft include the Saeta, Super Saeta and the Casa C–101 Aviojet. The F–104 Starfighter, notorious for its tendency to crash, is one in which Spanish pilots flew a record 10,000 hours without accidents.

On the runway you may see the bulbous Boeing *Guppy*, which flies part of the fuselage (made nearby) of the Airbus to its assembly plant in France.

In addition to aircraft, the museum provides information on the lives of famous aviators, and features displays of Air Force regalia, flight plans and models. There are also films, videos, drawings, documents, photographs and paintings.

Early Lufthansa aircraft at the Museo del Aire

Chinchón

Madrid. 4,200. *Plaza Mayor 3 (91 894 00 84).* Sat. *Semana Santa (Easter Week), San Roque (12–18 Aug).*

CHINCHÓN IS ARGUABLY Madrid province's most picturesque town. The 16th-century, typically Castilian, porticoed **Plaza Mayor** has a splendidly theatrical air. It comes alive for the Easter passion play *(see p34)*, acted out by the townspeople, and during the August bullfights. The 16th-century church, perched above the square, has an altar painting by Goya *(see p26)*, whose brother was a priest here. Just off the square an 18th-century Augustinian monastery has been converted into a parador with a peaceful patio garden *(see p150)*. There is a ruined 15th-century castle on a hill to the west of town. It is closed to the public but, from the outside, there are excellent views of Chinchón and the surrounding countryside.

Madrileños often come to the town at weekends to sample the superb chorizo and locally produced *anís (see p157)* in the town's many taverns.

Chinchón's unique porticoed Plaza Mayor, occasionally used for bullfights

Palacio Real de Aranjuez 16

Plaza de Parejas, Aranjuez. 91 891 07 40. 10am – 6:15pm Tue–Sun (Oct–Mar till 5:15pm). *(free Wed).*

THE ROYAL SUMMER PALACE and gardens of Aranjuez grew up around a medieval hunting lodge standing beside a natural weir, the meeting point of the Tagus and Jarama rivers.

Today's palace of brick and white stone was built in the 18th century to replace an earlier Habsburg palace which burned down. A guided tour takes you through numerous Baroque rooms, including the Chinese Porcelain Room, the Hall of Mirrors and the Smoking Room, modelled on the Alhambra in Granada. It is worth visiting Aranjuez for the simple pleasure of walking in the 300 hectares (740 acres) of shady royal gardens which

inspired Joaquín Rodrigo's *Concierto de Aranjuez*. The small Parterre Garden and Island Garden, between the rivers, survive from the original 16th-century palace.

Between the palace and the River Tagus is the 18th-century Prince's Garden, decorated with fountains and trees from the Americas. The Casa de Marinos (Sailors' House), is a small museum housing the boats once used by the royal family for trips along the river.

At the far end of the garden stands the Casa del Labrador (Labourer's Cottage), a decorative royal pavilion built by Carlos IV *(see p16)*.

The restaurants in the town of Aranjuez are very popular because of the high quality of local produce, in particular asparagus and strawberries. In

Pleasant grounds at the Palacio Real de Aranjuez

summer, a 19th-century steam train, built to take strawberries to the market in Madrid, runs between here and the capital.

Illescas 17

Toledo. 10,750. *Plaza Mayor 1 (925 51 10 51).* Thu. *Fiesta de Milagro (11 Mar), Fiesta Patronal (31 Aug).*

THE TOWN OF ILLESCAS was the summer venue for the court of Felipe II *(see p15)*. While there is little to see of the old town, it does have two interesting churches. The **Parroquial de la Asunción**, built between the 13th and 16th centuries, is easily identified by its Mudéjar tower, one of the best examples of its kind in the region. Nearby is the 16th-century church of the **Hospital de Nuestra Señora de la Caridad**, which boasts an important art collection. The church owns five outstanding works by El Greco *(see p139)*, the most famous being *The Virgin Dictating to Saint Ildefonso*. In its Chapel of Relics there is a portrait of Francisco Pacheco de Toledo by Pantoja de la Cruz and, in the sacristy, there is an original Ecce Homo by Luis de Morales.

Hospital de Nuestra Señora de la Caridad
Calle Cardenal Cisneros 2.
925 54 00 35.
daily.

Street-by-Street: Toledo ⑱

Damascene work, typical of Toledo

Picturesquely sited on a hill above the River Tagus is the historic centre of Toledo. Behind the old walls lies much evidence of the city's rich history. The Romans built a fortress on the site of the present-day Alcázar. The Visigoths made Toledo their capital in the 6th century AD, and left behind several churches. In the Middle Ages, Toledo was a melting pot of Christian, Muslim and Jewish cultures, and it was during this period that the city's most outstanding monument – its cathedral – was built. In the 16th century the painter El Greco came to live in Toledo, and today the city is home to many of his works.

The Iglesia de San Román, of Visigothic origin, now contains a museum relating the city's past under the Visigoths.

Puerta de Valmardón

0 metres　　　　　100
0 yards　　　　　　100

★ Iglesia de Santo Tomé
This church, with a beautiful Mudéjar tower, houses El Greco's The Burial of the Count of Orgaz.

Sinagoga de Santa María la Blanca; Monasterio de San Juan de los Reyes

Sinagoga del Tránsito; Casa-Museo de El Greco

CALLE DE SAN ROMÁN
CARDENAL LORENZANA
CALLE DE ALFONSO X
CALLE DE ALFONSO XII
CALLE DE LA TRINIDAD
CALLE

Archbishop's Palace

Taller del Moro
Once used as a workshop by craftsmen building the cathedral, this Mudéjar palace now houses a museum of Mudéjar ceramics and tiles.

STAR SIGHTS

★ Iglesia de Santo Tomé

★ Museo de Santa Cruz

★ Cathedral

The Puerta del Sol has a double Moorish arch and two towers.

Ermita del Cristo de la Luz
This small mosque, the city's only remaining Muslim building, dates from around AD 1000.

Tourist information;
Estación de
Autobuses & RENFE

VISITORS' CHECKLIST

Toledo. 🅿 67,000. ✈ 🚉
Paseo de la Rosa, 925 2230 99.
🚌 *Avenida de Castilla-La*
Mancha 3 (925 21 58 50).
🛈 *Puerta de Bisagra, 925 22*
08 43. 🗓 *Tue.* 🎉 *Corpus Christi*
(May/Jun), Virgen del Sagrario,
(15 Aug). **Iglesia de San Román**
⭘ *Tue–Sun.* 🎨 **Taller del**
Moro ⭘ *Tue–Sun.* 🎨

The Plaza de Zocodover
is named after the market which was held here in Moorish times. It is still the city's main square, with many cafés and shops.

PLAZA DE ZOCODOVER

ALFILERITOS

CALLE DEL COMERCIO

CUESTA DE CARLOS V

SIXTO RAMÓN PARRO

CARDENAL CISNEROS

★ Museo de Santa Cruz
The city's main fine arts collection includes several tapestries from Flanders. Among them is this 15th-century zodiac tapestry, with well-preserved rich colours.

KEY

– – – Suggested route

★ Cathedral
Built on the site of a Visigothic cathedral and a mosque, this impressive structure is one of the largest cathedrals in Christendom (see pp140–41). The Flamboyant Gothic high altar reredos (1504) is the work of several artists.

Alcázar
Inside the fortress, a statue of Carlos V portrays him triumphant over a Moor. The original is on display in the Museo de Prado.

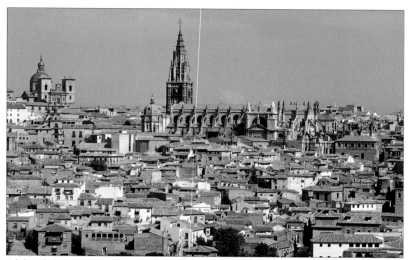

Toledo cathedral rising above the rooftops of the medieval part of the city

Exploring Toledo

Toledo is easily reached from Madrid by rail, bus or car, and is then best explored on foot. To visit all the main sights you need at least two days, but it is possible to walk around the medieval and Jewish quarters in a long morning. To avoid the heavy crowds, go midweek and stay for a night, when the city is at its most atmospheric.

♠ Alcázar

Cuesta de Carlos V. ▌ 925 22 30 38. ◯ Tue–Sun. ☒ (free Wed). ☒
The fortified palace of Carlos I (Holy Roman Emperor Charles V) stands on the site of former Roman, Visigothic and Muslim fortresses. Its severe square profile suffered fire damage before being nearly destroyed in 1936 when the Nationalists survived a 70-day siege by the Republicans. Restoration followed the original plans and the building now houses an army museum. The siege headquarters have been preserved as a monument to Nationalist heroism. Much is made of an alleged telephone conversation between the besieged Colonel Moscardó and his son, held by the Republicans and threatened with death unless his father surrendered. The Colonel refused, and his son was later killed, though not necessarily as a direct result of his father's refusal to capitulate.

⬛ Museo de Santa Cruz

Calle Cervantes 3. ▌ 925 22 10 36. ◯ daily. ☒
This museum is housed in a 16th-century hospital founded by Cardinal Mendoza. The building has some outstanding Renaissance features, including the main doorway, staircase and cloister. The four wings, in the shape of a Greek cross, are dedicated to the fine arts. The collection is strong in medieval and Renaissance works of art. There are also paintings by El Greco, including one of his last, *The Assumption* (1613), still in its original altarpiece. Displays include two typical Toledan crafts: armour and damascened swords, made by

***The Assumption* (1613) by El Greco in the Museo de Santa Cruz**

inlaying blackened steel with gold wire. Damascene work, including plates and jewellery (as well as swords), is still made in the city. Part of the museum is being renovated and will open in autumn 2000 with an exhibition on Carlos V.

⛪ Iglesia de Santo Tomé

Plaza del Conde 4. ▌ 925 25 60 98. ◯ daily. ☒
Visitors come to Santo Tomé mainly to admire El Greco's masterpiece, *The Burial of the Count of Orgaz*. An important patron of the church, the Count paid for much of the 14th-century building that stands today. The painting, commissioned in his memory by a parish priest, depicts the miraculous appearance of St Augustine and St Stephen at his burial, to raise his body to heaven. It has never been moved from the setting for which it was painted, nor restored. Nevertheless, it is remarkable for its contrast of glowing and sombre colours. In the foreground, allegedly, are the artist himself and his son (both looking out) as well as Cervantes. The church itself is thought to date back to the 12th century, and its tower is one of the best examples of Mudéjar architecture in the city.
    Nearby is the **Pastelería Santo Tomé**, a good place to buy locally made marzipan.

⛩ Sinagoga de Santa María la Blanca

Calle de los Reyes Católicos 4.
📞 925 22 72 57. ⬛ daily. 📷

The oldest and largest of the city's eight original synagogues, this monument dates back to the 12th century. In 1405 it was taken over as a church by the military-religious Order of Calatrava. Restoration has returned it as far as possible to its original beauty – finely carved stone capitals and wall panels stand out against plain white horseshoe arches and plasterwork. In the main chapel is a Plateresque altarpiece. In 1391 a massacre of Jews took place on this site, a turning point after years of religious tolerance in the city.

Mudéjar arches in the Sinagoga de Santa María la Blanca

⛩ Sinagoga del Tránsito

Calle Samuel Leví. 📞 925 22 36 65.
⬛ Tue–Sun. 📷

The most elaborate Mudéjar interior in the city is hidden behind the deceptively humble façade of this former synagogue, built in the 14th century by Samuel Ha-Leví, the Jewish treasurer to Pedro the Cruel. The interlaced frieze of the lofty prayer hall harmoniously fuses Islamic, Gothic and Hebrew geometric motifs below a wonderful coffered ceiling.

Adjoining the synagogue is an interesting museum dedicated to Sephardi (Spanish Jewish) culture. The manuscripts, tombstones, wedding costumes and sacred objects of worship on display date from both before and after the Jews' expulsion from Spain at the end of the 15th century.

Ornate ceiling in the Monasterio de San Juan de los Reyes

🔒 Monasterio de San Juan de los Reyes

Calle de los Reyes Católicos 17.
📞 925 22 38 02. ⬛ daily. 📷

A wonderful mixture of architectural styles, this monastery was commissioned by the Catholic Monarchs in honour of their victory over the Portuguese at the battle of Toro (near Salamanca) in 1476. Originally, it was intended to be their burial place, but they were actually laid to rest in Granada. Largely the work of Juan Guas, the church's main Isabelline structure was completed in 1492. Although it was badly damaged by Napoleon's troops in 1808 (see p16), it has been restored to its original splendour. It retains superb features such as a Gothic cloister (1510) – unique in the city – which has a beautiful multicoloured Mudéjar ceiling. Near to the church is a stretch of the Jewish quarter's original wall.

🏛 Casa-Museo de El Greco

Calle Samuel Leví. 📞 925 22 40 46.
⬛ Tue–Sun. 📷 (free Sat pm, Sun am).

It is not clear whether El Greco actually lived in or simply near to this house, in the heart of the Jewish quarter, which has been turned into a museum containing an important collection of his works. Canvases on display include *View of Toledo*, a detailed depiction of the city at the time, and the superb series *Christ and the Apostles*. Underneath the museum, on the ground floor, is a domestic chapel with a fine Mudéjar ceiling and a collection of art by painters of the Toledan School, such as Luis Tristán, a student of El Greco.

🔒 Iglesia de Santiago del Arrabal

This is one of Toledo's most beautiful Mudéjar monuments. It can easily be identified by its tower, reminiscent of a minaret, which is said to date back to the 12th-century Reconquest (see p13). The church, which was built slightly later, has a beautiful woodwork ceiling. The ornate Mudéjar pulpit and Plateresque altarpiece stand out against the otherwise plain Mudéjar interior.

⛩ Puerta Antigua de Bisagra

When Alfonso VI conquered Toledo in 1085, he entered it through this gateway, alongside El Cid. It is the only gateway in the city to have kept its original 10th-century military architecture. The huge towers are topped by a 12th-century Arab gatehouse.

EL GRECO

Born in Crete in 1541, El Greco ("the Greek") came to Toledo in 1577 to paint the altarpiece in the convent of Santo Domingo el Antiguo. Enchanted by the city, he stayed here, painting religious portraits and altarpieces for other churches. Although El Greco was trained in Italy and influenced by masters such as Tintoretto, his works are closely identified with the city where he settled. He died in Toledo in 1614.

Domenikos Theotocopoulos, better known as El Greco

Toledo Cathedral

T HE SPLENDOUR OF TOLEDO's massive cathedral reflects its history as the spiritual heart of the Spanish church and the seat of the Primate of all Spain. Still today, the Mozarabic Mass, which dates back to Visigothic times, is said here by papal permission. The present cathedral was built on the site of a 7th-century church. Work began in 1226 and spanned three centuries, until the completion of the last vaults in 1493. This long period of construction explains the cathedral's mixture of styles: pure French Gothic – complete with flying buttresses – on the exterior and Spanish decorative styles, such as Mudéjar and Plateresque work, in the interior.

Sacristy
El Greco's The Denuding of Christ, *above the marble altar, was painted especially for the cathedral. Also here are works by Titian, Van Dyck and Goya.*

The Cloister, on two floors, was built in the 14th century on the site of the old Jewish market.

View of Toledo Cathedral
Dominating the city skyline is the Gothic tower at the west end of the nave. The best view of the cathedral, and the city, is from the parador (see p151).

The belfry in the tower contains a heavy bell known as *La Gorda* ("the Fat One").

The Puerta del Mollete, on the west façade, is the main entrance to the cathedral. From this door, *mollete* (soft bread) was distributed to the poor.

★ **Monstrance**
In the Treasury is the 16th-century Gothic silver monstrance, over 3 m (10 ft) high. It is carried through the streets during the Corpus Christi celebrations (see p34).

STAR FEATURES

★ **Monstrance**

★ **Transparente**

★ **High Altar Reredos**

★ **Choir**

★ **Transparente**
This Baroque altarpiece of marble, jasper and bronze, by Narciso Tomé, is illuminated by an ornate skylight. It stands out from the mainly Gothic interior.

VISITORS' CHECKLIST

Calle Arco Palacio 2. 925 22 22 41. 8am–6:30pm daily. 8am, 8:30am, 9am, 10am, 5:30pm, 6:30pm daily (also 11am, noon & 1pm Sun).
Choir, Treasury, Sacristy and Chapterhouse 10:30am–6:30pm Mon–Sat, 2pm–6:30pm Sun.

Capilla de Santiago

The Capilla de San Ildefonso contains the superb Plateresque tomb of cardinal Alonso Carrillo de Albornoz.

Chapterhouse
Above beautiful 16th-century frescoes by Juan de Borgoña is this spectacular, multi-coloured Mudéjar ceiling.

Puerta de los Leones

★ **High Altar Reredos**
The polychrome reredos, one of the most beautiful in Spain, depicts scenes from Christ's life.

The Puerta del Perdón, or Door of Mercy, has a tympanum decorated with religious characters.

The Capilla Mozárabe has a beautiful Renaissance ironwork grille, carved by Juan Francés in 1524.

★ **Choir**
The carvings on the wooden lower stalls depict scenes of the fall of Granada. The alabaster upper ones show figures from the Old Testament.

TRAVELLERS' NEEDS

WHERE TO STAY

WHEN ALFONSO XIII *(see p17)* was married in 1906, he was embarrassed that his city, unlike other European capitals, did not have elegant hotels to accommodate his wedding guests. He decided to put things right, and personally instigated the building of the luxurious Ritz and Palace, which are still two of the best hotels in Europe. But, centuries before, Madrid

Hotel doorman

already had a strong tradition of more modest hostelries and guest houses offering shelter to the multitude of visitors from the provinces and from other countries. Today, the city continues to provide an abundance of comfortable lodgings, be they simple *pensiones*, pleasant three-star hotels in converted town houses, or palatial five-star establishments with every possible amenity.

Stately façade of the Reina Victoria *(see p147)* from the Plaza de Santa Ana

WHERE TO LOOK

CENTRAL MADRID has plenty of hotels, in every price category, close to the major sights. Some areas, such as Gran Vía and around Puerta del Sol, can be very noisy, both day and night, so soundproofing is a big consideration. If you are driving, parking in central Madrid is difficult, and a hotel with parking facilities is essential. If it is tranquillity you want, and you do not mind having to take a taxi or the metro to go sightseeing, there are some good hotels in the residential districts of Salamanca (east) or Chamberí (north). A few modern luxury hotels, aimed mainly at business travellers, are located along the Paseo de la

Castellana, and on the eastern side of the M30 ring road, convenient for those needing easy access to the airport.

GRADING AND FACILITIES

SPANISH HOTELS are rated from one to five stars. The top category is Gran Lujo (GL), indicated by five stars. Madrid has two hotels in this category – the Ritz *(see p148)* and the modern Villamagna *(see p149)*. Although the star-rating gives

Suite at the Ritz – one of Madrid's most exclusive and expensive hotels *(see p148)*

a rough indication of standards and prices, it is not an exact science. Three-star hotels, for example, can include anything from charmless grey establishments in need of repair, to real gems with friendly staff and interesting decor. Both four- and five-star hotels should have a good range of extra facilities, and they will be fairly smart, but often less so than a similarly-priced hotel located in a rural part of Spain. Most Madrid hotels in the three-to-five-star category have air conditioning and televisions. Very few have gardens or swimming pools.

One- and two-star hotels offer basic facilities, although most now have a telephone and television in the rooms, as well as individual bathrooms. The better ones will have friendly staff, high standards of cleanliness, direct-dial phones and air-conditioning, which is essential in summer.

Hotel-residencias (HR) are hotels without a meal service; otherwise, they are the same as other hotels. Accommodation with basic facilities is also offered in *hostales* (Hs) and *pensiones* (P) at much lower prices than hotels. The two types are essentially the same.

A double room for one person (*habitación doble uso individual*), which will cost slightly more than a single room, is an option for single travellers needing more space.

Some hotels have their own parking area. Those without often have an arrangement with neighbouring public parking garages. In either case, there is an additional charge for this service, and it can be quite expensive.

One of Madrid's many inexpensive *hostales* scattered around the centre

PARADORS

PARADORS ARE the deservedly famous state-run hotels in Spain. The best of them are located in converted historical buildings, and many are worth a visit in their own right. Madrid itself has none, but some of the most picturesque paradors are in striking distance of the city, including the first one to open, in 1928, in the Sierra de Gredos. A 17th-century palace in Chinchón *(see p150)*, a Moorish castle in Sigüenza *(see p151)* and a luxury parador in Segovia *(see p151)* offer unique accommodation.

Guest room in the spacious Crowne Plaza *(see p147)*

HOW TO BOOK

WHILE MADRID HAS ample hotel options, you never know whether an important trade fair or conference is going to cause greater demand, so prior booking is advisable. This can be done through a travel agent or directly by fax or phone. If you have any special requirements, such as a twin or double bed, interior room or one facing the street, make these known when booking. The receptionist will usually specify the hour until which your reservation will be held. Few hotels demand a credit card number or deposit to guarantee a booking. When checking in, you will be asked for ID (a national identity card or passport) and to sign a registration form. It is also a good time to deposit valuables in the safe and tip the porter a few hundred-peseta coins.

When leaving, rooms must be vacated before noon, but hotels will look after your luggage if your travel plans call for a later departure.

PAYMENT AND DISCOUNTS

PRACTICALLY ALL hotels take major credit cards, but not personal cheques. Rates are increased by seven per cent value-added tax (IVA). Madrid hotels often offer discounts on weekend stays and in August, and it is also possible to buy discount vouchers at travel agents. Companies can usually get a corporate rate – *precio de empresa* – which may mean a reduction of up to a third.

When booking, ask for the room rate, as this is often lower than the listed price. It is even worth asking for a discount.

SPECIAL NEEDS

ON THE WHOLE Spain is not wheelchair friendly, but newer hotels have ramps, wide elevators (lifts) and certain rooms adapted for disabled people. Enquire with the hotel beforehand, and be specific about your needs; a receptionist might think a ramp up the front steps makes the hotel "wheelchair accessible".

Few Madrid hotels, and only those with four or five stars, provide non-smoking rooms.

SELF CATERING

SOME HOTELS, known as *hotel apartamentos* or *apart-hotels*, contain a number of limited self-catering apartments (efficiency units). A few other establishments are entirely self-catering. These are called *apartamentos turísticos*, and usually require a minimum stay of one week.

CHILDREN

CHILDREN ARE WELCOME in most Madrid hotels, whatever the category. For small children, a cot or an extra bed will be put in the parents' room, often at no additional cost. But, as a rule, hotels provide few facilities for children, and only some of the more expensive offer babysitting – in Spain children tend to go everywhere with their parents.

HOSTELS

THE SPANISH *HOSTAL* is not a hostel, but a modest hotel. Youth hostels are known as *albergues juveniles*, and there are only two in Madrid: one on Calle de Santa Cruz de Marcenado in central Madrid, the other in the Casa de Campo *(see p114)*. Space is at a premium; to secure a place, book ahead through the **Instituto de Albergues Juveniles** on Gran Vía 10, 1st floor, telephone: 91 580 42 16.

The opulent Ritz hotel *(see p148)* facing Plaza Canovas del Castillo

Choosing a Hotel

THE HOTELS in this guide have been selected across a wide price range for excellent facilities and location. Many also have a highly recommended restaurant, pretty gardens or bedrooms with balcony views. The chart is divided into chapter areas for easy reference. For details on restaurants see pages 152–163.

	CREDIT CARDS	NUMBER OF ROOMS	PRIVATE PARKING	SWIMMING POOL	GARDEN OR TERRACE

OLD MADRID

HOSTAL BUENOS AIRES. Map 2 D5. ℗
Gran Vía 61, 28013. ☎ *91 542 01 02.* FAX *91 542 28 69.*
A simple and economical hotel conveniently located on the busy Gran Vía. The public rooms are pleasantly decorated, and each of the bedrooms has its own balcony or small terrace. 🛏 ▤ TV

| | AE DC MC V | 25 | | | |

HOSTAL MADRID. Map 4 F2. ℗
Calle de Esparteros 6, 2°, 28012. ☎ *91 522 00 60.* FAX *91 532 35 10.*
Inexpensive, central hotel in a mid-19th-century building between the Puerta del Sol and the Plaza Mayor. Rooms with balconies face Calle de Esparteros or Calle Postas; quieter rooms face the courtyard. 🛏 ▤ TV

| | AE DC MC V | 15 | | | |

REGENTE. Map 4 F1. @ info@hotelregente.com ℗℗
Calle de Mesonero Romanos 9, 28013. ☎ *91 521 29 41.* FAX *91 532 30 14.*
Convenient, centrally located hotel combining new facilities with old-style furniture. Rooms facing the Gran Vía can be noisy. 🛏 ▤ TV

| | AE DC MC V | 145 | | | |

REYES CATÓLICOS. Map 3 C4. ℗℗
Calle del Ángel 18, 28005. ☎ *91 365 86 00.* FAX *91 365 98 67.*
This modern, central hotel is popular and always very busy. Children are made welcome. The bedroom windows are double-glazed for soundproofing. There are views of the city from the roof terrace. 🛏 ▤ TV

| | AE DC MC V | 38 | ▣ | | ▣ |

CARLOS V. Map 4 E2. @ recepcion@hotelcarlosv.com ℗℗℗
Calle Maestro Vitoria 5, 28013. ☎ *91 531 41 00.* FAX *91 531 37 61.*
A city-centre hotel in a pedestrian street beside the Puerta del Sol, run by a family. There are interconnecting bedrooms, family rooms, rooms with balconies and top-floor rooms with sizeable sun terraces. 🛏 ▤ TV

| | AE DC MC V | 67 | | | |

REGINA. Map 7 A2. ℗℗℗
Calle de Alcalá 19, 28014. ☎ *91 521 47 25.* FAX *91 522 40 88.*
This modern hotel has a very elegant address near to the Real Academia de Bellas Artes on Calle de Alcalá, and close to the Puerta del Sol. 🛏 ▤ TV

| | AE DC MC V | 142 | ▣ | | |

TRYP CAPITOL. Map 4 E1. @ tryp@trypnet.com ℗℗℗
Gran Vía 41, 28013. ☎ *91 521 83 91.* FAX *91 521 77 29.*
Right in the middle of the action on the Gran Vía, next to the Plaza Callao, this hotel occupies one of Madrid's most architecturally interesting modern buildings. The rooms were renovated in 1998. 🛏 ▤ TV

| | AE DC MC V | 143 | | | |

TRYP MENFIS. Map 2 D5. @ tryp@trypnet.com ℗℗℗
Gran Vía 74, 28013. ☎ *91 547 09 00.* FAX *91 547 51 99.*
In a modern building right next to the Plaza de España, at the top end of the Gran Vía. The reception area is shiny and bright, the service professional, and the rooms were completely renovated in 1997. 🛏 ▤ TV

| | AE DC MC V | 120 | | | |

AROSA. Map 4 F1. @ arosa@hotelarosa.com ℗℗℗℗
Calle de la Salud 21, 28013. ☎ *91 532 16 00.* FAX *91 531 31 27.*
This central hotel is popular with international and business visitors to Madrid. All the bedrooms are comfortable and well soundproofed. 🛏 ▤ TV

| | AE DC MC V | 139 | ▣ | | |

TRYP GRAN VÍA. Map 4 F1. @ tryp@trypnet.com ℗℗℗℗
Gran Vía 25, 28013. ☎ *91 522 11 21.* FAX *91 521 24 24.*
A chain hotel located in one of the city's busiest streets. Some of the furniture is in the style of the 1960s and 1970s. 🛏 ▤ TV

| | AE DC MC V | 174 | | | |

TRYP REX. Map 4 E1. @ tryp@trypnet.com ℗℗℗℗
Gran Vía 43, 28013. ☎ *91 547 48 00.* FAX *91 547 12 38.*
A chain hotel in an old building between the Plaza del Callao and the Plaza de España, close to a large public car park. It has spacious public rooms and well-equipped bedrooms, each with its own safe. 🛏 ▤ TV

| | AE DC MC V | 144 | | | |

			CREDIT CARDS	NUMBER OF ROOMS	PRIVATE PARKING	SWIMMING POOL	GARDEN OR TERRACE

Price categories for a standard double room per night, with tax, breakfast and service included:

Ⓟ under 12,000 ptas
ⓅⓅ 12,000–17,000 ptas
ⓅⓅⓅ 17,000–22,000 ptas
ⓅⓅⓅⓅ 22,000–27,000 ptas
ⓅⓅⓅⓅⓅ over 27,000 ptas

CREDIT CARDS
Indicates which credit cards are accepted: *AE* American Express; *DC* Diners Club; *MC* MasterCard/Access; *V* VISA.
PARKING
Parking provided by the hotel in a private car park or a private garage on the hotel site or very close by. Some hotels charge for use of private parking facilities.
SWIMMING POOL
Hotel pool outdoors unless otherwise stated.
GARDEN
Hotel with garden, courtyard or terrace, often providing tables for eating outdoors.

Hotel	CREDIT CARDS	NUMBER OF ROOMS	PRIVATE PARKING	SWIMMING POOL	GARDEN OR TERRACE
CROWNE PLAZA. Map 2 D5. @ reservas@crowneplaza.es ⓅⓅⓅⓅⓅ Gran Via 84, 28013. 📞 91 547 12 00. FAX 91 548 23 89. Newly refurbished, American-style hotel in the Edificio España, facing the Plaza de España. Close to the action on the Gran Vía. Spacious common areas and large rooms. 🔌 ▤ TV ♿	AE DC MC V	306	■		
EMPERADOR. Map 4 E1. @ hemperador@sevillaespanaitalia.es ⓅⓅⓅⓅⓅ Gran Via 53, 28013. 📞 91 547 28 00. FAX 91 547 28 17. A popular hotel, ideally placed for exploring the city centre. The spacious bedrooms are quiet, and there is a rooftop swimming pool. 🔌 ▤ TV	AE DC MC V	246		●	■
SANTO DOMINGO. Map 4 D1. ⓅⓅⓅⓅ Plaza de Santo Domingo 13, 28013. 📞 91 547 98 00. FAX 91 547 59 95. Stylish, mid-1990s establishment one block south of the Gran Vía and close to the Puerta del Sol and the Teatro Real. Modern interior decor. Each room is different; some non-smoking rooms. 🔌 ▤ TV	AE DC MC V	120	■		■
TRYP AMBASSADOR. Map 4 D1. @ tryp@trypnet.com ⓅⓅⓅⓅ Cuesta de Santo Domingo 5, 28013. 📞 91 541 67 00. FAX 91 559 10 40. Modern hotel in a 19th-century palace. Stylish and comfortable, with large rooms. Close to the Teatro Real and the Palacio Real *(see pp54–7)*. Pleasant greenhouse-style bar with tropical plants. 🔌 ▤ TV	AE DC MC V	181			
TRYP REINA VICTORIA. Map 7 A3. @ tryp@trypnet.com ⓅⓅⓅⓅⓅ Plaza de Santa Ana 14, 28012. 📞 91 531 45 00. FAX 91 522 03 07. Ernest Hemingway once lodged in this historic hotel, a graceful edifice and a traditional haunt of bullfighting aficionados. 🔌 ▤ TV ♿	AE DC MC V	201	■		

BOURBON MADRID

Hotel	CREDIT CARDS	NUMBER OF ROOMS	PRIVATE PARKING	SWIMMING POOL	GARDEN OR TERRACE
HOSTAL-RESIDENCIA LISBOA. Map 7 A2. Ⓟ Calle de Ventura de la Vega 17, 28014. 📞 91 429 46 76. FAX 91 429 46 76. Clean, functional and centrally located near the Plaza de Santa Ana and one block east of Calle Echegaray. The rooms are simply furnished. 🔌 TV	AE DC MC V	25			
MEDIODÍA. Map 7 C4. Ⓟ Plaza del Emperador Carlos V 8, 28012. 📞 91 527 30 60. FAX 91 527 30 66. This great bargain hotel lies in a stately 19th-century building near the Centro de Arte Reina Sofía *(see pp86–9)*. Comfortable, wooden-floored rooms, some with splendid views over Atocha station, and friendly service. 🔌 TV	AE MC V	165			
MORA. Map 7 C4. Ⓟ Paseo del Prado 32, 28014. 📞 91 420 15 69. FAX 91 420 05 64. This 1930s hotel has an attractive entrance. Its rooms and facilities are functional, but its prices are low and it is centrally located, near the Jardín Botánico and the Museo del Prado *(see pp80–83)*. 🔌 ▤ TV	MC V	63			
SANTANDER. Map 7 A3. Ⓟ Calle de Echegaray 1, 28014. 📞 91 429 46 44. FAX 91 369 10 78. This small, friendly family hotel offering neat, comfortable, simple rooms has been popular with travellers since it opened in the 1920s. Good location – close to the Puerta del Sol and handy for the sights in central Madrid. 🔌 TV	AE DC MC V	35			
INGLÉS. Map 7 A3. ⓅⓅ Calle de Echegaray 8, 28014. 📞 91 429 65 51. FAX 91 420 24 23. A good-value, family-run hotel with its own garage. The bedrooms facing the street are sunny but the back rooms are quieter. 🔌 TV	AE DC MC V	58	■		
MERCATOR. Map 7 C4. ⓅⓅ Calle de Atocha 123, 28012. 📞 91 429 05 00. FAX 91 369 12 52. Comfortable, reasonably priced, somewhat old-fashioned hotel just one block from the Centro de Arte Reina Sofía *(see pp86–9)*. The quietest rooms are those facing the parking area. 🔌 ▤ TV	AE DC MC V	89	■		

For key to symbols see back flap

				CREDIT CARDS	NUMBER OF ROOMS	PRIVATE PARKING	SWIMMING POOL	GARDEN OR TERRACE

Price categories for a standard double room per night, with tax, breakfast and service included:

P under 12,000 ptas
PP 12,000–17,000 ptas
PPP 17,000–22,000 ptas
PPPP 22,000–27,000 ptas
PPPPP over 27,000 ptas

CREDIT CARDS
Indicates which credit cards are accepted: *AE* American Express; *DC* Diners Club; *MC* MasterCard/Access; *V* VISA
PARKING
Parking provided by the hotel in a private car park or a private garage on the hotel site or very close by. Some hotels charge for use of private parking facilities.
SWIMMING POOL
Hotel pool outdoors unless otherwise stated.
GARDEN
Hotel with garden, courtyard or terrace, often providing tables for eating outdoors.

Hotel	Credit Cards	Rooms	Private Parking	Swimming Pool	Garden or Terrace
AGUMAR. Map 8 E5. PPP Paseo de la Reina Cristina 7, 28014. 91 552 69 00. FAX 91 433 60 95. A stylish hotel near the big museums, with its own collection of good paintings and carpets from the Real Fábrica de Tapices.	AE DC MC V	245	■		
EL PRADO. Map 7 B3. @ prado@green-hoteles.com PPPP Calle del Prado 11, 28014. 91 369 02 34. FAX 91 429 28 29. Modern and efficiently run small hotel with spacious rooms, located along a narrow street close to Plaza de Santa Ana. Business facilities.	AE DC MC V	47	■		
SUITE PRADO. Map 7 A3. PPPP C/ Manuel Fernández y González 10, 28014. 91 420 23 18. FAX 91 420 05 59. A stylish apartment hotel of luxurious suites a short distance from the Prado *(see pp80–83)* and the Museo Thyssen-Bornemisza *(see pp70–73).*	AE DC MC V	18			
NH ALCALÁ. Map 8 E1. @ nhalcala@nh-hoteles.com PPPPP Calle de Alcalá 66, 28009. 91 435 10 60. FAX 91 435 11 05. A hotel with a friendly atmosphere across the street from the Parque del Retiro. The back bedrooms overlook a pretty garden.	AE DC MC V	146	■		■
HOTEL PALACE. Map 7 B2. @ palace1@mol.es.com PPPPP Plaza de las Cortes 7, 28014. 91 360 80 00. FAX 91 360 81 00. This gracious Belle Epoque hotel *(see p69)*, with a glass dome and a colonnade, has accommodated statesmen as well as the spy Mata Hari. The bedrooms are elegant and the service welcoming.	AE DC MC V	440	■		
HOTEL RITZ. Map 7 C3. @ press@ritz.es PPPPP Plaza de la Lealtad 5, 28014. 91 521 28 57. FAX 91 532 87 76. Inaugurated in 1910 as a hotel for aristocrats, the Ritz is still one of Spain's most elegant hotels *(see p68)*. It has an ornate, circular foyer and a terrace garden, and offers musical teas and brunches.	AE DC MC V	158	■		■
SUECIA. Map 7 B2. @ hotelsuecia@genio.infor.es PPPPP Calle del Marqués de Casa Riera 4, 28014. 91 531 69 00. FAX 91 521 71 41. Centrally located near the Puerta del Sol, the Suecia has a small, seventh-floor terrace where guests can relax and soak up the sun.	AE DC MC V	128	■		■
VILLA REAL. Map 7 B2. @ villareal@derbyhotels.es PPPPP Plaza de las Cortes 10, 28014. 91 420 37 67. FAX 91 420 25 47. A stylish hotel near the Prado *(see pp80–83)*, built in the 19th-century. The public areas have mahogany furniture and embroidery.	AE DC MC V	115	■		

AROUND LA CASTELLANA

Hotel	Credit Cards	Rooms	Private Parking	Swimming Pool	Garden or Terrace
DON DIEGO. Map 6 F4. P Calle de Velázquez 45, 28001. 91 435 07 60. FAX 91 431 42 63. Reasonably priced, friendly hotel in the elegant Salamanca district *(see p99)*. Some rooms have balconies; interior rooms are quieter.	MC V	58			
HOSTAL SANTA BÁRBARA. Map 5 B4. P Plaza de Santa Bárbara 4, 28004. 91 446 93 08. FAX 91 446 23 45. A simple and clean low-budget option in one of the liveliest spots in Madrid. Some rooms have balconies with views. The interior rooms are quieter.	AE DC MC V	14			
HOSTAL SIL. Map 5 A5. P Calle de Fuencarral 95, 28004. 91 448 89 72. FAX 91 447 48 29. In a lively part of town, this is a comfortable, convenient hotel with quality bedroom and bathroom furnishings, but low prices.	AE DC MC V	20			
MÓNACO. Map 7 B1. P Calle de Barbieri 5, 28004. 91 522 46 30. FAX 91 521 16 01. The decor of this hotel, formerly Madrid's most famous high-class brothel, is unashamedly kitsch. The bedrooms retain some decadent features.	MC V	32			

GALIANO. Map 6 D4. ₧₧₧
Calle de Alcalá Galiano 6, 28010. **(** 91 319 20 00. FAX 91 319 99 14.
A surprising little hotel in a Neo-Classical building, one block west of Plaza de Colón. Quirky service, but spacious and comfortable rooms. 🛏 ▤ TV

| | AE DC MC V | 29 | ▨ | | |

TRYP STYLE ESCULTOR. Map 6 D2. @ ottoresc@trypnet.com ₧₧₧₧
Calle de Miguel Ángel 3, 28010. **(** 91 310 42 03. FAX 91 319 25 84.
Good price for a hotel of this category in this location, one block west of the Paseo de la Castellana in the prosperous Chamberí area. All the rooms in this modern hotel have balconies. 🛏 ▤ TV

| | AE DC MC V | 63 | ▨ | | |

CASTELLANA INTERCONTINENTAL. Map 6 D1. ₧₧₧₧
Paseo de la Castellana 49, 28046. **(** 91 310 02 00. @ madrid@interconti.com
This hotel in Madrid's commercial centre is a favourite with business travellers. Guests can choose between two restaurants. 🛏 ▤ TV 🛗

| | AE DC MC V | 313 | ▨ | | ▨ |

OCCIDENTAL MIGUEL ÁNGEL. Map 6 D1. ₧₧₧₧₧
Calle de Miguel Ángel 31, 28010. **(** 91 442 81 99.
Located beside the Paseo de la Castellana, the Miguel Ángel combines modern comfort with classic style. One of the hotel's two fine restaurants holds dinner dances until 3am. 🛏 ▤ TV 🛗 @ hma@occidental-hoteles.com

| | AE DC MC V | 271 | ▨ | ● | ▨ |

SANTO MAURO. Map 5 C2. @ ac-hoteles@ac-hoteles.com ₧₧₧₧₧
Calle de Zurbano 36, 28010. **(** 91 319 69 00. FAX 91 308 54 77.
This palace, built in 1894 in one of Madrid's most elegant streets, has housed embassies. It has a swimming pool beneath a vaulted basement ceiling, and a restaurant occupies the former library. 🛏 ▤ TV

| | AE DC MC V | 37 | ▨ | ● | |

NH SANVY. Map 6 D4. @ nh@nh-hoteles.com ₧₧₧₧₧
Calle de Goya 3, 28001. **(** 91 576 08 00. FAX 91 575 24 43.
This very modern hotel, in a side street off Plaza de Colón, is the flagship of the NH chain, which caters for the business traveller. Modern and functional. Facilities for business meetings. Non-smoking rooms. 🛏 ▤ TV

| | AE DC MC V | 149 | ▨ | | ▨ |

TRYP FENIX. Map 6 D4. @ recfen@trypnet.com ₧₧₧₧₧
Calle de Hermosilla 2, 28001. **(** 91 431 67 00. FAX 91 576 06 61.
This is one of Madrid's most elegant addresses. The communal areas are stylish, and the lobby has a magnificent spiral staircase. Most rooms have good views of the Paseo de la Castellana or Plaza de Colón. 🛏 ▤ TV 🛗

| | AE DC MC V | 228 | ▨ | | ▨ |

VILLAMAGNA. Map 6 D3. @ hotel@villamagna.es ₧₧₧₧₧
Paseo de la Castellana 22, 28046. **(** 91 587 12 34. FAX 91 575 95 04.
The Villamagna combines 18th-century decor with modern luxury, and is ringed by gardens. It is popular with business people. 🛏 ▤ TV 🛗

| | AE DC MC V | 182 | ▨ | | ▨ |

WELLINGTON. Map 8 F1. @ hotel>wellington@hotel-wellington.com ₧₧₧₧₧
Calle de Velázquez 8, 28001. **(** 91 575 44 00. FAX 91 576 41 64.
A stylish hotel built in the early 1950s close to the Parque del Retiro. It is a meeting place for people interested in bullfighting. 🛏 ▤ TV

| | AE DC MC V | 288 | ▨ | ● | ▨ |

FURTHER AFIELD

RAMÓN DE LA CRUZ ₧₧
C/ de Don Ramón de la Cruz 94, 28006. **(** 91 401 72 00. FAX 91 402 21 26.
Very good value at this hotel in a quiet street off Plaza Manuel Becerra, at the top of Calle de Alcalá and close to the Ventas bullring *(see p110)*. Rooms are large, comfortably furnished and have wooden floors. 🛏 ▤ TV

| | DC MC V | 103 | ▨ | | |

PUERTA DE TOLEDO. Map 3 C5. ₧₧
Glorieta Puerta de Toledo 4, 28005. **(** 91 474 71 00. FAX 91 474 07 47.
Functional, reasonably priced hotel facing the Glorieta Puerta de Toledo. Close to El Rastro *(see p61)*, typical Spanish taverns in Cava Alta and Cava Baja and a short walk from the Palacio Real *(see pp54–7)*. 🛏 ▤ TV 🛗

| | MC V | 152 | ▨ | | |

TIROL ₧₧
Calle del Marqués de Urquijo 4, 28008. **(** 91 548 19 00. FAX 91 541 39 58.
A good-value hotel, conveniently located off the Plaza de España and near the student district. The bedrooms are spacious and clean. 🛏 ▤ TV

| | AE DC MC V | 97 | | | |

GRAN ATLANTA @ hatlanta@arrakis.es ₧₧₧
Calle del Comandante Zorita 34, 28020. **(** 91 553 59 00. FAX 91 533 08 58.
A large, bright, attractively decorated lobby welcomes you to this modern hotel in the heart of Madrid's business district. Catering mainly to business travellers, it is near some of Madrid's best-known restaurants. 🛏 ▤ TV

| | AE DC MC V | 180 | ▨ | | |

For key to symbols see back flap

Price categories for a standard double room per night, with tax, breakfast and service included:

Ⓟ under 12,000 ptas
ⓅⓅ 12,000–17,000 ptas
ⓅⓅⓅ 17,000–22,000 ptas
ⓅⓅⓅⓅ 22,000–27,000 ptas
ⓅⓅⓅⓅⓅ over 27,000 ptas

CREDIT CARDS
Indicates which credit cards are accepted: *AE* American Express; *DC* Diners Club; *MC* MasterCard/Access; *V* VISA
PARKING
Parking provided by the hotel in a private car park or a private garage on the hotel site or very close by. Some hotels charge for use of private parking facilities.
SWIMMING POOL
Hotel pool outdoors unless otherwise stated.
GARDEN
Hotel with garden, courtyard or terrace, often providing tables for eating outdoors.

	CREDIT CARDS	NUMBER OF ROOMS	PRIVATE PARKING	SWIMMING POOL	GARDEN OR TERRACE
ARISTOS ⓅⓅⓅⓅ Avenida de Pio XII 34, 28016. ☎ 91 345 04 50. FAX 91 345 10 23. If pleasant, tranquil surroundings take precedence over proximity to the centre, this delightful small hotel in a leafy northern residential area is a good choice. Its restaurant serves modern Mediterranean cuisine. 🔧 ▤ TV	AE MC V	23	■		■
COLÓN @ fiesta-colon@eurociber.es ⓅⓅⓅⓅ Calle del Doctor Esquerdo 119, 28007. ☎ 91 573 59 00. FAX 91 573 08 09. A comfortable hotel in a tower block between the Parque del Retiro and the Parque de Roma. It has a gym and business facilities. 🔧 ▤ TV	AE DC MC V	389	■		
CONDE DE ORGAZ @ condeorgaz@zenithoteles.com ⓅⓅⓅⓅ Avenida del Moscatelar 24, 28043. ☎ 91 748 97 60. FAX 91 388 00 09. A modern hotel, with big, comfortable bedrooms, near to the airport and the Campo de las Naciones Exhibition Centre. 🔧 ▤ TV 🔧	AE DC MC V	90	■		
NH BALBOA @ nh@nh-hoteles.es ⓅⓅⓅⓅ Núñez de Balboa 112, 28006. ☎ 91 563 03 24. FAX 91 562 69 80. Modern and comfortable, with an efficient, professional staff, this hotel on the corner of Núñez de Balboa and General Oráa is in the elegant Salamanca district (*see p99*) near the fashionable shops. 🔧 ▤ TV	AE DC MC V	122	■		
NH ZURBANO @ nh@nh-hoteles.es ⓅⓅⓅⓅ Calle de Zurbano 79–81. ☎ 91 441 45 00. FAX 91 441 32 24. Modern, efficient and comfortable, if somewhat impersonal, this hotel is located in two separate buildings one block from La Castellana, on a quiet street. It is very popular with business travellers. 🔧 ▤ TV 🔧	AE DC MC V	266	■		
RAFAEL VENTAS @ hotel@rafaelventas.es ⓅⓅⓅ Calle de Alcalá 269, 28027. ☎ 91 326 16 20. FAX 91 326 18 19. Sleek, modern, four-floor building with marble exterior, purpose-built as a hotel in 1994, and efficiently run. Convenient for the airport and a favourite with business travellers. 🔧 ▤ TV 🔧	AE DC MC V	111	■	●	■
BAUZA @ mas@hotelbauza.com ⓅⓅⓅⓅ Calle de Goya 79, 28001. ☎ 91 435 75 45. FAX 91 431 09 43. The lobby of this hotel, a short walk from the Plaza de Colón or the Parque del Retiro, has been remodelled in a modernist style. 🔧 ▤ TV	AE DC MC V	177	■		
CUZCO @ hotelcuzco@mundivia.es ⓅⓅⓅⓅ Paseo de la Castellana 133, 28046. ☎ 91 556 06 00. FAX 91 556 03 72. Flashy, American-style hotel near the Santiago Bernabeu stadium. Occupies a high-rise block in the business district on La Castellana. Spacious common areas, health centre, sauna and gym, and modern, large rooms. 🔧 ▤ TV	AE DC MC V	330	■		
TRYP MONTE REAL @ hotelcuzco@mundivia.es ⓅⓅⓅⓅ Camino del Arroyo del Fresno 17, 28035. ☎ 91 316 21 40. FAX 91 316 39 34. Situated in a residential area near the Puerta de Hierro golf course, this imposing modern hotel has a peaceful atmosphere. Its balconies overlook the swimming pool and gardens. 🔧 ▤ TV 🔧	AE DC MC V	80	■	●	■

BEYOND MADRID

	CREDIT CARDS	NUMBER OF ROOMS	PRIVATE PARKING	SWIMMING POOL	GARDEN OR TERRACE
ALAMEDA DEL VALLE: *La Posada de Alameda* ⓅⓅ Calle Grande 34, 28749. ☎ 91 869 13 37. FAX 91 869 01 63. A sensitively restored farmhouse in the tranquil Lozoya valley, about an hour's drive from Madrid. All the bedrooms are well equipped and some have views of the countryside. Two are in converted silos. 🔧 TV	MC V	22	■		
CHINCHÓN: *Parador de Chinchón* @ chinchon@parador.es ⓅⓅⓅ Avenida del Generalísimo 1, 28370. ☎ 91 894 08 36. FAX 91 894 09 08. This converted 17th-century monastery with immensely thick walls is built round an airy courtyard. Delightful tiles, frescoes and antiques. 🔧 ▤ TV	AE DC MC V	38	■	●	■

GUADALAJARA: *España* ℗
Calle Teniente Figueroa 3, 19001. 【 949 21 13 03. FAX 949 21 13 05.
Family-run hotel in a 19th-century mansion in the city centre. Modern interior with original touches, such as the mural on the staircase. 🛏 TV 🚻
AE DC MC V · 40

PEDRAZA DE LA SIERRA: *El Hotel de la Villa* ℗℗
Calle Calzada 5, 40172 (Segovia). 【 921 50 86 51. FAX 921 50 86 53.
All the rooms in this charming hotel are exquisitely decorated with floral wallpaper and furnished with antiques and four-poster beds. 🛏 ▤ TV
AE DC MC V · 24

PEDRAZA DE LA SIERRA: *La Posada de Don Mariano* ℗℗
Calle Mayor 14, 40172 (Segovia). 【 921 50 98 86. FAX 921 50 98 86.
It is hard to nominate the best hotel in this lovely village. Every room here looks like something out of a decor magazine. 🛏 TV
AE DC MC V · 18

RASCAFRÍA: *Santa María de El Paular* ℗℗℗℗
Carretera C604 km 25.6, El Paular, 28740. 【 91 869 10 11. FAX 91 869 10 06.
Hotel occupying part of a Benedictine monastery in the Guadarrama mountains. The bar offers an informal alternative to the dining room. ● Jan. 🛏 TV
AE DC MC V · 44

SAN LORENZO DE EL ESCORIAL: *Victoria Palace* ℗℗℗
Calle Juan de Toledo 4, 28200. 【 91 896 98 90. FAX 91 896 98 96.
A short walk from the 16th-century palace of El Escorial, this stylish and elegant hotel offers magnificent views from the bedrooms. 🛏 TV
AE DC MC V · 87

SAN LORENZO DE EL ESCORIAL: *El Botánico* ℗℗℗℗
Timoteo Padrós 16, 28200. 【 91 890 78 79. FAX 91 890 81 58.
A small and pleasant hotel near the famous palace of El Escorial *(see pp122–5).* Some rooms have good views of the palace. 🛏 ▤ TV
AE DC MC V · 20

SEGOVIA: *Infanta Isabel* ℗℗
Plaza Mayor, 40001. 【 921 46 13 00. FAX 921 46 22 17.
This modern hotel in *fin de siècle* style is complemented by traditional Segovian decor. The bedrooms are cosy. 🛏 ▤ TV
AE DC MC V · 27

SEGOVIA: *Los Linajes* ℗℗
Calle Doctor Velasco 9, 40003. 【 921 46 04 75. FAX 921 46 04 79.
Hidden behind an ancient half-timbered, red-brick façade is a modern hotel which steps down the hillside beside the city walls in eight levels. The higher your room level, the better the view. 🛏 TV 🚻
AE DC MC V · 53

SEGOVIA: *Parador de Segovia* ℗℗℗
Carretera de Valladolid, 40003. 【 921 44 37 37. FAX 921 43 73 62.
Luxury parador strategically sited just outside Segovia where guests can enjoy splendid views from the gardens. Gym and indoor pool. 🛏 ▤ TV 🚻
AE DC MC V · 113

SIGÜENZA: *Parador de Sigüenza* ℗℗℗
Plaza del Castillo, 19250 (Guadalajara). 【 949 39 01 00. FAX 949 39 13 64.
Sigüenza's massive castle overlooks the town from a hilltop. Its former VIP guests include the Catholic Monarchs *(see p20).* It is furnished in regal style and the bedrooms surround a courtyard. 🛏 ▤ TV 🚻
AE DC MC V · 81

TOLEDO: *La Almazara* ℗
Carretera Toledo-Argés, 45080. 【 925 22 38 66. FAX 925 25 05 62.
This 16th-century country house hotel is high on a wooded hilltop outside Toledo, and has a magnificent view. Obliging and informal staff compensate for simple bedrooms and limited facilities. 🛏 🚻
AE DC MC V · 21

TOLEDO: *Hostal del Cardenal* ℗℗
Paseo de Recaredo 24, 45004. 【 925 22 49 00. FAX 925 22 29 91.
Now a historic hotel by the city walls, this 18th-century mansion was formerly the residence of the archbishop of Toledo. It has splendid, sculpted ceilings and pretty brick courtyards. 🛏 ▤ TV
AE DC MC V · 27

TOLEDO: *Pintor El Greco* ℗℗
Calle Alamillos del Tránsito 13, 45002. 【 925 21 42 50. FAX 925 21 58 19.
A 17th-century house in Toledo's former Jewish quarter has been discreetly extended behind the original façade and patio. Wrought iron and traditional ceramics add character to the hotel. 🛏 ▤ TV 🚻
AE DC MC V · 33

TOLEDO: *Parador de Toledo* ℗℗℗
Cerro del Emperador, 45002. 【 925 22 18 50. FAX 925 22 51 66.
There is a spectacular view of Toledo from the terrace of this parador on the brow of a hill overlooking the city. Popular with photographers. 🛏 ▤ TV
AE DC MC V · 76

RESTAURANTS, CAFÉS AND BARS

VEN IF MADRID didn't have its wealth of fabulous museums, palaces and monuments, it would be worth coming here just to experience its abundance of restaurants, cafés and bars. *Madrileños* spend a significant amount of time away from home with family, friends or colleagues, enjoying breakfast, pre-meal *tapas (see pp30–31)* or lunch. For the visitor, it is very easy to slip into this unhurried style of eating and drinking.

Tiles at La Chata, a bar in Old Madrid's Calle de la Cava Baja

Regional food from all over Spain is served in picturesque *tabernas (see pp28–9)*, including some of the oldest existing in Europe, modest *casas de comidas* (local restaurants) and some of the continent's most elegant and creative culinary establishments. Whatever the ambience, whatever the price, tasty food is guaranteed – a restaurant serving mediocre fare is unlikely to survive long in this city of discerning eaters.

Interior view of the finely polished bar at El Espejo (see p160)

RESTAURANTS AND BARS

MADRID IS POPULATED by legions of executives and white-collar workers who are the mainstay of the city's restaurant trade. They demand good food, fast service and like to linger at the table after the meal. Lunchtime and the *sobremesa* – the casual conversation that follows the meal – is sacred in this city. To serve this market, there are hundreds of places to eat, from simple bistros that offer home cooking and daily menus at low prices, to some of Europe's most stylish establishments.

Some of the most famous restaurants are run by Basques, the acknowledged gastronomic masters of Spain. Every other Spanish region is represented as well, and Madrid also has restaurants serving international food, from Japanese to Russian, but to a lesser degree than other major European cities.

As the majority of their clients are business people, most restaurants close on Sunday. Many close Saturday lunchtime too, and a large number close for the whole of August.

FAST FOOD

IN ADDITION TO home-grown bars serving Spanish *tapas*, Madrid has branches of most of the familiar international franchises, offering American-style hamburgers. Successful Spanish chains include Pans & Co (sandwiches) and Telechef (salads). One of the best is the Museo del Jamón (ham museum), which serves cured ham and sausages *(see p161)*.

EATING HOURS IN SPAIN

MADRID IS NOTORIOUS for its late meal times, with lunch around 3pm and dinner around 11pm. For the majority of travellers, eating times here take some getting used to.

Madrileños usually have two breakfasts *(desayunos)*. The first may be a perfunctory coffee at home. The second, around 10 or 11am, is often eaten in a bar or a café. It might consist of coffee with *churros* – sticks of fried batter for dunking, a thick slice of *tortilla* (potato omelette) or a sandwich *(bocadillo)*. Most hotels offer either a continental breakfast of coffee or tea with a roll, or a breakfast buffet.

At lunchtime *Madrileños* adjourn to a bar for a *tapa* – an appetizer served with beer or a *copa* (glass of wine). This is followed by the midday *comida* or *almuerzo* (lunch), often eaten at a restaurant.

A late-afternoon *merienda* (tea) of sandwiches or pastries with coffee, tea or juice tides *Madrileños* over until the time comes for a second round of *tapas* at a bar in the evening, before returning home for the *cena* (dinner) or enjoying another meal at a restaurant.

Dining room at Hostería Pintor Zuloaga in Pedraza de la Sierra (see p163)

An enticing place to rest – a terrace bar on Paseo de Recoletos

READING THE MENU

THE SPANISH WORD *menú* refers to the attractively-priced daily fixed menu. Some gourmet restaurants also offer a *menú de degustación* – a sampler menu which might include several small portions of the house specialities.

On a set day of the week some restaurants may serve an elaborate, traditional dish such as *fabada* (bean stew) or *cocido madrileño*, the classic hearty local dish *(see p155)*.

The Spanish word for menu is *la carta*. It starts with *sopas* (soups), *entremeses* (hors d'oeuvres), *ensaladas* (salad), *huevos y tortillas* (eggs and omelettes) and *verduras y legumbres* (vegetable dishes). The *plato principal* (main course) may be *pescados y mariscos* (fish and shellfish) or *carnes y aves* (meat and poultry). Dessert is *postre*.

PRICES AND TIPPING

ALL SPANISH RESTAURANTS must offer a *menú del día*, a comparatively inexpensive daily fixed-price menu comprising two courses and a dessert. Some restaurants do not reveal their daily menu unless it is requested.

Certain dishes, especially seafood, are not priced on the menu. They might be labelled as *según peso* (according to weight) or *según mercado* (according to the market price that day). It is a good idea to ask for an estimate. Seven per cent value-added tax (IVA) is added to *la cuenta* (the bill)

as well as service, but tips in cash are customary – around five per cent of the bill. Almost all restaurants take credit cards, though MasterCard and VISA are the most commonly used.

Bodega de Angel Sierra, a local bar in the Plaza de Chueca *(see p92)*

BOOKING

AS A RULE, BOOKING is essential in Madrid, especially at midday. Phoning a few hours ahead will usually secure a table. At the most popular or fashionable restaurants, however, you should reserve a table one or more days in advance. Arriving early may be no guarantee of a place.

ETIQUETTE AND SMOKING

APART FROM THE inexpensive and the tourist restaurants, smart casual dress is best in most places, and smart dress should be worn in more exclusive establishments, especially in the evening. Few restaurants have non-smoking sections.

CHILDREN

CHILDREN ARE WELCOME in most restaurants, even the more exclusive during the day, but they do not receive the royal treatment they get in other parts of Spain, nor are children's menus or high chairs likely to be offered. Children might feel happiest in an informal restaurant, especially if it has an outdoor terrace.

DISABLED PERSONS

FACILITIES FOR disabled people are rare in Spanish restaurants and it is always worth phoning in advance (or asking the hotel staff to phone) to enquire about their provision.

WINE CHOICES

YOUR WAITER MIGHT offer you an *aperitivo* (aperitif), in which case an excellent choice would be a sherry – a pale, dry *fino* or darker *oloroso* – accompanied perhaps by olives or a *tapa*. Wine is usually served with the main course. Spain has a formidable selection of wines *(see pp156–7)*. Although there is a significant mark-up in restaurants, they can still be reasonably priced, especially *vino de la casa* (house wine).

VEGETARIANS

WITH FEW VEGETARIAN establishments in Madrid, you may decide to opt for the egg, salad or vegetable dishes at an ordinary restaurant, but always check the ingredients first.

The entrance to Combarro, with its medieval charm *(see p162)*

What to Eat in Madrid

Throughout Madrid's history, people have flocked to the capital from every region of Spain, bringing their recipes with them. Thus, Madrid's restaurants offer the perfect chance for a complete culinary tour of Spain. In addition to Madrid's own classics, such as *cocido madrileño* or *besugo a la madrileña* (red bream), you'll find seafood as fresh as any in Galicia, *paella* as tasty as Valencia's, refreshing Andalusian *gazpacho*, filling *fabada* from Asturias, roast suckling-pig from Castile and culinary delights from the Basque country. Spanish cuisine is based on the freshest of ingredients. A first course may consist of a rich soup or vegetable dish, followed by fish or meat. The choice of desserts, however, is often limited to fruit, *flan* (caramel custard) or ice cream.

Garlic

Fritura de pescado *is a typical dish from Málaga and Cádiz, where fried fish and* squid (calamares) *are served with wedges of fresh lemon.*

Fish and seafood *are popular ingredients in many Spanish recipes and in a vast range of tapas (see pp30– 31). It is never a problem to find high quality fish* (pescado) *and seafood* (mariscos), *even in a city like Madrid which is a long way from the sea. Although it tends to be on the expensive side, it is a price worth paying.*

**Scallops
(veneras)**

**Spider crab
(centollo)**

Pimientos rellenos, *the regional dish of Navarra, are the local spicy pointed red peppers stuffed with fish, seafood or meat* (carne).

**Prawns
(gambas)**

**Saffron rice
(arroz con
azafrán)**

**Mussels
(mejillones)**

Fabada *is stew from Asturias with broad beans* (fabes), *salt pork* (tocino), *black sausage* (morcilla), *spicy* chorizo *sausage and ham.*

**Peppers
(pimientos)**

Paella
This Valencian rice dish is cooked in a large, shallow pan, tra- ditionally over an open fire. Short-grain Spanish saffron rice is simmered with a variety of colourful ingredients: seafood, chick- en, rabbit (conejo), *pork* (cerdo), *tomatoes, peppers and beans.*

Pisto, *which originated in La Mancha, is the Spanish version of* ratatouille. *It is a delicious combination of pep- pers, tomatoes, onions, garlic and zucchini* (courgettes).

COCIDO MADRILEÑO

The *cocido*, a full meal cooked in a pot, is available in one variation or another in many Spanish regions, but nowhere is it as revered as in Madrid, where *cocido madrileño* occupies a special place in people's hearts – and on their tables. To prepare this traditional dish, all the ingredients – *garbanzos* (chickpeas), *puerros* (leeks), cabbage, potatoes, *nabos* (turnips) and *zanahorias* (carrots), sausages, beef, chicken, *jamón serrano* (cured ham), bay leaves, cloves, and more – simmer together for many hours. The broth is served as a first course, then the vegetables and meat as a second course. As it takes so long to cook and cannot be prepared in small quantities, Madrid restaurants tend to offer *cocido* on a particular day of the week, usually Thursday.

Sopa de ajo *is a warming garlic soup thickened with bread. The Spanish often eat this soup with a poached egg and some paprika.*

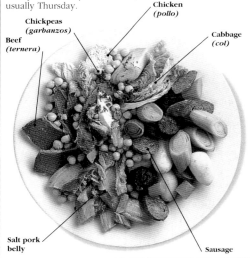

Chicken (*pollo*)
Chickpeas (*garbanzos*)
Beef (*ternera*)
Cabbage (*col*)
Salt pork belly
Sausage

Rabo de toro *is the tail of a bull braised with vegetables and red wine. Of all the dishes that use bull's meat, this is one of the best.*

Pollo al ajillo *is fried chicken with garlic. It is served with a white wine or sherry sauce made with the juices from the chicken.*

Red pepper
Cold *gazpacho* soup
Croutons
Cucumber

Gazpacho *is a chilled raw soup that is made by pounding bread and garlic with tomatoes, cucumber and peppers. Olive oil makes it creamy and vinegar gives it a refreshing tang. It is usually garnished with diced vegetables and croutons.*

Tocino de cielo, *which is translated as "heavenly bacon", is the richest and most mouthwatering delicious of Spain's custard and caramel desserts.*

What to Drink in Madrid

Spain is one of the world's largest wine-producing countries and many fine wines are made here, in addition to the famous sherries of southern Spain and the *cavas* (sparkling wines) of Catalonia. Beer is produced throughout Spain, and Madrid's *cervecerías* (beer bars) are especially adept at pulling a refreshing half pint. Some offer *sidra* (apple cider) from northern Spain. The full range of non-alcoholic drinks is available, including mineral water. Spanish coffee is rich and strong and, to round off a meal, many restaurants offer traditional liqueurs such as brandy and *anís*.

Customers enjoying a pre-meal drink at an outdoor terrace bar

Hot chocolate

A plate of *churros* (batter sticks)

Café con leche

Camomile   **Lime flower**

Hot Drinks

Coffee served in Spanish bars is usually espresso. The traditional start to the day is a big cup of *café con leche* (with milk). *Café cortado* has a dash of milk, *café solo* is black and *café americano* is weaker. Another popular breakfast drink is thick hot chocolate served with *churros* (fried batter sticks). A good cup of tea is hard to find, but herbal teas to try are *manzanilla* (camomile) and *tila* (lime flower).

Cold Drinks

Madrid's tap water is safe to drink, but Spaniards prefer bottled water *(agua mineral)*, either still *(sin gas)* or sparkling *(con gas)*. Summer favourites include Valencian *horchata*, a sweet milky drink made from ground *chufas* (earth almonds), and *granizado de limón* (iced lemon). *Gaseosa*, or sparkling lemonade, can be drunk either on its own or as *tinto de verano*, mixed with red wine *(see Mixed Drinks)*. Soft drinks and orange juice *(zumo de naranja)* are also widely available.

Horchata, made from *chufas*

Sparkling and still mineral water

Wine

Spain produces some of the best wines in the world. The key standard for the industry is the *Denominación de Origen (DO)* classification, a guarantee of a wine's origin and quality. *Vino de la Tierra* is a classification of wines below that of DO in which over 60 per cent of the grapes come from a specified region. *Vino de Mesa*, the lowest category, covers basic unclassified wines. Spanish *cavas* include best-selling sparkling wines, Freixenet and Codorníu, which are *brut* (dry) or *semi-seco* (slightly sweet). In restaurants, wine is served by the glass, bottle or half-bottle. House wines are sometimes decanted into a carafe.

Penedès white wine   **Rioja red wine**   **Sparkling wine (*cava*)**

Spirits and Liqueurs

Not all of Spain's grapes go into making wine. Much of the harvest is distilled to make clear spirits, the basis of Spain's many liqueurs. These include the aniseed flavoured which can either be throat-shrivellingly dry *(seco* or *orujo)* or syrupy sweet *(dulce)*. Brandy *(coñac)* de Jeréz, an aged wine spirit, is another popular digestive; the price is a good indication of quality. Fruits are also used to flavour liqueurs. One of the most popular variations is *pacharán*, a Navarrese drink using sloes. Spain, and especially the Canary Islands, has always produced *ron* (rum) from sugar cane that grows in the south. *Ginebra* (gin) was introduced by the British when they occupied the island of Menorca in the 18th century. Whisky is also a favourite, though imported Scotch is preferred to the domestic brands. A popular drink with younger people is *cuba-libre*, a rum with cola *(see Mixed Drinks)*.

Anís   *Pacharán*

Beer

Spaniards love their *cerveza* (beer) and Mahou is a popular brand in Madrid. Bars serve *cerveza del barril* (draught beer) in a *caña* (small glass) or larger *jarra*. Beer also comes in bottles of 25 cl, 33 cl or one litre *(litronas)*. Alcohol-free lager *(cerveza sin alcohol)* is sold in many bars.

Bottled beers

Two brands of *fino* sherry

Sherry

Sherry is produced in *bodegas* in Jeréz de la Frontera, Sanlúcar de Barrameda and El Puerto de Santa María. Similar wines are produced in Montilla near Córdoba, although they are not officially called sherry. Pale *fino* is dry and light and makes an excellent aperitif. Amber *amontillado* (aged *fino*) has a strong earthy taste while *oloroso* is full-bodied and ruddy.

Mixed Drinks

Sangría is a refreshing blend of red wine and *gaseosa* (lemonade). Other ingredients include pieces of freshly chopped fruit, sugar and liqueurs. Another favourite drink is *Agua de Valencia*, which is an invigorating combination of *cava* (sparkling wine) and orange juice. A wide range of cocktails is available, including the ever popular *cuba-libre*.

Red wine and lemonade

Sangría

Cuba-libre   *Tinto de verano*

How to Read a Wine Label

As well as the wine's name and its producer, the label will tell you the region it comes from, usually a *Denominación de Origen,* and the vintage year. Wines labelled *cosecha* are recent vintages and the least expensive, while *crianza* and *reserva* wines are aged a minimum of two or three years, part of that time in oak casks. *Blanco* (white) can be *seco* (dry), *semi-seco* (semi-dry) or *dulce* (sweet). *Rosado* is rosé and *tinto* is red. The label also gives the content (usually 75 cl), the alcohol level (around 12–13 per cent volume) and sometimes specifies the grape variety.

Brand name   **Company's crest**

Capacity of the bottle

Estate-bottled rather than cooperative

The wine's *Denominación de Origen*

The vintage   **Symbol for region**

Choosing a Restaurant

THE RESTAURANTS in this guide have been selected across a wide range of price categories for their good value, exceptional food and interesting location. Some offer tables outside and special menus. The restaurants are listed by area, starting with Old Madrid, then Bourbon Madrid, Around La Castellana, Further Afield and Beyond Madrid.

OLD MADRID

	Credit Cards	Tapas Bar	Fixed-Price Menu	Good Wine List	Outdoor Tables
La Trucha. Map 7 A3. ℗ Calle de Núñez de Arce 6. ☎ *91 532 08 90.* This inexpensive restaurant one block from Plaza de Santa Ana offers simple Spanish fare, including three recipes for *trucha* (trout). The *verbena de ahumados* (selection of smoked fish) is famous. ● *Sun & Mon.* ▤	AE DC MC V	●	▨		
Malacatín. Map 4 E4. ℗ Calle de la Ruda 5. ☎ *91 365 52 41.* This old bar in the centre of the Rastro has only one item on the menu: *cocido madrileño (see p155)*, served in three separate stages. The price includes wine and dessert. Book a day ahead. ● *Sun & Aug.* ▤		●	▨		
Café de Oriente. Map 3 C2. ℗℗ Plaza de Oriente 2. ☎ *91 547 15 64.* Splendidly located opposite the Palacio Real *(see pp54–7)*. As well as a large interior bar and cafeteria, there is a comfortable dining room serving innovative Basque-French cuisine. Reservations essential. ▤	AE DC MC V	●	▨	●	▨
Casa Ciriaco. Map 3 C3. ℗℗ Calle Mayor 84. ☎ *91 548 06 20.* A traditional tavern near the Palacio Real, renowned for its *gallina en pepitoria* (a chicken stew with egg and saffron). ● *Wed & Aug.* ▤ &	MC V	●	▨	●	
Casa Labra. Map 4 F2. ℗℗ Calle de Tetuán 12. ☎ *91 531 00 81.* In 1879 the Spanish Socialist party was founded in this small, classic Madrid tavern, also famous for its *tapas* of croquettes and fried codfish. The oak-panelled dining room serves traditional Spanish dishes. ● *Sun & Aug.* &	AE MC V	●	▨		
Casa Patas. Map 7 A3. ℗℗ Calle de Cañizares 10. ☎ *91 369 04 96.* Known for its flamenco shows in the evening, Casa Patas has a well-stocked *tapas* bar and unbeatable fixed-price menu. ● *Sun.* ▤ &	AE DC MC V	●	▨	●	
Cornucopia. Map 4 E2. ℗℗ Calle de la Flora 1. ☎ *91 547 64 65.* Pleasant dining rooms in a 19th-century building facing the Monasterio de las Descalzas Reales *(see p52)*. Creative cuisine with an American influence, friendly service and excellent value menu of the day. ● *Mon.* ▤	AE DC MC V		▨		
El Grill de la Opera. Map 4 D2. ℗℗ Vergara 3. ☎ *91 548 10 05.* Also known as Chez Margot, this tiny French restaurant off Plaza Isabel II has yet to be discovered by Madrid's gastronomic set. The pâté de foie gras makes a tasty starter, followed by fish or meat. ● *Sun.* ▤ &	AE DC MC V				
El Schotis. Map 4 D4. ℗℗ Calle de la Cava Baja 11. ☎ *91 365 32 30.* The speciality at this bar with rustic restaurant is steak on a hot clay slab – it continues cooking to your liking. Popular at night. ● *Sun dinner.* ▤ &	AE DC MC V	●	▨		
El Sobrino del Botín. Map 4 E3. ℗℗ Calle de los Cuchilleros 17. ☎ *91 366 42 17.* Reputedly the oldest restaurant in the world, dating back to 1725. The original wood-burning oven is still used to cook the traditional Castilian roast lamb and suckling pig. Reasonable fixed-price menu. ▤	AE DC MC V		▨	●	
La Barraca. Map 7 A1. ℗℗ Calle de la Reina 29. ☎ *91 532 71 54.* Over ten different Valencia-style rice dishes and paellas are on offer here, made with first-class ingredients. Good home-made desserts. ▤	AE DC MC V		▨	●	

							CREDIT CARDS	TAPAS BAR	FIXED-PRICE MENU	GOOD WINE LIST	OUTDOOR TABLES

Price categories for a three-course evening meal for one, including a half-bottle of house wine, tax and service:

Ⓟ under 3,000 ptas
ⓅⓅ 3,000–5,000 ptas
ⓅⓅⓅ 5,000–7,000 ptas
ⓅⓅⓅⓅ over 7,000 ptas

CREDIT CARDS
Indicates which credit cards are accepted: *AE* American Express; *DC* Diners Club; *MC* MasterCard/Access; *V* VISA.
TAPAS BAR
In addition to the main dining room, there is a bar serving *tapas (see pp30–31)* and *raciones* (larger portions).
FIXED-PRICE MENU
A good-value menu is offered, usually with three courses.
GOOD WINE LIST
Denotes a wide range or specialized selection of wines.
OUTDOOR TABLES
Facilities for eating on a terrace, or in a garden or courtyard.

Restaurant	Price	Credit Cards	Tapas Bar	Fixed-Price Menu	Good Wine List	Outdoor Tables
LA BOLA. Map 4 D1. Calle de la Bola. 📞 91 547 69 30. A true bastion of the *cocido madrileño (see p155)*, this restaurant dates back to 1870. Since then, little has changed in the preparation of the hearty stew, served at lunchtimes only. ● *Sat dinner & Sun in Jul, Aug.* ▤ ♿	ⓅⓅ			■	●	
RASPUTIN. Map 3 C2. Calle de San Nicolás 8. 📞 91 542 49 49. This well-known Russian restaurant is decorated with lace curtains and regal red drapes and carpets, evoking Imperial Russia. ● *Tue.* ▤	ⓅⓅ	MC V		■		
ASADOR FRONTÓN. Map 4 F3. Tirso de Molina 7. 📞 91 369 23 25. One of Madrid's oldest Basque *asadors* (roasting houses). The decor is simple and the menu features an enormous *chuletón de buey*, or beef chop (it's okay to share), and fish dishes. ● *Sun dinner & every Sun in Aug.* ▤	ⓅⓅⓅ	AE DC MC V				
CASA LUCIO. Map 4 D3. Calle de la Cava Baja 35. 📞 91 365 32 52. This historic tavern serves Castilian specialities. The fried eggs with potatoes are exquisite and the rice pudding renowned. ● *Sat lunch, Aug.* ▤	ⓅⓅⓅ	AE DC MC V	●		●	
GURE-ETXEA. Map 4 D3. Plaza de la Paja 12. 📞 91 365 61 49. Quality Basque cooking in a vaulted dining room. The *piperrada*, made with scrambled eggs, red peppers, green beans and ham, goes well with the sharp white Basque wine, *txacoli*. ● *Sun, Mon lunch & Aug.* ▤ ♿	ⓅⓅⓅ	AE DC MC V		■		
JULIÁN DE TOLOSA. Map 4 D3. Calle de la Cava Baja 18. 📞 91 365 82 10. The menu at this restaurant, pleasingly decorated in wood and unrendered brick, is quite small. Specialities include roast peppers and beef chops, but there is always something for fish eaters. ● *Sun.* ▤	ⓅⓅⓅ	AE DC MC V				
LA POSADA DE LA VILLA. Map 4 D4. Calle de la Cava Baja 9. 📞 91 366 18 60. Colourful restaurant, with extensive menu, in a building dating from 1642. One of the rooms has a dome-shaped roasting oven where lamb and roast suckling pig are cooked. A classic Madrid experience. ● *Sun dinner & Aug.* ▤	ⓅⓅⓅ	AE DC MC V		■		
LHARDY. Map 4 F2. Carrera de San Jerónimo 8. 📞 91 521 33 85. Established in 1839 and conserving its true character with chandeliers, mirrors and dark wood-panelled walls, this restaurant serves what is arguably the most classic *cocido madrileño (see p155)*. ● *Sun dinner & Aug.* ▤	ⓅⓅⓅⓅ	AE DC MC V	●	■	●	

BOURBON MADRID

Restaurant	Price	Credit Cards	Tapas Bar	Fixed-Price Menu	Good Wine List	Outdoor Tables
CHAMPAGNERÍA GALA. Map 7 B3. Calle Moratín 22. 📞 91 429 25 62. Admire the indoor patio and chandeliers and enjoy a generous set menu with Catalan specialities at an unbelievably reasonable price. ▤	Ⓟ		●	■		■
MUSEO THYSSEN-BORNEMISZA. Map 7 C2. Paseo del Prado 8. 📞 91 429 27 32. The restaurant in the basement of the Museo Thyssen-Bornemisza *(see pp70–73)* offers a small menu of straightforward dishes, some with a Catalan touch, which are surprisingly good value. ● *Mon.* ▤ ♿	Ⓟ	AE DC MC V	●	■		
EDELWEISS. Map 7 B2. Calle de Jovellanos 7. 📞 91 532 33 83. Reputedly a hangout for spies during World War II, this popular German restaurant includes pork knuckles among its specialities. ● *Sun dinner.* ▤ ♿	ⓅⓅ	AE DC MC V	●	■	●	

For key to symbols see back flap

Price categories for a three-course evening meal for one, including a half-bottle of house wine, tax and service: ℗ under 3,000 ptas ℗℗ 3,000–5,000 ptas ℗℗℗ 5,000–7,000 ptas ℗℗℗℗ over 7,000 ptas	**CREDIT CARDS** Indicates which credit cards are accepted: *AE* American Express; *DC* Diners Club; *MC* MasterCard/Access; *V* VISA. **TAPAS BAR** In addition to the main dining room, there is a bar serving *tapas (see pp30–31)* and *raciones* (larger portions). **FIXED-PRICE MENU** A good-value menu is offered, usually with three courses. **GOOD WINE LIST** Denotes a wide range or specialized selection of wines. **OUTDOOR TABLES** Facilities for eating on a terrace, or in a garden or courtyard.

	CREDIT CARDS	TAPAS BAR	FIXED-PRICE MENU	GOOD WINE LIST	OUTDOOR TABLES
NICOLAS. Map 8 D1. ℗℗℗ Calle de Villalar 4. 91 431 77 37. This cosy, modern restaurant, panelled in wood, offers attentive service and good value fare. It serves Spanish classics such as *rabo de toro* (bull's tail) and *kokotxas de bacalao* (cod morsels). ● *Sun, Mon & Aug.* ▤ ⬇	AE DC MC V			●	
PARADIS. Map 7 B2. ℗℗℗ Calle del Marqués de Cubas 14. 91 429 73 03. This restaurant is part of a successful Catalan chain offering quality Mediterranean cuisine. The grilled vegetables or rice dishes make delicious starters. ● *Sat lunch & Sun.* ▤ ⬇	AE DC MC V			●	
PALACIO DE LINARES. Map 8 D1. ℗℗℗℗ Paseo de Recoletos 2. 91 575 45 40. Set in the sumptuous Palacio de Linares *(see p66)*, this stylish restaurant features quality Catalan and Mediterranean dishes. ● *Sat lunch & Sun.* ▤	AE DC MC V			●	▤
VIRIDIANA. Map 8 D2. ℗℗℗℗ Calle de Juan de Mena 14. 91 523 44 78. Innovative Spanish cuisine complemented by an encyclopedic wine list is offered in this restaurant decorated with stills from Luis Buñuel's film *Viridiana*. The creative menu changes frequently. ● *Sun & Aug.* ▤	AE MC V			●	

AROUND LA CASTELLANA

	CREDIT CARDS	TAPAS BAR	FIXED-PRICE MENU	GOOD WINE LIST	OUTDOOR TABLES
TONY ROMA'S. Map 5 C4. ℗ Calle de Génova 17. 91 310 14 88. An American-style rib house, popular with young Spaniards and a good place to take the children. Informal, fun atmosphere. ▤	AE MC V				
BOCAÍTO. Map 7 B1. ℗℗ Calle de la Libertad 4–6. 91 532 12 19. The combination bar and kitchen dominates this small, noisy restaurant. Good *tapas*; meals are served in the rear dining area. ● *Sat lunch & Sun.* ▤	MC V	●	▤		
CARMENCITA. Map 7 B1. ℗℗ Calle de la Libertad 16. 91 531 66 12. What was once a neighbourhood tavern (founded in 1850) patronized by impoverished intellectuals has become fashionable, serving refined home cooking. The menu of the day is excellent value. ● *Sat lunch & Sun.* ▤	AE DC MC V		▤		
CENTRO RIOJANO. Map 6 E5. ℗℗ Calle de Serrano 25. 91 575 03 37. This is a social club for people from the Rioja region, but its restaurant is open to the public. Basic decor, large quantities of Rioja country cooking (and wine), and very good value. Packed at lunchtime. ● *Sun.* ▤ ⬇	DC MC V		▤		
EL ESPEJO. Map 6 D5. ℗℗ Paseo de Recoletos 31. 91 308 23 47. This café offers a striking decorative blend of Toulouse Lautrec and Art Deco with plenty of mirrors. The dining room, behind, serves international cuisine. There is also a conservatory-style restaurant at the front. ▤	AE DC MC V	●	▤		▤
EL PUCHERO. Map 5 A4. ℗℗ Calle de Larra 13. 91 445 05 77. Popular, unfussy restaurant offering hearty, home-style cooking. The baby broad beans with ham, the roast suckling pig and the game stews are legendary, along with the cantankerous waitresses. ● *Sun & Aug.* ▤	AE MC V			●	
ALKADE. Map 6 E5. ℗℗℗ Calle Jorge Juan 10. 91 576 33 59. Try Basque specialities in the dining room or at the *tapas* bar, such as spider crab soup and *chipirones* (squid in its own ink). ● *Sat & Sun in Jul & Aug.* ▤	AE DC MC V	●	▤	●	

AL MOUNIA. Map 6 D5.   ₱₱₱   AE DC MC V
Calle de Recoletos 5. **[** 91 435 08 28.
Madrid's finest Moroccan restaurant serving authentic couscous and *tajine* (lamb stew). If you have room, there is the rich house dessert, made with honey, almonds and orange blossom water. ● *Sun, Mon & Aug.* 📋 ♿

LA GASTROTECA DE STEPHANE Y ARTURO. Map 5 B5.   ₱₱₱   AE DC MC V
Plaza de Chueca 8. **[** 91 532 25 64.
In this unusual restaurant, decorated with dark colours and modern art, the extrovert owner assists customers with their choices, while his wife cooks dishes in keeping with the arty atmosphere. ● *Sat lunch; Sun in Aug.* 📋 ♿

LA GIRALDA. Map 6 E5.   ₱₱₱   AE DC MC V
Calle de Claudio Coello 24. **[** 91 576 40 69.
Andalusian cuisine is served in a restaurant decorated in Moorish style. Try the *pescado frito* (an assortment of fried fish). ● *Sun dinner.* 📋 ♿

LA TRAINERA. Map 6 F4.   ₱₱₱   AE DC MC V
Calle de Lagasca 60. **[** 91 576 80 35.
A narrow, crowded and lively restaurant, specializing exclusively in fresh seafood. Typical fishing decor and a great ambience. ● *Sun & Aug.* 📋

TEATRIZ. Map 6 E4.   ₱₱₱   AE DC MC V
Calle de Hermosilla 15. **[** 91 577 53 79.
A restaurant in the stalls of an old theatre, with a cocktail bar on the stage. Italian-inspired food, such as a salmon and sole *carpaccio.* 📋 ♿

ARCE. Map 5 A5.   ₱₱₱₱   AE MC V
Calle de Augusto Figueroa 32. **[** 91 522 04 40.
Stylish restaurant serving innovative, creative cuisine. Interesting wine list. Full of executives at lunchtime; more intimate at night. ● *Sat lunch & Sun.* 📋

EL AMPARO. Map 6 E5.   ₱₱₱₱   AE MC V
Callejón de Puigcerdá 8. **[** 91 431 64 56.
New Basque Cuisine in what many consider to be Madrid's nicest setting, with a skylight that lets you gaze up at the stars. The tuna mousse with lobster and parsley oil is just one creation. ● *Sat lunch, Sun, Aug & Easter.* 📋

JOCKEY. Map 6 D4.   ₱₱₱₱   AE DC MC V
Calle de Amador de los Ríos 6. **[** 91 319 10 03.
Among Madrid's top five restaurants, frequented by gourmets and celebrities, Jockey offers a seasonal menu. Excellent poultry and game dishes and a superb wine list. Smart dress only. ● *Sat lunch, Sun & Aug.* 📋 ♿

FURTHER AFIELD

CASA MINGO. Map 3 A1.   ₱
Paseo de la Florida 2. **[** 91 547 79 18.
Rambunctious, loft-like establishment reminiscent of a German bierkeller, except that here the drink is Asturian cider. The menu is limited to roast chicken, salad and braised sausages, but people crowd its long tables.

MUSEO DEL JAMÓN.   ₱   MC V
Calle de Alcalá 155. **[** 91 431 72 96.
Countless hams hang from the rafters at the "Ham Museum", which specializes in *jamón serrano* (cured ham). There is a large bar, but meals are served in the separate dining room. Inexpensive fare in an informal atmosphere. 📋

BADEN   ₱₱   AE DC MC V
Calle General Rodrigo 17. **[** 91 553 87 96.
Combining a bustling tapas bar and a cosy restaurant, Baden serves excellent *chuletón de ternera* (veal chop) and the best pizzas in Madrid. 📋

CASA RICARDO   ₱₱   DC MC V
Calle de Fernando El Católico 31. **[** 91 447 61 19.
This typical Spanish bar offers unpretentious and good, home-style dishes at a very reasonable price. The oxtail soup is delicious as are the baby squid prepared in their ink. ● *Sun dinner.* 📋 ♿

DON SANCHO   ₱₱   AE DC MC V
Calle de Bretón de los Herreros 58. **[** 91 441 37 94.
This is a small, pretty dining room in the tranquil Chamberí neighbourhood. Its short and varied menu is served in a relaxed atmosphere. ● *Sun & Mon dinner, Aug & public hols.* 📋

For key to symbols see back flap

	CREDIT CARDS	TAPAS BAR	FIXED-PRICE MENU	GOOD WINE LIST	OUTDOOR TABLES

Price categories for a three-course evening meal for one, including a half-bottle of house wine, tax and service:

Ⓟ under 3,000 ptas
ⓇⓇ 3,000–5,000 ptas
ⓇⓇⓇ 5,000–7,000 ptas
ⓇⓇⓇⓇ over 7,000 ptas

CREDIT CARDS
Indicates which credit cards are accepted: *AE* American Express; *DC* Diners Club; *MC* MasterCard/Access; *V* VISA.
TAPAS BAR
In addition to the main dining room, there is a bar serving *tapas (see pp30–31)* and *raciones* (larger portions).
FIXED-PRICE MENU
A good-value menu is offered, usually with three courses.
GOOD WINE LIST
Denotes a wide range or specialized selection of wines.
OUTDOOR TABLES
Facilities for eating on a terrace, or in a garden or courtyard.

Restaurant	CREDIT CARDS	TAPAS BAR	FIXED-PRICE MENU	GOOD WINE LIST	OUTDOOR TABLES
EL BUEY — Calle del General Pardiñas 7810. 91 578 11 54. ⓇⓇ. A small restaurant specializing in steaks, but fish is always on offer, too. It has a hugely popular bar, serving Ribera del Duero wine and *tapas*. ▤	AE V	●	▤		
LA TABERNA DE LA DANIELA — Calle del General Pardiñas 21. 91 575 23 29. ⓇⓇ. Short but well-chosen menu. At lunchtimes, only *cocido madrileño (see p155)* is served, or *tapas* at the bar. Good home-made desserts. ▤	V	●			
PAULINO — Calle de Alonso Cano 34. 91 441 87 37. ⓇⓇ. Known as "the Poor Man's Zalacaín", this popular restaurant serves creative dishes at reasonable prices. The food always impresses. ● *Sun; Aug.* ▤ ♿	AE DC MC V		▤		
ALBORÁN — Calle de Ponzano 39–41. 91 399 21 50. ⓇⓇⓇ. This tastefully decorated restaurant in northwest Madrid offers Andalusian-style seafood, including *pescaíto frito* (batter-fried fish). ● *Sun dinner.* ▤ ♿	AE DC MC V			●	
SACHA — Calle de Juan Hurtado de Mendoza 11 (entrada posterior). 91 345 59 52. ⓇⓇⓇ. Decorated like a cosy bistro, this restaurant serves traditional specialities such as partridge with rice and mushrooms. ● *Sun & Aug.* ▤ ♿	AE DC MC V			●	▤
CABO MAYOR — Calle de Juan Ramón Jiménez 37. 91 350 87 76. ⓇⓇⓇⓇ. One of Madrid's finest seafood restaurants, with Cantabrian-Navarrese cuisine. Try the delicious fresh pasta and prawn salad or the monkfish with mushrooms. Excellent wines and desserts. ● *Sat lunch & Sun.* ▤	AE DC MC V		▤	●	▤
COMBARRO — Calle de la Reina Mercedes 12. 91 554 77 84. ⓇⓇⓇⓇ. The day's offerings are displayed in the window of one of Madrid's best seafood restaurants. Relaxed yet elegant. ● *Sun dinner, Easter & Aug.* ▤	AE DC MC V	●			
CURRITO — Pabellon Vizcaya, Casa del Campo. 91 464 57 04. ⓇⓇⓇⓇ. Traditional Basque specialities – meat and fish grilled over charcoals – are served at this restaurant installed in a pavilion in the Casa del Campo. Large terrace for dining outdoors in warm weather. ● *Sun dinner.* ▤	AE DC MC V			●	▤
EL BARRIL DE GOYA — Calle de Goya 86. 91 578 39 98. ⓇⓇⓇⓇ. Patrons crowd the bar of this popular restaurant, and the dining room, with its fishing motifs and big picture windows, is equally busy. The speciality is fresh fish and seafood of every description. ● *Sun dinner.* ▤ ♿	AE DC MC V	●			
EL OLIVO — Calle del General Gallegos 1. 91 359 15 35. ⓇⓇⓇⓇ. Top of the line Mediterranean cuisine, with olive oil as the underlying culinary theme. The owner will advise you on which of the 40 different olive oils will best accompany your meal. ● *Sun, Mon, late Aug & Easter.* ▤	AE DC MC V		▤	●	
GOIZEKO KABI — Calle del Comandante Zorita 37. 91 533 01 85. ⓇⓇⓇⓇ. Traditional Basque cuisine in a refined setting. Excellent fresh produce and seafood, good wine list and delectable desserts. ● *Sun.* ▤ ♿	AE DC MC V			●	
PEDRO LARUMBE. Map 6 E3. — Calle de Serrano 61. 91 575 11 12. ⓇⓇⓇⓇ. This elegant, spacious restaurant with a palatial entrance offers creative cuisine. The fish dishes are especially good. ● *Sat lunch & Sun.* ▤	AE MC V		▤	●	

ZALACAÍN ℗℗℗
Calle de Álvarez de Baena 4. ☎ 91 561 48 40.
Considered to be Madrid's finest restaurant, Zalacaín lives up to its
reputation with a luxurious setting, attentive service and above all,
delicious Basque-oriented cuisine. Smart dress only. ● Sun & Aug. ▦ ♿

AE
MC
V

BEYOND MADRID

ARANJUEZ: *Casa Pablo.* ℗℗
Calle Almíbar 42. ☎ 91 891 14 51.
A centrally located tavern offering solid home cooking. Try the pheasant
with grapes or the fresh asparagus and strawberries. ● Aug. ▦ ♿

AE
MC
V

CHINCHÓN: *Mesón de la Virreina.* ℗℗
Plaza Mayor 28. ☎ 91 894 00 15.
Traditional Castilian food, including *sopa castellana* (a garlic soup with
chickpeas) and classic roast lamb, is prepared in this 16th-century
building. The local *anís* makes an excellent *digestif.* ▦ ♿

AE
DC
MC
V

GUADALAJARA: *Minaya.* ℗℗
Calle Mayor 23. ☎ 949 21 22 53.
A wonderful 16th-century palace with period furniture. The short,
seasonal menu has an emphasis on grilled meats and roast kid. ● Sun. ▦

AE
MC
V

GUADALAJARA: *Amparito Roca.* ℗℗℗
Calle Toledo 19. ☎ 949 21 46 39.
This pleasantly decorated house offers traditional Spanish cuisine with
innovative touches. Try the venison sirloin served in a mushroom sauce
and the scrambled eggs with potato and salmon. ● Sun & Aug. ▦ ♿

AE
MC
V

LA GRANJA DE SAN ILDEFONSO: *Hilaria.* ℗℗
Carretera Valladolid–Madrid, Valsaín (Segovia). ☎ 921 47 02 92.
The owners of this family-run restaurant still use an original recipe for
their white bean stew. Good roast suckling lamb and pig. ● Mon. ▦ ♿

AE
DC
MC
V

PEDRAZA DE LA SIERRA: *Hostería Pintor Zuloaga.* ℗℗
Calle Matadero 1 (Segovia). ☎ 921 50 98 35.
Located in a former Inquisition house, this restaurant serves traditional
Castilian fare such as roast pork and lamb, and hearty stews. ● Tue. ▦

AE
DC
MC
V

SAN LORENZO DE EL ESCORIAL: *Taberna La Cueva.* ℗℗
Calle San Antón 4. ☎ 91 890 15 16.
Juan de Villanueva, architect of the Prado, designed this 18th-century
inn whose specialities include the *huevos a la cueva* (fried eggs and
ham served in a nest of straw potatoes). ● Mon.

MC
V

SEGOVIA: *Mesón de Cándido.* ℗℗
Plaza del Azoguejo 5. ☎ 921 42 81 03.
Don't leave town without visiting Mesón de Cándido, *the* place to eat in
Segovia. The restaurant has good views of the Roman aqueduct and
serves local specialities such as roast lamb and suckling pig. ▦ ♿

AE
DC
MC
V

SIGÜENZA: *El Motor.* ℗℗
Avenida Juan Carlos I (Guadalajara). ☎ 949 39 08 27.
As well as the typical roast suckling pig and lamb you can also try the
fried breadcrumbs *(migas)* or the garlic soup *(sopa castellana).* ▦ ♿

AE
DC
MC
V

TOLEDO: *Hostal del Cardenal.* ℗
Paseo de Recaredo 24. ☎ 925 22 08 62.
Once the summer residence of Cardinal Lorenzana, this 18th-century
palace retains its beautiful garden, enclosed by the city walls. It serves
garlic soup, suckling pig and the famous Toledo *mazapán* (marzipan). ▦

AE
MC
V

TOLEDO: *La Lumbre.* ℗℗
Calle Real de Arrabal 3. ☎ 925 22 03 73.
A lovely old house with wooden beams, next to the Puerta de Bisagra.
The meat dishes, such as roast suckling pig and lamb, are especially good,
and there is delicious *manchego* cheesecake for dessert. ● Sun & Jul. ▦

AE
MC
V

TOLEDO: *Adolfo.* ℗℗℗
Calle de Granada 6. ☎ 925 22 73 21.
Set in the heart of the Jewish quarter, the Adolfo, with its tiles, columns,
antiques and a wonderful 15th-century Mudéjar coffered ceiling, serves game
in winter and fresh trout from the Río Tajo. ● Sun dinner & late Jul. ▦ ♿

AE
DC
MC
V

SHOPPING IN MADRID

From SHERRY TO SEAFOOD, the finest goods in Spain have always made their way across the country to the capital. Madrid still lives off that heritage, despite increasing competition from other parts, especially arch rival Barcelona. Many products are basic Castilian commodities – Manchego cheese, olive oil and leather goods – whose quality lies in the excellent raw materials. Since the swinging 1980s, fashion design has flourished in Madrid. New-look, home-grown fashion outlets now dot Madrid's different shopping areas from the city centre to the upmarket district of Salamanca *(see p99)*. The latest street-wear is available in the Chueca area *(see p94)*. There are colourful food markets all over the city, and in the heart of Old Madrid you'll find superb speciality food and wine stores. Don't miss the El Rastro flea market *(see p61)* on Sundays.

The logo of Spain's best known department store

OPENING HOURS

SPANISH SHOPPING HOURS are not like anywhere else in Europe, thanks to Spanish mealtimes. Most shops are open from 10am to 2pm and from 5pm to 8pm, with only department stores staying open during the lunch break. Small shops often close on Saturday afternoons. Sunday opening in Madrid is largely restricted to tourist shops and delicatessens, and to the rush from before Christmas until 5 January, eve of the Feast of the Epiphany.

HOW TO PAY

BOTH CASH and credit cards are popular methods of payment in Madrid, whereas cheques are hardly ever accepted. Small shops may sometimes reject credit cards which charge them high commission, so it's always worth double-checking that your card is acceptable. A passport or photo ID may be required when you pay by credit card. Some tourist shops accept payment in US dollars.

VAT EXEMPTION AND TAX

A VALUE-ADDED TAX (IVA) is applied to most goods. The standard rate of 16 per cent is charged on clothes and most other products, while the rate for most food-stuffs is seven per cent. A reduced rate of four per cent is applied to basic foods such as cheese and fruit, as well as printed matter and materials for the disabled. At shops with a "Tax-free for Tourists" sign, non-EU residents can claim tax refunds on all purchases over 15,000 pesetas, except food, drink, tobacco, motor bikes, cars and medicines.

SALES

SPANISH SALES ARE a popular institution, taking place in January and July. Beginning after the Feast of the Epiphany on 6 January, the New Year sales go on well into February. In July the summer fashion sales can turn up some real bargains, especially useful as Madrid's hot season often lasts well into September. Look out for signs advertising , *Rebajas, Traspaso* or *Liquidación.*

High fashion on Calle de Serrano, Madrid's smartest shopping street

SHOPPING CENTRES

SHOPPING CENTRES, or *centros comerciales*, have grown rapidly in Madrid. Among the best for upmarket fashion are the **Jardín de Serrano** and **ABC Serrano**, both set in the elegant neighbourhood of Salamanca. Beneath the Hotel Palace *(see p69)*, the **Galería del Prado** has been going through a change of management, but the popular centre is expected to be operational again soon. If you want to find everything under one roof, go to the huge **La Vaguada** mall on the north side of Madrid.

The department store **El Corte Inglés** is a national institution. Gigantic branches all over the city sell clothes, food, household goods and almost everything else. They offer photo-developing and shoe repair services, too.

Madrid also boasts a number of hypermarkets, mostly located off the M30 ring road.

Entrance to the Museo del Jamón *(see p170)*

Display of hand-painted ceramics in Toledo

MARKETS

THE LEGENDARY **El Rastro** flea market is held on Sundays and public holidays. It is located between the Plaza de Cascorro and streets leading off the Ribera de Curtidores. Do not expect to stumble across a painting by Velázquez, but you will find everything else from valuable antiques to second-hand clothes, jewellery, records, collector items, mountain gear and statues for your garden. This is probably the only market in Madrid where it is possible to knock two-thirds off the starting price. Many shops and stalls in the area are open on weekdays for more relaxed browsing.

Also on Sundays, the **Mercadillo de Sellos y Monedas** is a small coin, stamp and postcard market held under the arches of the Plaza Mayor. If you like browsing through old books, visit the wooden stands of the **Mercado del Libro**, on the south side of the Real Jardín Botánico (see p84). Both new and second-hand books are sold here. On Sundays the stalls are thronged, but most open on weekdays, too.

ANNUAL FAIRS

FOR MANY MADRILEÑOS, the passing of the year is marked by popular annual fairs, many of them outdoors.

The contemporary art fair **ARCO** takes place in February. Whether you want to buy or just browse, it provides a great opportunity to catch up on the latest trends in the art world. In the week prior to Madrid's Fiestas de San Isidro (see p34), which begin on 15 May, you can buy earthen cookware and wine jugs at the **Feria de la Cerámica** in the colourful district of Malasaña (see p103). A sure sign that summer is just around the corner is the arrival of hundreds of book stalls along the leafy avenues of Parque del Retiro (see p77), where publishers and book-shop owners exhibit their wares at the **Feria del Libro** over several weeks, beginning at the end of May.

On the Paseo de Recoletos the **Feria de Artesanos** takes place every December. Craft items from ceramics and jewellery to leather goods, glassware and silks make it ideal for Christmas shopping. Throughout December, the Plaza Mayor is the venue for a traditional Christmas fair, the **Mercado de Artículos Navideños**. Christmas trees are for sale, as well as cork-wood and moss for use in homemade nativity scenes. Stallholders sell figurines, including joke items such as the Catalan *caganers* – bare-bottomed shepherd figures traditionally placed behind the manger.

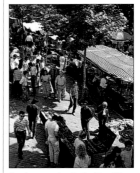

Sunday morning in the busy El Rastro flea market

DIRECTORY

SHOPPING CENTRES

ABC Serrano
Calle de Serrano 61.
Map 6 E3.
91 577 50 31.

El Corte Inglés
Calle de Preciados 1–3.
Map 4 F2.
91 379 80 00.
One of several branches.

Galería del Prado
Plaza de las Cortes 7.
Map 7 B2.
91 360 80 80.

Jardín de Serrano
Calle de Goya 6–8.
Map 6 E4.
91 577 00 12.

La Vaguada
Avenida Monforte de Lemos 36.
91 730 10 00.

MARKETS

El Rastro
Calle de la Ribera de Curtidores. **Map** 4 E4.

Mercadillo de Sellos y Monedas
Plaza Mayor (Sun only).
Map 4 E3.

Mercado del Libro
Calle de Claudio Moyano.
Map 8 D4.

ANNUAL FAIRS

For information on outdoor events call city information:
010.

ARCO
Parque Ferial Juan Carlos I.
91 722 51 80.

Feria de Artesanos
Paseo de Recoletos.
Map 6 D5.

Feria de Cerámica
Plaza de las Comendadoras.
Map 2 D4.

Feria del Libro
Paseo de Coches del Retiro, Parque del Retiro.

Mercado de Artículos Navideños
Plaza Mayor.
Map 4 E3.

What to Buy in Madrid

Traditional fan

I F FLAMENCO FRILLS and kitsch bulls are not to your taste, you can find a satisfying reminder of your visit in many traditional Spanish goods. Strongly scented saffron, matured ewe's cheese or a fruity extra-virgin olive oil all make prized gifts. Leather goods are particularly sought-after. The beautifully crafted Loewe bags are in a league of their own, but most leather, especially shoes, is extremely good value. Traditional crafts, such as woven baskets, are harder to find, but lovely and inexpensive ceramics are widely available. By looking around, you may even pick up an original piece of clothing.

Chulapo Dolls
These typically Spanish dolls with their endearing pout are dressed in the traditional costume of Madrid's castizos (see p105).

Phineas T-shirt
T-shirts make great gifts, and Phineas (see p169) offers a wide range of unique designs.

Leather Handbag
The best bags come from Majorca, and are stocked at Piamonte (see p168), although many other shops sell leather, too.

Mantón de Manila
Classical, beautifully embroidered silk shawls, like this one, are easy to find and come in a wide range of colours.

Turrón
Luxury nougat and almond paste, pressed into almond-shaped shells, comes in a wooden gift box at Casa Mira (see p170).

Saffron (Azafrán)
Hand-picked azafrán comes from the autumn crocus. Introduced by the Moors, it is the world's most expensive spice.

Queso Manchego
Used in tapas or served with quince jelly (membrillo) at the end of a meal, Manchego cheese also makes an ideal gift. It is widely regarded as Spain's greatest cheese.

Barquillera
Filled with wafer biscuits, this old-fashioned cookie (biscuit) tin has a children's roulette game on the lid. Barquilleras are sold in the pastry departments of El Corte Inglés and Mallorca (see p170).

Modern Fan
A wide range of fans, from the traditional delicate lace variety to colourful, simple modern versions, can be found throughout Madrid. This fan was bought from Tucán (see p170).

Modern fan

Traditional Ceramics
The art of hand-painting ceramics with traditional colours and designs continues to thrive in Madrid. The attractive plates and tiles make memorable keepsakes.

Antique ceramic tiles

Decorative ceramic plates

Painted modern candlesticks

Modern Ceramics
Those in search of 20th-century ceramics will not need to look far. As well as traditional designs, Madrid offers a wide range of entirely modern craftwork.

SAUSAGES AND HAMS

Spain has a deep-rooted tradition of pork products, ranging from whole hams to sausages of every shape and size. The annual *matanza*, when pigs were killed and families spent the day preparing food for the months ahead, was an important date on the country calendar. Today, most products are made in a factory. *Jamón serrano* is cured ham, served thinly sliced as a *tapa* or used diced as an ingredient in numerous recipes. The best, and most expensive ham, is *ibérico*, from the small, black-hoofed, free-ranging Iberian pig. Many sausages are seasoned with Spain's favourite spice – paprika; they are called *chorizo*. Those without paprika are called *salchichón*. Other types of sausage are *longaniza* (long, thin sausages), *morcilla* (blood sausage or black pudding, made with rice, onions or potatoes) and *chistorras* (small Basque sausages, often flambéed). *Caña de lomo* is cured pork loin.

Jamón serrano

Morcilla

Salchichón

Caña de lomo

Chorizo

Fashion and Accessories

SPANIARDS ARE CELEBRATED for their elegance. No woman will leave the house, even if it is simply to go to the market, without dressing impeccably. The most popular styles tend towards classic cuts, with the occasional Baroque flounce. Madrid's cultural boom in the 1980s impacted the fashion world with a look based on sleek, understated design and sophisticated accessories. Footwear and clothing boutiques carry all the well-known international designer labels but, if you want something a little bit different, look out for the Spanish designers.

SHOES

THE BEST SHOES are made in Mallorca, with classic footwear by Yanko at the very top of the range. Yanko shoes are so soft and comfortable that they feel like slippers. **Bravo** shoe shops carry many top Mallorcan makes, including Yanko, Lotusse and Barratts.

Another Mallorcan export is the young and comfortable **Camper** shoe. Outlets exist all over Madrid, with customer-friendly displays. The **Geltra** chain stocks the Camper brand in addition to its own good quality range of shoes.

For sophisticated designs – and prices – go to **Farrutx**. For a more avant-garde style, it is worth trying the Catalan shoe outlet **Excrupulus Net**.

If you forgot your trainers, or need to get out of rain-soaked shoes cheaply, try the shops along the Calle de Fuencarral, or go to **Los Guerrilleros** in the heart of Madrid's "kilometre 0" – the area around the Puerta del Sol. Jot down the reference number of the shoe in the showcase and you will get efficient service inside.

Brightly coloured espadrilles are sold in most areas but, for an old-world feel, visit **Casa Hernanz** off the Plaza Mayor.

HANDBAGS AND OTHER LEATHER GOODS

THE ULTIMATE in Spanish bags and leather clothing goes by the prestigious name of **Loewe**. Established over a century ago by a German tanner who settled in Spain, Loewe bags are sold all over the world. At the Loewe shop in Calle de Serrano, you can feast your eyes, if nothing else.

Around the corner you will find **Lotusse** selling wallets, bags and coats, as well as its famous shoes. The Mallorcan connection continues nearby at **Boxcalf**, with an enticing range of quality leather clothing and accessories.

Piamonte, in the Chueca district, has become synonymous with attractive bags at affordable prices. They also have belts and an interesting selection of jewellery.

For a touch of Andalusian chic, see the handbags and belts for sale at **El Caballo**. **Manuel Herrero** offers value for money in what feels like a bazaar crammed with leather and suede, visitors and persuasive salespeople.

A delightful outlet for classic gloves is the small, but well-stocked **Guante Varade**.

JEWELLERY

MADRID IS FULL of small shops, stacked with trays of 18-carat gold studs, chains and bracelets, and grand jewellers – whether you walk down the Gran Vía or Calle de Serrano. Most Spanish women adore gold – and the heavier the better – and pearls. Popular, man-made "Majorica" pearls, as well as the cultivated variety, can be found all over Madrid. **Las Perlas** on Gran Vía sells all categories of pearls, starting at good prices.

Del Pino on Calle de Serrano is fun for its variety of costume jewellery across the price range, and the Catalans' innovative **Tous** outlet in Madrid should not be missed.

If you are interested in new creations, visit internationally acclaimed jeweller **Joaquín Berao**. His shop is like a miniature art gallery devoted to thoughtfully understated and tasteful design.

At **La Oreja de Plata**, designer Chus Burés displays his own work and that of other jewellers he has discovered. **Helena Rohner**, whose silver, bronze and enamel jewellery can be found in **Piamonte** (see Handbags), is also becoming a popular name. You can visit her workshop, but it is best to call first.

WOMEN'S FASHIONS

THE BEST OF SPANISH and international fashion is located on Calle de Serrano and Calle de José Ortega y Gasset, as well as in adjacent streets. The best place to find the work of young designers is the Chueca district, in and around Calle del Almirante, with shops such as **Ararat**. If you want original "street" fashion, go to **Glam** in busy Calle de Fuencarral, a street full of fun shops for the young.

In the designer category, **Adolfo Domínguez** – doyen of Madrid's minimalist look – and **Roberto Verino** offer excellent value for money. The more eccentric should try **Agatha Ruiz de la Prada**'s unique creations – also for children – in her shop off the Paseo de la Castellana. And for a dress made of ties or a bag made of zippers, go to **Vacas Flacas**, but do not expect a bargain for this kind of recycled clothing.

Another creation in a league of its own is the traditional **Seseña** cape, exclusive to the Madrid fashion house of the same name which also makes more modern versions.

The chain store **Zara** has become a national phenomenon, offering easy-to-wear clothes for women, men and children at very good prices.

Fine lingerie is part of a Spanish tradition, and lingerie shops – called corseterías in the more expensive parts of town – are everywhere. A cotton nightdress can be an expensive affair but, for a select choice of sleepwear as well as bed linen, visit **¡Oh qué luna!** for original and attractive designs.

Not to be forgotten, Spain is big on babies, and **Prenatal** is well worth a visit for expectant women and for mothers with very young children.

MENSWEAR

MEN'S FASHIONS can be found in the same areas of Madrid as women's. The traditional tailored look lives on, but Spanish men also like styles from abroad. You will find that many shops which sell off-the-peg clothes have Italian- or English-sounding names, but only sell home-produced merchandise. Prices and quality vary. For a more

interesting purchase, check out the menswear at **Roberto Verino**, **Adolfo Domínguez** or **Zara** *(see Women's Fashions)*. At the top end, **Loewe**'s store for men has beautiful clothes, adapting fashion trends to its own look. A Loewe silk tie with a Spanish art motif makes a rewarding purchase.

In the Calle del Almirante, **Pedro Morago** has stylish clothes for men on the move. Even though the young and fashionable stars of Spanish cinema and sports shop here, prices are accessible.

Another name to look out for is Antonio Miró and his famous shirts, available in

Gallery, which hosts a range of top international labels.

For casual wear, **Phineas** has become a very popular Madrid label and there are clothes for women, too. Its outlets throughout the city offer quality cottonwear with original designs that come in attractive colours.

When it comes to cotton, a Portuguese label, intriguingly named **Throttleman**, has set up shop in Madrid, offering shirts and fantasy boxer shorts. And for outdoor clothes, which cater for anything between a walk in the park and a safari, go to **Coronel Tapioca** for comfort at a reasonable price.

DIRECTORY

SHOES

Bravo
Calle de Serrano 42.
Map 6 E4.
91 435 27 29.

Camper
Gran Vía 54.
Map 4 E1.
91 547 52 23.

Casa Hernanz
Calle de Toledo 18.
Map 4 E3.
91 366 54 50.

Excrupulus Net
Calle del Almirante 7.
Map 5 C5.
91 521 72 44.

Farrutx
Calle de Serrano 7.
Map 8 D1.
91 576 94 93.

Geltra
Gran Vía 33.
Map 4 F1.
91 531 13 53.

Los Guerrilleros
Puerta del Sol 5.
Map 4 F2.
91 521 27 08.

HANDBAGS AND OTHER LEATHER GOODS

Boxcalf
Calle de Jorge Juan 14.
Map 6 E5.
91 435 34 29.

El Caballo
Calle de Lagasca 55.
Map 6 E5.
91 576 40 37.

Guante Varade
Calle de Serrano 54.
Map 6 E3.
91 575 67 41.

Loewe
Calle de Serrano 26.
Map 6 E4.
91 577 60 56.

Lotusse
El Jardin de Serrano,
Calle de Goya 6–8.
Map 6 E4.
91 577 20 14.

Manuel Herrero
Calle de Preciados 7 & 16.
Map 4 F2.
91 521 29 90.

Piamonte
Calle del Marqués de Monasterio 5.
Map 5 C5.
91 308 48 62.

JEWELLERY

Del Pino
Calle Ayala 46.
Map 6 E3.
91 435 26 70.

Helena Rohner
Calle del Almendro 4.
Map 4 D3.
91 365 79 06.

Joaquín Berao
Calle del Conde de Xiquena 13.
Map 5 C5.
91 310 16 20.

La Oreja de Plata
Calle de Jorge Juan 39.
Map 6 F5.
91 576 39 01.

Las Perlas
Gran Vía 33.
Map 4 E1.
91 521 18 44.

Tous
Calle de Ayala 26.
Map 6 E4.
91 575 53 86.

WOMEN'S FASHIONS

Adolfo Domínguez
Calle de Serrano 18.
Map 6 E5.
91 577 82 80.

Agatha Ruiz de la Prada
Calle del Marqués de Riscal 8.
Map 6 D3.
91 310 44 83.

Ararat
Calle del Almirante 10.
Map 5 C5.
91 531 81 56.

Glam
Calle de Fuencarral 35.
Map 7 A1.
91 522 80 54.

¡Oh que luna!
Calle de Ayala 32.
Map 6 F4.
91 431 37 25.

Prenatal
Calle Goya 99.
Map 7 A1.
91 431 59 30.

Roberto Verino
Calle de Serrano 33.
Map 6 E4.
91 426 04 75.

Seseña
Calle de la Cruz 23.
Map 7 A2.
91 531 68 40.

Vacas Flacas
Calle de Claudio Coello 24.
Map 6 E5.
91 575 64 83.

Zara
ABC Serrano, Calle de Serrano 61. **Map** 6 E3.
91 575 63 34.

MENSWEAR

Coronel Tapioca
Calle del Carmen 12.
Map 4 F2.
91 531 59 29.

Gallery
Calle de Jorge Juan 17.
Map 6 E5.
91 576 79 31.

Loewe
Calle de Serrano 34.
Map 6 E4.
91 435 30 56.

Pedro Morago
Calle del Almirante 20.
Map 5 C5.
91 521 66 28.

Phineas
Calle Mayor 10. **Map** 4 E2.
91 366 52 28.

Throttleman
Calle de Ayala 28.
Map 6 E4.
91 577 87 92.

Antiques, Crafts and Gifts

S PAIN'S RICH AND VARIED POPULAR ART makes it relatively easy to pick up an original piece of handicraft. It is often possible to obtain the same item, be it a ceramic mortar or a silk shawl, as an antique, a reproduction or even a stylized update. Genuine articles at good prices can still be found, but many rural crafts are fast disappearing. Fortunately, they do not include the age-old arts of producing Manchego cheese, cured ham and wines. Spain's musical tradition is very much alive, and a CD of flamenco-jazz fusion can be a spellbinding gift.

ANTIQUES

S TROLLING DOWN the Calle de Claudio Coello, in elegant Salamanca, you will pass some outstanding antique shops. The streets around are also full of specialist outlets for rare antiques, ranging from 18th-century lacquered furniture at **María Gracia Cavestany**, to 15th-century Flemish paintings at **Theotokopoulos**, or rustic tools at **Collector**. Some of Madrid's top dealers, such as Pedro Alarcón and Luis Carabe, can be found under one roof at the **Centro de Anticuarios**.

Calle del Prado is lined with antique shops crammed with Castilian-style furniture, books, old tiles, religious artifacts and antique jewellery. Shops on neighbouring Calle de las Huertas deal in old prints.

Hidalgo in El Rastro (see p61) sells collectors' items, such as keys and corkscrews, while reasonably priced bric-à-brac (including some reproductions) can be found at **La Trastienda de Alcalá**, just northeast of the Parque del Retiro (see p77).

Casa Postal, near Plaza de Cibeles, specializes in old postcards and has a great selection of old signs and posters.

MODERN ART, PRINTS AND PHOTOGRAPHS

W HEN IT COMES TO modern art, new trends and new talent, the galleries around Calle de Claudio Coello are well worth visiting. The **Juan Gris** gallery always has works from established as well as up-and-coming artists. **Juana de Aizpuru**, a relative newcomer, has rapidly become one of the most influential

galleries in Madrid. Also well known for promoting young artists are **Fúcares** and **Soledad Lorenzo**. You can find sketches by artists such as Picasso, Chillida, Tàpies and Miró at **Estiarte**. Most galleries are closed on Mondays.

CRAFTS

A WIDE CHOICE of ceramics is offered at **Cántaro**, near the Plaza de España (see p53). Well stocked in regional styles, the shop also carries so-called "extinct" ceramics – pottery which is no longer produced. **El Caballo Cojo**, in Old Madrid, offers a bewildering array of ceramics from the 1960s and 1970s, as well as "extinct" pottery. In all shops, some of the attractive pottery is likely to be Moroccan.

The Spanish are proud of their embroidered linen, but hand-embroidered tablecloths or shawls at ridiculously low prices probably come from China. **Casa Bonet** offers the real thing, but at a premium.

One of the best shops for mantones (silk shawls) and linen – hand- and machine-made – is **Borca**, just off the Puerta del Sol (see p44).

Basket shops tend to offer Asian imports, but you will still find traditional wares at **Joaquín Fernández**. And for fine hand-made guitars, visit **Guitarrería F Manzanero**.

BOOKS AND MUSIC

T HERE IS AN AMPLE stock of foreign language titles at **Casa del Libro** on Gran Vía. French-owned **FNAC**, nearby, offers a wide choice of books both in English and in other languages. **Booksellers**, a

little further afield, has classics but only a limited choice of new books. The second-hand bookstalls of the **Mercado del Libro** behind the Ministerio de Agricultura (see p84) are good for cheap paperbacks and, sometimes, rare volumes.

Art books can be found at **Crisol** branches, while one of the best specialist art bookshops is **Gaudí**, near Chueca.

For all types of music, go to the FNAC or **El Corte Inglés** branches in Calle de Preciados or Paseo de la Castellana. Flamenco buffs must drop in to **El Flamenco Vive**.

GIFTS

F OOD GIFTS FROM Madrid are always appreciated, and olive oil or "green gold" from Catalonia to Andalusia is available at **Patrimonio Comunal Olivarero**, a specialist olive oil shop near Chueca. The **El Corte Inglés** Club du Gourmet on the 4th floor of its Calle de Serrano branch also carries a wide selection of olive oil and other typical Spanish produce, such as sherry vinegar.

At **Casa Mira** you can get turrón – Spain's traditional Christmas sweet – all year round. An almond speciality, turrón comes in a hard or a soft version. For a less sticky, bite-size treat of soft turrón pressed into almond-shaped wafer shells, try almendras imperiales (imperial almonds).

For assorted cakes in the centre of Madrid go to **Horno de San Onofre**; for a first-class selection of wines visit **Mariano Madrueño**. Various categories of cured ham are available at **Museo del Jamón** outlets. One of the best cheese shops is **La Boulette** inside the Mercado de la Paz, just off Calle de Serrano. **Mallorca**, Madrid's finest delicatessen, carries the very best of foodstuffs to eat in or take away.

El Arco de los Cuchilleros is one of Madrid's most tasteful gift shops, with jewellery, leather goods and ceramics, while **Así**, conveniently located in the city centre, sells all kinds of dolls as well as reasonably priced household goods.

The Spanish share a national passion for cologne, and there are *perfumerías* (toiletry and cosmetic shops) everywhere.

SOUVENIRS

For a superior tourist shop, go to **La Tienda de Madrid**, which is attached to Madrid's Museo Municipal *(see p103)*.

You will find souvenirs such as *barquilleras* (traditional biscuit or cookie tins), also sold at **El Corte Inglés** pastry shops and **Mallorca** *(see Gifts)*.

Dolls in typical Madrid costume are available at the **Sanatorio de Muñecos**.

Between the Puerta del Sol and Plaza Mayor, especially on Calle Postas, are outlets for

religious artifacts. **Palomeque** specializes in postcards and reproductions of religious art.

Almoraima, on the Plaza Mayor, sells a vast range of fans. For a T-shirt that will remind you of your stay, but will not make you feel too touristy, try **El Tintero** in Chueca, which does designs and messages in Spanish.

ENTERTAINMENT IN MADRID

FEW EUROPEAN CITIES take their entertainment as seriously as Madrid. The city is an international mecca for cultural events, putting a great deal of energy into providing its citizens and visitors with the best in traditional and modern entertainment throughout the year. World-famous orchestras, ballets and operas, including Madrid's own *zarzuela*, are daily staples. Dozens of mainstream and alternative theatres offer everything from Spanish Golden Age classics to experimental drama. The country's best flamenco acts bring their southern

Street performer in Parque del Retiro

Spanish art to Madrid's international audiences. Some of Europe's liveliest cafés and bars are found here. The afternoon siesta, once a civilized way to escape the Spanish heat, is now either an excellent remedy for the previous night's revelry, or a way to prepare for the one ahead. Most bars and dance clubs are crowded four nights a week, from Thursday through Sunday, and smaller venues offer jazz, rock, salsa and world music on an almost nightly basis. Be prepared for late nights, however, because most activities begin well after midnight and often continue until after breakfast.

Façade of the Teatro Real *(see p58)*, fronted by a statue of Felipe IV

PRACTICAL INFORMATION

THE FIRST STOP for visitors to Madrid should be at one of several tourist information offices, where English will be spoken and free information on events and venues can be obtained. For those interested in exploring Madrid with a professional guide, contact **A.P.I.T.** or **COSITUR**. These agencies supply guides with a comprehensive and intimate knowledge of the city.

Most Spaniards speak some English and are usually willing to help confused foreigners. Unfortunately, however, most of the city's entertainment guides are published exclusively in Spanish. *Lookout* is one informative English-language magazine relied upon by Madrid's expatriate community. Another is *In Madrid*, a free monthly publication that can be found in many bookshops, Irish bars and record shops.

You can also pick up a copy at most embassies and at the tourist information office at **Barajas Airport** *(see p192)*.

Of the Spanish options, the most complete entertainment guide is the weekly *Guía de Ocio*, which hits newsstands and bookstores on Friday and is usually sold out by Sunday. It covers every kind of entertainment on offer.

Madrid's top three daily newspapers – *El Mundo*, *El País* and *ABC* – have weekly entertainment supplements. These are more geared towards entertainment features, but their listings are broad and sometimes include last-minute events that you may not find in the *Guía de Ocio*. The *El País* and *ABC* supplements appear on Friday, while *El Mundo* tries to get a head start with a Thursday publication.

BOOKING TICKETS

THE EASIEST WAY to purchase tickets to major events, especially theatre, opera and concerts, is by telephone. **TeleTicket** and **Tel-Entradas** are the two main agents. Both accept VISA and MasterCard. Their services are provided free of charge and your tickets will be waiting for you at the venue's ticket booth.

SEASONS AND TICKETS

WHILE THERE IS never a shortage of top events year-round in Madrid, the main concert and theatre seasons run from September to June. During May's Fiestas de San Isidro *(see p34)* and the Festival de Otoño *(see p36)*, from September to November, the authorities

A full house at the Joy Eslava dance club *(see p176)*

Children enjoying the adventure playground in the Plaza de Oriente

like to splurge by booking top Spanish and international names in music, theatre and dance. Special events listings can be picked up at tourist offices and at most branches of the Caja Madrid bank.

The **Madrid Rock** record shop and **FNAC** sell most big-venue concert tickets, while the **TEYCI** agency sells tickets for most other events, but charges up to 20 per cent commission.

Other agencies that sell tickets for a wide variety of events include **El Corte Ingles** and **Caja Madrid (Venta de Entradas)**.

FACILITIES FOR THE DISABLED

To find out about wheelchair accessibility, you are advised to telephone the venue itself. *El País* provides a 1–4 rating for some venues in its daily listing: '1' means totally accessible while '4' indicates considerable difficulty.

Getting to and from events is easier. Each bus route runs several low-level vehicles with a wheelchair symbol. **Radio-teléfono Taxi** (91 547 82 00) provides special cars – book well in advance and ask for Eurotaxis. The Metro does not cater for disabled people.

CHILDREN'S ACTIVITIES

There is no shortage of activities in Madrid for visitors with children. To give them some space, head for the Casa de Campo *(see p114)*. Simply getting to this park can be fun if you take the high-flying **Teleférico** cable car. The park is home to the **Zoo-Aquarium**, the modern **Parque de Atracciones** amusement park, a boating lake and several swimming pools. In the centre of Bourbon Madrid is the popular Parque del Retiro *(see p77)* with magic shows, jugglers, clowns and a lake.

The main children's theatre is **Sala San Pol**, but numerous fringe theatres also hold performances for young people.

Flamenco guitarist in the Parque del Retiro

Relaxing at a street café in the Plaza del Dos de Mayo *(see p103)*

Traditional Entertainment

THE SPANISH TAKE PARTICULAR pride in their cultural
heritage, and attending a performance at one of
Madrid's theatres, opera houses, music auditoriums or
cabarets is one of the best ways of sharing the experience
and traditions of Spain. Madrid plays host to a wide
variety of classical art performances, which equal the
best on offer in other European cities, but it also provides
plenty of opportunities for savouring the traditional art
forms of the Spanish people. These include the sponta-
neity of flamenco, the three-act drama of the *corrida* or
bullfight *(see p111)*, and *zarzuela*, Madrid's particular
version of the Spanish operetta *(see p75)*.

CLASSICAL MUSIC

THE NEWLY RENOVATED **Teatro
Real de Madrid** is prob-
ably best known as the home
of the city's opera company,
but it is also the venue for
top national and international
classical music concerts.

The two concert halls of
the **Auditorio Nacional de
Música** also host international
classical music performances,
along with programmes by
the national orchestra, the
Orquesta Nacional de España.
The Orquesta Nacional is
frequently accompanied by
Spain's national choir, the
Coro Nacional de España.

The **Teatro Monumental**
is the main venue for the
excellent Orquesta Sinfónica y
Coro de RTVE, the orchestra
and choir of Spain's state
radio and television company.
The **Auditorio Conde
Duque** also hosts a variety
of classical concerts.

OPERA AND ZARZUELA

A VISIT TO THE Spanish capital
would not be complete
without spending a night at
the *zarzuela*, Madrid's own
variety of comic opera. The
best productions are those
staged at the **Teatro de la
Zarzuela**. Other venues
include the **Teatro Albéniz**
and the newly reopened
**Teatro Príncipe – Palacio
de las Variedades**. Several
other theatres offer *zarzuela*
productions in the summer.

The best place to see
national and international
opera, including Madrid's
own opera company, is
the **Teatro Real de Madrid**,

appropriately located next to
the Ópera Metro station. The
Teatro Calderón also hosts
some excellent classical and
modern opera productions.

DANCE

THERE ARE SEVERAL venues in
Madrid that stage performances of classical and modern
dance, in addition to those that
put on larger flamenco productions. The **Teatro Albéniz**
is one of the main places to
see good international dance
companies as well as the top
national acts. The three other
major venues are the **Teatro
Madrid**, the **Teatro Español**
and the **Teatro Olimpia**.

FLAMENCO

A SPONTANEOUS musical art
form, flamenco has its
roots in the gypsy culture of
Andalusia. However, many of
the best exponents are now
based in the capital.

Flamenco is a late-night art
form with shows usually taking
place through the evening and
into the early hours of the
morning. Most venues offer
dinner and a show, which
may be singing only, or both
singing and dancing. Although
the familiar rhythmic dancing
is often a part of flamenco,
the purest form of the art
consists of a solo singer
accompanied by a guitar.

Casa Patas is still the best
place to catch the raw power
of genuine flamenco guitar
and *cante* singing. Dancing
often, but not always, accom-
panies the singing. Both music
and dance can be enjoyed at
Café de Chinitas. Other

venues offering high-quality
flamenco performances are
Arco de Cuchilleros, **Corral
de la Morería**, **Candela** and
Torres Bermejas.

THEATRE

MADRID'S MOST prestigious
theatres are the **Teatro
de la Comedia** and the **Teatro
María Guerrero**. The former
is the home of the Compañía
Nacional de Teatro Clásico,
which stages classic works
by Spanish playwrights. The
Teatro María Guerrero hosts
foreign productions as well as
modern drama in Spanish.
Many other theatres, including
Teatro Español, **Teatro
Alcázar**, **Teatro Muñoz Seca**
and **Teatro Reina Victoria**,
also stage drama productions.

As well as drama, Teatro
Muñoz Seca and Teatro Reina
Victoria also offer comedy
productions, as do **Teatro
Lara** and **Teatro La Latina**,
which specializes in *Madrileño*
comedy productions. **Centro
Cultural de la Villa** presents
popular theatre. Madrid also
has a thriving network of alter-
native venues, most notably
Cuarta Pared, **Ensayo 100**
and **Teatro Afil**. Teatro de la
Abadía, **Teatro Lope de
Vega** and **Teatro Nuevo
Apolo** often stage musicals.

An enormous range of both
Spanish and international
theatrical talent, from established companies to radical
new fringe groups, gathers
in the city during the annual
Festival de Otoño *(see p36)*.

BULLFIGHTING

BULLFIGHTING continues to
be a popular spectacle in
Madrid *(see p111)*, as throughout the country, but it is not
for the squeamish. The **Plaza
de Toros de Las Ventas**
bullring is the most important
in the world, and holds
corridas every Sunday from
March through to October.
During the May Fiestas de
San Isidro *(see p34)* there are
fights every day. Each fight is
made up of six 15-minute
faenas of three acts, the last
of which ends with the kill-
ing of the bull or, on very
rare occasions, the matador.

FOOTBALL

WINNERS OF the European Cup on many occasions, **Real Madrid** are the local aristocrats of football. Their Bernabéu stadium, which has a capacity of 105,000, is one of the great theatres of the game. Real Madrid's cross-town rivals are **Atlético de Madrid**. They play at the Vicente Calderón stadium, a smaller and cheaper venue along the Manzanares River, which often has a better atmosphere. Madrid's third team is **Rayo Vallecano**, who are constantly shifting up and down between the first and second divisions.

DIRECTORY

CLASSICAL MUSIC

Auditorio Conde Duque
Calle del Conde Duque 11.
Map 2 D4.
(91 588 57 35.

Auditorio Nacional de Música
Calle del Príncipe de Vergara 146.
(91 337 01 00.

Teatro Monumental
Calle de Atocha 65.
Map 7 A3.
(91 429 81 19.

Teatro Real de Madrid
Plaza de Oriente.
Map 3 C2.
(91 516 06 06.

OPERA AND ZARZUELA

Teatro Albéniz
Calle de la Paz 11.
Map 4 F3.
(91 521 99 98.

Teatro Calderón
Calle de Atocha 18.
Map 4 F3.
(91 632 01 14.

Teatro de la Zarzuela
Calle de Jovellanos 4.
Map 7 B2.
(91 524 54 00.

Teatro Príncipe – Palacio de las Variedades
Calle de las Tres Cruces 8.
Map 4 F1.
(91 521 83 81.

Teatro Real de Madrid
(see Classical Music)

DANCE

Teatro Albéniz
(see Opera and Zarzuela)

Teatro Español
Calle del Príncipe 25.
Map 7 A3.
(91 429 62 97.

Teatro Madrid
Avenida de la Ilustración.
(91 740 52 74.

Teatro Olimpia
Plaza de Lavapiés.
Map 7 A5.
(91 527 46 22.

FLAMENCO

Arco de Cuchilleros
Calle de Cuchilleros 7.
Map 4 E3.
(91 364 02 63.

Café de Chinitas
Calle de Torija 7.
Map 4 D1.
(91 547 15 02.

Candela
Calle del Olivar 2.
Map 7 A4.
(91 467 33 82.

Casa Patas
Calle de Cañizares 10.
Map 7 A3.
(91 369 04 96.

Corral de la Morería
Calle de la Morería 17.
Map 3 C3.
(91 365 84 46.

Torres Bermejas
Calle de Mesonero Romanos 11.
Map 4 F1.
(91 532 33 22.

THEATRE

Teatro Alcázar
Calle de Alcalá 20.
Map 7 A2.
(91 532 06 16.

Teatro Afil
Calle del Pez 10.
Map 2 F5.
(91 521 58 27.

Centro Cultural de la Villa
Plaza de Colón.
Map 6 D5.
(91 575 60 80.

Teatro de la Comedia
Calle del Príncipe 14.
Map 7 A3.
(91 521 49 31.

Cuarta Pared
Calle de Ercilla 17.
(91 517 23 17.

Teatro Español
(see Dance)

Ensayo 100
Calle de Raimundo Lulio 20.
Map 5 A2.
(91 447 94 86.

Teatro La Latina
Plaza de la Cebada 2.
Map 4 D4.
(91 365 28 35.

Teatro Lara
Calle Corredera Baja de San Pablo 15.
Map 2 F5.
(91 521 05 52.

Teatro Lope de Vega
Gran Vía 57.
Map 4 E1.
(91 547 20 11.

Teatro de la Abadía
Calle Fernandez de los Rios 42.
Map 2 E1.
(91 448 16 27.

Teatro María Guerrero
Calle de Tamayo y Baus 4.
Map 5 C5.
(91 319 47 69.

Teatro Muñoz Seca
Plaza del Carmen 1.
Map 4 F1.
(91 523 21 28.

Teatro Nuevo Apolo
Plaza de Tirso de Molina 1.
Map 4 F3.
(91 369 06 37.

Teatro Reina Victoria
Carrera de San Jerónimo 24.
Map 7 A2.
(91 429 58 90.

BULLFIGHTING

Plaza de Toros de las Ventas
Calle de Alcalá 237.
(91 356 22 00.

FOOTBALL

Atlético de Madrid
Estadio Vicente Calderón, Paseo de la Virgen del Puerto 67.
(91 366 47 07.

Rayo Vallecano
Nuevo Estadio de Vallecas, Avenida de la Albufera 132.
(91 478 22 53.

Real Madrid
Estadio Santiago Bernabéu, Avenida de Concha Espina.
(91 344 00 52.

Modern Entertainment

MADRID'S NIGHTLIFE starts to rumble at dusk in the city's numerous *tapas* bars and cafés. After a quick bite and yet another *caña* (small glass of beer), you may decide to head off to one of the city's palatial movie houses to see a film, or perhaps you would prefer to hit a lively night spot for a little rock, jazz or salsa to warm up your dancing shoes. The younger *Madrileños*, who may well have to go to school the next day, begin to head for the Metro stations at about 1:30am to catch the last train home, clearing the way for the multitudes of over-20s to take over the dance clubs until daybreak.

CINEMA

SPANISH CINEMA has been undergoing a renaissance in recent years as a new crop of film-makers tries to follow in the footsteps of internationally acclaimed film director Pedro Almodóvar, famous for his *Women on the Verge of a Nervous Breakdown (see p104)*.

For those with a grasp of the language, Spanish cinema is a rewarding experience, especially if enjoyed at one of the vast movie houses along Gran Vía *(see p48)*, such as the the **Capitol**, **Amaya** or 1,500-seat **Coliseum**. At the weekends many cinemas have late-night film programmes which begin only after midnight.

For those with no knowledge of Spanish, Hollywood productions and independent films can be seen in their original-language version at **Alphaville**, **Luna**, **Ideal Multicines** and **California**. These cinemas have sprung up over the years to cater to Madrid's foreign residents and Spaniards who wish to enjoy productions in their purest form with Spanish subtitles. Films shown in their original version are listed in the film section of newspapers and various listings magazines as *VO (versión original)*.

CAFÉS AND BARS

WITH SUCH a vast array of cafés and bars in Madrid, you'd think supply would outstrip demand. But Madrid's social life revolves around the city's endless watering holes, which are also great places for people-watching and encounters. The large, historic **Café**

Comercial is a Madrid landmark. Its comfortable turn-of-the-century ambience is authentic and its proximity to the popular night spots in the Bilbao-Malasaña area makes it an excellent meeting point. The **Café del Círculo de Bellas Artes** is a cultural institution overlooking the busy Gran Vía, and the view of the Palacio Real *(see pp54–7)* from the **Café de Oriente** is without equal.

Overlooking the lively Plaza de Santa Ana *(see p47)* are the well established **Cervecería Alemana** and **Cervecería Santa Ana** bars. Irish bars have become very popular in Madrid, as in other parts of Europe. They tend to be run by English speakers and frequented by English-speaking Spaniards, who like chatting with foreigners. Two of the best are the **Irish Rover** and **O'Neill's**, which includes an oyster bar among its facilities.

And then, of course, there are the *tabernas (see pp28–9)*, the quintessential ingredient of any visit to Madrid. One of the most popular *tabernas* is **Los Gabrieles**, although **Viva Madrid** draws in a healthy crowd of young *Madrileños* attracted by the nightly activity around the Plaza de Santa Ana. For a more bohemian flavour, try **Casa Carmencita**, famous for its association with writers and artists in the 1920s. **Casa Labra** was the birthplace of the Spanish socialist party in the late 19th century and, as well as its clandestine history, you can savour its tasty *tapas*. For sheer character born from centuries-old history, visit **Casa Alberto**, **La Bola** and

Taberna Antonio Sanchez. The elegant surroundings of the **Taberna Casa Domingo** exude a more modern feel, whereas **Taberna del Foro** actually is modern but has succeeded in recreating an authentic feel of "Old Madrid".

NIGHTCLUBS

THERE IS A HIGH price to pay for dancing until dawn at one of Madrid's many night-clubs as entrance fees tend to be expensive. Two that are very much in vogue at the moment are **Nells** and **Joy Eslava**. For something slightly different, however, you might like to try **Berlin Cabaret** where dance is mixed with cabaret acts.

The roomy and somewhat up-market dance club **Pachá** contrasts with the rest of the music bars in Malasaña, which tend to be reasonably priced but rather claustrophobic. A particular favourite with tourists is the **Villa Rosa** dance club in Old Madrid, or the Madrid de los Austrias. The decorative mosaics of this one-time café are exceptional.

Famous Spanish actor Javier Bardém is the proprietor of the nightclub **El Torero**, where you can dance to Latin and Flamenco style music upstairs, or head downstairs for some funky House. The club **Suristán** also plays mainly Latin style music. Nightclubs stay open until after 6am.

ROCK, JAZZ AND WORLD MUSIC

FOR THOSE WHO would rather seek out good live music, there is no shortage of venues in Madrid. For rock music, **Sala Riviera** has hosted some internationally famous bands, while **Moby Dick** and **Siroco** are good places to see some of the more vibrant local and national talent. **Café Central** is considered the best place to enjoy jazz in a wonderfully elegant setting. The nearby **Populart** is an excellent venue too. Formerly a pottery shop, it is a relaxed and busy venue. Both the Café Central and Populart are also near to some of the best Latin music clubs in Madrid, where you can see live bands and dance to the sinuous rhythms of salsa into the early hours of the morning. The much larger **Clamores** hosts a range of musical performers, from jazz and tango to pop and blues.

Maravillas holds some of the city's best rock concerts, so keep an eye out for posters advertising forthcoming events.

Needless to say, this partially-covered venue located next to the Manzanares river *(see p114)* is more popular during the warm summer months.

GAY CLUBS

THE HEART OF the gay scene is located in the Chueca district *(see p94)* of central Madrid. **Why Not** is a small bar that caters mostly to locals and plays music from the 1970s and '80s. There's not much in the way of leather at **New Leather**, but it is still one of the most popular gay bars in the city. **Ambient** is a lesbian disco bar in the Alonso-Martínez area and, for mixed crowds, **La Lupe** is a favourite hangout that puts on frequent cabaret shows.

DIRECTORY

CINEMA

Alphaville
Calle de Martín de los Heros 14.
Map 1 A1.
91 559 38 36.

Amaya
Gral. Martinéz Campos 9.
Map 5 C1.
91 448 41 69.

California
C/ de Andrés Mellado 53.
91 544 00 58.

Capitol
Gran Vía 41.
Map 4 E1.
91 570 66 33.
902 33 32 31 (tickets).

Coliseum
Gran Vía 78.
Map 2 D5.
91 547 66 12.

Ideal Multicines
Calle del Doctor Cortezo 6.
Map 4 F3.
91 369 25 18.

Luna
Calle de la Luna 2.
Map 2 E5.
91 522 47 52.

CAFÉS AND BARS

Café Comercial
Gta. de Bilbao 7.
91 521 56 55.

Café del Círculo de Bellas Artes
Calle del Marqués de Casa Riera 2.
Map 7 B2.
91 531 77 00.

Café de Oriente
Plaza de Oriente 2.
Map 3 C2.
91 541 39 74.

Casa Alberto
Calle de las Huertas 18.
Map 7 A3.
91 429 93 56.

Casa Carmencita
Calle de la Libertad 16.
Map 7 B1.
91 521 59 66.

Casa Labra
Calle de Tetuán 12.
Map 4 F2.
91 531 00 81.

Cervecería Alemana
Plaza de Santa Ana 10.
Map 7 A3.
91 429 70 33.

Cervecería Santa Ana
Plaza de Santa Ana 10.
Map 7 A3.
91 429 43 56.

Irish Rover
Avenida del Brasil 7.
(no telephone).

La Bola
C/ Bola 5. **Map** 4 D1.
91 547 69 30.

Los Gabrieles
Calle de Echegaray 17.
Map 7 A3.
91 429 62 61.

O'Neill's
Calle del Príncipe 12.
Map 7 A3.
91 521 20 30.

Taberna Antonio Sanchez
C/ Mesón de Paredes 13.
Map 4 F5.
91 539 78 26.

Taberna Casa Domingo
Calle de Alcalá 99.
Map 8 F1.
91 576 01 37.

Taberna del Foro
Calle de San Andrés 38.
Map 2 F4.
91 445 37 52.

Viva Madrid
Calle de Manuel Fernández y González 7.
Map 7 A3.
91 429 36 40.

NIGHTCLUBS

Berlin Cabaret
Costanilla de San Pedro 11. **Map** 4 D3.
91 366 20 34.

El Torero
Calle de la Cruz 26.
Map 4 F3.
91 523 11 29.

Joy Eslava
Calle del Arenal 11.
Map 4 E2.
91 366 37 33.

Nells
C/ López de Hoyos 25.
91 562 49 54.

Pachá
Calle de Barceló 11.
Map 5 A4.
91 447 01 28.

Suristán
Calle de la Cruz 7.
Map 4 F3.
91 532 39 09.

Villa Rosa
Plaza de Santa Ana 15.
Map 7 A3.
91 521 36 89.

ROCK, JAZZ AND WORLD MUSIC

Café Central
Plaza del Angel 10.
Map 7 A3.
91 369 41 43.

Clamores
Calle de Alburquerque 14.
Map 5 A3.
91 445 79 38.

Maravillas
Calle de San Vicente Ferrer 35.
Map 2 E4.

Moby Dick
Avenida del Brasil 5.
91 555 76 71.

Populart
Calle de las Huertas 22.
Map 7 A3.
91 429 84 07.

Sala la Riviera
Paseo de la Virgen del Puerto.
91 365 24 15.

Siroco
Calle de San Dimas 3.
Map 2 E4.
91 593 30 70.

GAY CLUBS

Ambient
Calle de San Mateo 21.
Map 5 A4.
(no telephone).

La Lupe
Calle de Torrecilla del Leal 12.
Map 7 A4
91 527 50 19.

New Leather
Calle de Pelayo 42.
Map 5 B5.
91 308 14 62.

Why Not
Calle de San Bartolomé 7.
Map 7 A1.
91 523 05 81.

OUTDOOR ACTIVITIES

A VAST WILDERNESS, ranging from the gentle to the dramatic, lies on the doorstep of Madrid. A scant hour's drive from the city centre will bring you to granite peaks, pine forests, glacial lakes and wild pastureland. Against this backdrop there are endless possibilities for hiking, climbing, horse riding, camping, swimming, skiing or simply finding tranquillity. Stretching across central Spain, the Sierra de Guadarrama and the Sierra de Gredos form a 250-km (155-mile) chain of craggy peaks dipping down to lush

Cycling in Madrid

pastureland, where you can track a mountain stream in spring, ski in winter or picnic in the wilderness in summer. Within Madrid, golf and tennis facilities are on hand, and waterworlds have begun to appear everywhere in response to the hot summers. Beyond Madrid, the area surrounding Toledo is famous for its hunting and, further afield, Cuenca's river gorges and ravines are an ideal setting for adventure sports. Details on all outdoor activities are available at **Comunidad de Madrid Tourist Information** offices.

Enjoying a game of golf amid the attractive countryside of El Escorial

GOLF AND TENNIS

M ADRID'S FINEST sports grounds are to be found at the semi-private **Club de Campo**. The entrance fee for non-members is high, but the excellent facilities and lovely setting make it well worth the

A pleasant break from sightseeing at one of Madrid's tennis courts

cost for weary tourists who need a day away from the museums. Tennis, squash and golf are all on offer here. The club also provides designated play areas for children. Tennis courts can be reserved over the telephone, but for golf you must turn up at the club in person. When deciding which day to plan your activities, it is worth bearing in mind that admission prices rise at the weekends.

El Olivar de la Hinojosa is a new golf course that has opened just off the road to Barajas airport *(see p192)*. It accepts reservations over the telephone. At both the Club de Campo and El Olivar you can rent golf equipment.

If you want a game of tennis in the centre of town, you can reserve a court at the **Canal de Isabel II** sports centre. This

modern, attractively designed complex, which is conveniently located in north-central Madrid, boasts excellent facilities as well as a pleasant bar and restaurant. The **Puerta de Hierro** complex, alongside the Río Manzanares *(see p114)*, also has tennis courts.

WALKING AND CYCLING

F OR KEEN WALKERS, there are numerous day hikes within easy access of the city – even if you don't have a car. Just an hour away by train, Cercedilla is an excellent starting point for trails into the Valle de la Fuenfría. One such trail is the old Roman road *(calzada romana)*. Dating from around the 1st century AD, the road once ran over the mountain to Segovia. A tram which links Cercedilla with the area's ski resorts climbs to the Puerto de Navacerrada for more substantial trails higher up.

Further east, the regional park which encompasses Manzanares el Real *(see p126)* leads into a valley of fast-flowing streams and pools, climbing sharply to the source of the Río Manzanares. The valley tends to attract large numbers of picnickers – one good reason for an early start.

Because only limited roadside bicycle trails are available, many cyclists opt for mountain biking instead. **Karacol Sport** near Atocha Station *(see p85)* rents bicycles which can then be taken by train to Cercedilla. For other destinations, check

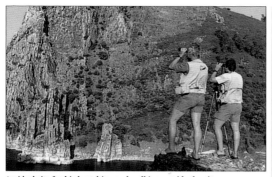

An ideal site for birdwatching and walking outside the city

with RENFE first *(see p196)*. In addition to organizing walks, **Sport Natura** and other specialist outlets provide bikes and transport at weekends to areas such as the Sierra Pobre, east of the Guadarrama.

Remember to take sensible precautions when walking or cycling in the intense Spanish summer heat. It is essential to wear a hat and a high-factor suncream and to take an adequate supply of water with you. Walkers venturing into high-mountain areas should always check the weather forecast first, as conditions here can change very rapidly.

HORSE RIDING

THE SIERRAS and *cañadas* (old sheep trails) surrounding Madrid are ideal for horse riding. Spaghetti westerns were once filmed in this wild region of the country. At the **Club de Campo**, on the edge of the city, horses can be hired for rides through Madrid's expansive Casa de Campo *(see p114)*. You can also hire a steed by the hour or even for the day at the **Escuela de Equitación Pozuelo**.

Most riding centres, such as the **Centro Equestre de la Comunidad de Madrid** on

the edge of the Manzanares regional park, are off the beaten track, but it is quite easy to reach them by bus, followed by a short walk.

High up on the route from Cercedilla to the Puerto de Navacerrada, set back from the tram line, **Picadero los Ciruelos** also offers a wide choice of day routes or even longer outings. In the rugged Sierra Pobre near Buitrago del Lozoya, **Rutas Equestres Sierra Norte** organizes routes from Braojos de la Sierra, which is accessible by direct bus once a day from Madrid.

For an overnight stay or longer stays, the Sierra de Gredos offers superb horse riding set against imposing peaks. You can hire horses at **Turismo Ecuestre Almanzor**, down the road from the Parador Nacional de Gredos. Further along, **Gredos Rutas a Caballo (GRAC)** also organizes day- or week-long outings. During holiday periods, especially Easter week, you should book your accommodation well in advance. Also make sure the riding centre is open on the day you plan to go, and specify your riding level.

Rugged terrain of the sierras – perfect for horse riding

Skiing at the popular resort of the Puerto de Navacerrada

SKIING

I N A YEAR of good snowfall, skiing through pine trees under an azure sky can be a glorious experience. The most popular resort near Madrid is the **Puerto de Navacerrada**. It has 15 slopes and a daunting chairlift up to the "Bola del Mundo" at 2,200 m (7,200 ft). Further away, **Valdesquí** offers better snow conditions and 24 slopes, while **La Pinilla** in the Segovia region is probably the least crowded. All the equipment you need, including skis, snowboards and sleds, can be rented at the resorts.

On weekends during the skiing season, the route to the Puerto de Navacerrada tends to be congested with traffic. Avoid driving if you can and take the tram from Cercedilla. A reliable source of information is **ATUDEM** (Asociación Turística de Estaciones de Esquí y Montaña), a group that specializes in alpine skiing and will provide details on any of the resorts.

MOUNTAINEERING AND CLIMBING

S OME PERFECT DROPS for novice climbers can be found at La Pedriza de Manzanares, as well as at La Cabrera at the eastern end of the Guadarrama mountains. Patones, in the Sierra Pobre, offers ideal rock

Climbing at Escalada en Patones

faces. For the experienced mountaineer, the huge granite needles and walls in the Sierra de Gredos present a higher degree of challenge. Information on courses and guides is available at the **Escuela Madrileña de Alta Montaña**. **Club Ibérico de Expediciones** organises four-wheel drive (4WD) trips out of Madrid for weekends. They take care of the accommodation and the food and also offer tuition in driving the 4WD off-road vehicles. A company called **Gente Viajera** organizes weekend courses near Cuenca in which those with a seriously robust constitution can be taught the exciting art of rappelling (abseiling) down river gorges.

SHOOTING

L IKE THE REST OF Spain, the rugged terrain surrounding Madrid is ideal for hunting. But, unless you are fortunate enough to hunt on one of the many private estates, you will not find much game in the remaining free shooting zones. The best option is to go to Toledo or Ciudad Real, both of which are rich in game, from birds to wild boar and deer. To avoid hassles for permits, contact **Cacerías Ibéricas** in advance. They will do the paperwork, organize the outing and provide equipment. **Viajes Marsans** will do everything except provide your equipment.

WATER SPORTS

M ADRID'S SIZZLINGLY hot summers make watering holes a dire necessity. There is a splendid swimming pool at the **Club de Campo** although, in spite of its great size, it can be uncomfortably full on a hot day. The sports complex at **Puerta de Hierro** has a huge, neck-deep basin just for cooling off, as well as a proper lane pool for swimmers. By far the best pool in Madrid is the **Centro de Natación M-86**, but it is only open to the public from June to the end of August. The **Canal de Isabel II** sports complex, which is also conveniently situated in town, has a much-appreciated outdoor pool, as well as an Olympic-size indoor

One of the reservoirs on the outskirts of Madrid – ideal for canoeing

Causing a splash outside Madrid

pool and a children's pool. There are also a number of large reservoirs outside Madrid, which are perfect for sailing, windsurfing and canoeing.

Contact **Sport Natura**, which provides equipment and transport at weekends to its centre at Embalse del Atazar near El Berrueco.

THEME PARKS

NEARLY 500 ANIMALS run wild at **Safari Madrid** outside Aldea del Fresno, making this a great outing for children. There is also a daily show of birds of prey. A nearby added attraction is the park and beach along the Alberche river.

Aquópolis, a 40-minute drive from the city, is Madrid's most complete waterworld, with slides and innumerable other water features. Bring a picnic, and enjoy a day out for the family. Free buses leave from the Plaza de España.

Another waterworld, the **Aquamadrid** in San Fernando de Henares, boasts a huge pool with a water chute and waves. It is worth bearing in mind, however, that anywhere near water on a hot Sunday in July or August will be extremely crowded.

The thrilling **Parque de Atracciones** (see p114) has the latest stomach-churning rides from roller coasters to vertical drops, as well as all the old favourites. There is also a zone for small children.

DIRECTORY

Comunidad de Madrid Tourist Information
Calle del Duque de Medinaceli 2, Madrid.
Map 7 B3.
📞 91 429 49 51.

GOLF AND TENNIS

Canal de Isabel II
Avenida de Filipinas 54, Madrid.
📞 91 533 17 91.

Club de Campo
Carretera de Castilla, km 2, Madrid.
📞 91 550 20 18 (tennis).
📞 91 550 20 27 (water sports).
📞 91 549 50 56 (riding school).

El Olivar de la Hinojosa
Campo de las Naciones, Avenida de Dublin, Madrid.
📞 91 721 18 89.

Puerta de Hierro
Carretera de El Pardo, km 1, Madrid.
📞 91 316 15 47.

WALKING AND CYCLING

Karacol Sport
Calle de Tortosa 8, Madrid.
Map 7 C5.
📞 91 539 96 33.

Sport Natura
Avenida Donostiarra 4 posterior, Madrid.
📞 91 403 61 61.

HORSE RIDING

Centro Ecuestre de la Comunidad de Madrid
Camino del Mediano, Soto del Real.
📞 91 847 83 58.

Club de Campo
See Golf and Tennis.

Escuela de Equitación Pozuelo
Calle de la Vereda del Cansino 24, Pozuelo de Alarcón.
📞 91 351 13 23.

Gredos Rutas a Caballo (GRAC)
Calle de los Guijuelos 13, Hoyos del Espino (Avila).
📞 920 34 90 85.

Picadero los Ciruelos
Camino los Ciruelos 30, Carretera Camorritos, Cercedilla.
📞 91 852 07 67.

Rutas Ecuestres Sierra Norte
Calle Generalísimo 13, Braojos de la Sierra.
📞 91 868 09 44.

Turismo Ecuestre Almanzor
Barajas de Gredos, Navarredonda de Gredos (Avila).
📞 920 34 80 47.

SKIING

ATUDEM
Calle del Padre Damián 43, 2nd Floor 26, Madrid.
📞 91 359 75 26.

La Pinilla
📞 921 55 03 04.

Puerto de Navacerrada
📞 91 852 33 02.

Valdesquí
📞 91 852 04 16.

MOUNTAINEERING AND CLIMBING

Escuela Madrileña de Alta Montaña
Calle de Apodaca 16, Madrid.
Map 5 A4.
📞 91 593 80 74.

Club Iberico de Expediciones
Avenida Complutense 16 Camarma de Esteruelas.
Map 8 D1.
📞 606 72 94 21.

Gente Viajera
Calle de Santa Alicia 19, Madrid.
📞 91 478 01 11.

SHOOTING

Cacerías Ibéricas
Calle de San Pedro el Verde 49.3, Toledo.
📞 925 21 25 52.

Viajes Marsans
Gran Vía 59, Madrid.
Map 4 E1.
📞 91 547 73 00.

WATER SPORTS

Canal de Isabel II
See Golf and Tennis.

Club de Campo
See Golf and Tennis.

Centro de Natación M-86
Calle de José Martínez de Velasco 3, Madrid.
📞 91 409 53 51.

Puerta de Hierro
See Golf and Tennis.

Sport Natura
See Walking and Cycling.

THEME PARKS

Aquamadrid
Carretera N-II, km 15.5, San Fernando de Henares.
📞 91 673 10 13.

Aquópolis
Avenida de la Dehesa, Villanueva de la Cañada.
📞 91 815 69 11.

Parque de Atracciones
Casa de Campo, Madrid.
📞 91 463 29 00.

Safari Madrid
N-V Salida 32, Aldea del Fresno.
📞 91 862 23 14.

SURVIVAL GUIDE

PRACTICAL INFORMATION

SPAIN HAS FINALLY begun to market itself beyond the attractions of its coastline, and now has a solid tourist infrastructure. In Madrid there are national tourist offices, while the smaller towns have regional offices. All offer help with finding accommodation, restaurants and activities in their area. One of Madrid's best offices is at Calle del Duque de Medinaceli.

PLAZA DE SAN MIGUEL

Old street sign

August is Spain's vacation (holiday) period, during which many businesses close. Roads are very busy at the beginning and end of the month. Find out in advance whether your visit coincides with Madrid's many fiestas because, although these are attractions, they often entail widespread closures. It is a good idea to plan leisurely lunches, as most of Spain stops from 2pm to 5pm.

LANGUAGE

SPAIN'S OFFICIAL LANGUAGE is *castellano* (Castilian). It is spoken by everyone and is certainly the language you will experience most frequently in Madrid. There are three main regional languages – *català* (Catalonia), *euskera* (Basque country) and *gallego* (Galicia). Places that deal with tourists usually employ at least one English-speaker.

MANNERS

MADRILEÑOS are a warm, open, spirited people who are justly proud of their city. Drawn to the capital from all parts of the country, they have brought with them a strong and varied cultural tradition. As a result, this lively city teems with culture and the arts.

It is common for the Spanish to greet and say goodbye to strangers at bus stops and in elevators (lifts), shops and other public places. They often talk to people they do not know. People shake hands when introduced and subsequently whenever they meet. Women usually kiss on both cheeks when they meet; friends and family members embrace or kiss. In bars or restaurants, it is unusual to sit at someone else's table.

VISAS AND PASSPORTS

VISAS ARE NOT required by citizens of EU countries, Iceland or Norway. A list of entry requirements, which is available from Spanish embassies, specifies 35 other countries, including Canada, New Zealand and the US, whose nationals do not need a visa for visits of less than 90 days. For an extension, apply to the *Gobierno Civil* (a local government office) with proof of employment or of sufficient funds to support yourself for a long stay. Visitors from all other countries need a valid visa. British visitors are no longer able to travel on a Visitor's Passport; a full passport must be obtained.

TAX-FREE GOODS AND CUSTOMS INFORMATION

NON-EU RESIDENTS can reclaim IVA (VAT) on single items worth over 15,000 pesetas and bought in shops displaying a "Tax-free for Tourists" sign. Food, drink, tobacco, cars, motorcycles and medicines are

TAX FREE FOR TOURISTS

Sign indicating tax-free goods

exempt. You pay the full price and ask the sales assistant for a *formulario* (tax exemption form). When you leave Spain, ask customs to stamp your *formulario* (this must be within six months of purchase). You will receive the refund by mail or as a credit on your credit card account.

Branches of Spain's Banco Exterior at Madrid's Barajas Airport give refunds on *formularios* that have been stamped by customs.

TOURIST INFORMATION

MADRID AND ALL MAJOR historic towns in the vicinity have *oficinas de turismo* (tourist information offices). On arrival, it is worth visiting the tourist office at **Barajas Airport**'s international terminal (Terminal One) where there is also a hotel reservation desk and a RENFE *(see p192)* desk offering information on rail travel. Tourist information offices provide maps of the town, transport details, lists of hotels (including rural retreats)

MADRID TIME

Madrid is one hour ahead of Greenwich Mean Time (GMT) and 6 hours ahead of Eastern Standard Time (EST). Spain uses the 24-hour clock, so 1pm = 13:00 hours.

City and Country	Hours ahead or behind Spain	City and Country	Hours ahead or behind Spain
Athens (Greece)	+ 1	Moscow (Russia)	+ 2
Auckland (New Zealand)	+ 11	New York (US)	– 6
Bangkok (Thailand)	+ 6	Paris (France)	0
Berlin (Germany)	0	Perth (Australia)	+ 7
Cape Town (South Africa)	+ 1	Rome (Italy)	0
Chicago (US)	– 7	Sydney (Australia)	+ 9
Dublin (Ireland)	– 1	Tokyo (Japan)	+ 8
Hong Kong (China)	+ 7	Toronto (Canada)	– 6
London (UK)	– 1	Vancouver (Canada)	– 9
Los Angeles (US)	– 9	Washington DC (US)	– 6

◁ **The start of Madrid's sweeping Gran Vía with its relentless flow of traffic** and restaurants. They also provide information on local sights, activities and special events. They are usually open Monday to Friday from 8am or 9am until 7 or 8pm, and on Saturday from 9am until 1pm. They are closed on Sundays.

OPENING HOURS

MOST MUSEUMS and monuments close daily from 2pm to 5pm, as well as Sunday afternoons and all day Monday. Major art museums do not close over lunch. Churches have more restricted opening hours; some open only for services.

FACILITIES FOR THE DISABLED

COCEMFE sign for disabled access

SPAIN'S NATIONAL association for the disabled, **Confederación Coordinadora Estatal de Minusválidos Físicos de España (COCEMFE)**, operates Servi-COCEMFE – a tour company which publishes guides to disabled facilities in Spain and can help plan a vacation (holiday) to your requirements.

Tourist information offices and the social services supply information on local conditions and facilities. Metro maps and other information in Braille are available from the Spanish national organization for the blind, **Organización Nacional de Ciegos (ONCE)**. If you prefer to let someone else do the work, the Spanish travel agent **Viajes 2000** specializes in vacations for the disabled. In the United States, the **Society for the Advancement of Travel for the Handicapped (SATH)** publishes the useful *ACCESS to Travel* magazine which deals with destinations, attractions, accommodation, transportation and other information for disabled people.

STUDENT INFORMATION

HOLDERS OF THE International Student Identity Card (ISIC) are entitled to benefits, such as discounts on travel and reduced admission to museums and galleries. Information is available from all international student organizations and, in

Students in Madrid

Madrid, from the government-run youth information centre, **Centro de Información Juvenil (CIJ)**. One company that specializes in student travel is **Turismo y Viajes Educativos (TIVE)**.

ELECTRICAL ADAPTOR

SPAIN'S ELECTRICITY supply is 220 volts, but the 125-volt system still operates in some old buildings. Plugs for both have two round pins.

A three-tier, standard travel converter will enable you to use appliances from abroad on both supplies. Hair dryers, however, should be used only with 220-volt sockets.

Personal Security and Health

IN MADRID, AS IN OTHER cities with a high concentration of tourists, you should take steps to guard against theft. Carry credit cards, money and a photocopy of your passport in a money belt, and never leave anything visible in your car when you park it. If you lose your documents, contact your embassy *(see p185)* and the police. If you are unwell, there will always be a local pharmacy *(farmacia)* open. In Spain, pharmacists are qualified to advise and sometimes even to prescribe.

Spanish pharmacy sign

IN AN EMERGENCY

THE NEW TELEPHONE number for all emergency services is 112. Depending on the nature of the problem you have, ask for *policía* (police), *ambulancia* (ambulance) or *bomberos* (fire brigade).

In cases of medical emergency, hospitals will accept admissions to the *urgencias* (casualty department).

Sign identifying a *Cruz Roja* (Red Cross) emergency treatment centre

MEDICAL TREATMENT

ANY EU NATIONAL who becomes ill in Madrid is entitled to Spanish social security cover. To be able to claim for medical treatment, UK citizens must obtain Form E111 from the Department of Health or from a post office before travelling. This form must be given to anyone who treats you, so take several copies. The accompanying booklet, *Health Advice for Travellers*, explains what health care you are entitled to, and where and how to claim. Not all treatments are covered by Form E111, so you are also advised to arrange private medical insurance before travelling.

If you want private health care, ask at your hotel, embassy or tourist office for the name of a doctor. If necessary, ask for an English-speaker.

Visitors from the US should check with their insurance companies before leaving home to be sure they are covered if medical care is

needed. Many medical facilities require payment for treatment in full at the time of service. Get an itemized bill to submit to your insurance company. In some cases, insurance companies require you to provide an official translation before they reimburse you. Travellers may wish to take out extra private travel insurance for emergency hospital care, doctors' fees and repatriation. Have your policy at hand when requesting medical assistance.

PHARMACIES

FOR NON-EMERGENCIES, a pharmacist *(farmacéutico)* can advise and, out a doctor's consultation. Some medicines available only on prescription at home may be sold over the counter in Spain. The *farmacia* sign is an illuminated green cross. The addresses of those open at night or at weekends are displayed in the windows of all the local pharmacies or may be found in local newspapers.

Guardia Civil   **Policía Municipal**

PERSONAL SECURITY

ALTHOUGH VIOLENT CRIME is rare in Madrid, it is wise to take sensible precautions when out and about, as you would in any city with which you are unfamiliar.

To guard against theft, wear your purse, bag or camera strapped across your body, not on your shoulder, and always keep your possessions in sight, especially at the airport.

At night, avoid walking alone in poorly lit areas and, if possible, take a taxi back to your lodgings late at night.

SPANISH POLICE

THERE ARE ESSENTIALLY three types of police in Spain. The first is the *Guardia Civil* (paramilitary Civil Guard) who mainly police rural areas, country roads, highways and state buildings and take part in anti-terrorist operations. Their uniform is olive green in colour, but their black patent leather tricorns, for which they are renowned, are now donned only on ceremonial occasions.

The *Policía Nacional* wear a blue uniform and they deal mainly with national security, terrorism and major crime in towns with a population of more than 30,000. They also police immigration, work permits and residence documents. There is a special female department in Puerta del Sol which has been set up specifically to deal with crimes perpetrated against women.

The third and final branch of the Spanish police force is the *Policía Municipal*. They are involved for the most part with traffic regulation, the imposition of fines and the policing of local communities.

Patrol car of the Policía Nacional, Spain's main urban police force

Cruz Roja (Red Cross) ambulance

Spanish fire engine

DIRECTORY

EMERGENCY SERVICES

Police *(Policía)*
Ambulance *(Ambulancia)*
Fire Brigade *(Bomberos)*
[112 for all emergency services.

Red Cross *(Cruz Roja)*
[91 522 22 22.

LEGAL ASSISTANCE

SOME INSURANCE POLICIES cover legal costs – after an accident, for instance. If you are not covered, telephone your embassy. They should be able to provide you with a list of bilingual lawyers.

If you are arrested, you have the right to telephone your embassy. The *Colegio de Abogados* (Lawyers' Association) can also inform you where best to obtain legal advice or representation.

If you require an interpreter, it is best to consult either your embassy *(see p185)* or the *Páginas Amarillas* (Yellow Pages) telephone directory under *Traductores* (Translators) or *Intérpretes* (Interpreters). Both *Traductores Oficiales* and *Traductores Jurados* are qualified to translate legal and official documents.

PUBLIC CONVENIENCES

PUBLIC PAY-TOILETS have sprung up on some streets in Madrid but, on the whole, public conveniences are rare. Most people walk into a bar or café, a department store or a hotel and ask for *los servicios*, although it would be preferable to be a customer. On highways (motorways), there are toilets at service stations. Women often have to ask for the key *(la llave)*. Always carry toilet tissue with you as it is often not provided.

PERSONAL PROPERTY

VACATION (HOLIDAY) insurance is there to protect you financially in the event of the loss or theft of your property,

but it is always advisable to take preventative measures – by making use of hotel safes, for example, and playing down the obvious tourist image.

It should not be necessary to carry large sums of money with you, as Spain has more ATMs (cashpoints) than any other country in Europe, and they take EuroCard and all major credit cards. If you have more than one card, do not carry them together. Travellers' cheques are another option, but you will need your passport with you to cash them.

If you discover a loss or theft, report it to the local *comisaría* (police station). To claim insurance you must do this immediately, as many companies give you only 24 hours. You must make a *denuncia* (formal written statement) to the police and obtain a copy to give to your insurers. The process can take some time.

If you lose your passport, your embassy can supply a replacement but cannot provide financial assistance.

Sometimes lost property is found and handed in. If this is the case, it will probably end up at Madrid's main post office in the Plaza de Cibeles or at your embassy, so it is worth checking these two places.

OUTDOOR HAZARDS

SPAIN IS PREY in summer to forest fires fanned by winds and fuelled by bone-dry vegetation. Avoid fire hazards by extinguishing cigarettes in car ashtrays and taking empty bottles away with you.

The sign *coto de caza* in woodland areas identifies a hunting reserve where you must follow the country code. *Toro bravo* means fighting bull – do not approach. A *camino particular* sign indicates a private driveway.

If climbing or hiking, go properly equipped and tell someone when you expect to return. You can also keep in touch by cellular (mobile) phones, which work in most parts of the country.

Banking and Local Currency

YOU MAY ENTER SPAIN with any amount of money, but if you intend to export more than one million pesetas, you should declare it. Eurocheques are widely accepted in Spain. Traveller's cheques may be exchanged at banks, *cajas de cambio* (foreign currency exchanges), some hotels and shops. Banks generally offer the best exchange rates. The cheapest exchange may be offered on your credit or debit card, which may be used in cash dispensers (ATMs) displaying the appropriate sign.

BANKING HOURS

ALTHOUGH SPANISH BANKS are beginning to extend their opening hours throughout the country, expect extended hours only at the large central branches in the city centre.

As a general rule, banks are open from 8am to 2pm on weekdays. Some are also open until 1pm on Saturdays, except in the month of August when most are closed on Saturdays.

Foreign currency exchange

CHANGING MONEY

MOST BANKS HAVE a foreign exchange desk with the sign *Cambio* or *Extranjero*. Always take your passport as ID to effect any transaction.

You can draw up to 50,000 pesetas on major credit cards at a bank. If you bank with **Barclays Bank** it is possible to cash a cheque in the usual way at one of their branches in Spain.

Foreign currency exchange offices (bureaux de change), with the sign *Caja de Cambio* or "Change", invariably charge higher rates of commission than banks, but are often open outside normal hours. They are easy to find in the popular tourist areas.

Cajas de Ahorro (savings banks) also exchange money. They open from 8:30am to 2pm on weekdays and also on Thursday afternoons from 4:30pm to 7:45pm.

CHEQUES AND CARDS

TRAVELLER'S CHEQUES can be purchased at American Express, Thomas Cook or your bank. All are accepted in Spain. If you exchange AmEx cheques at an AmEx office, commission is not charged. You can purchase cheques in pesetas from any bank.

You can write a cheque in pesetas using Eurocheques, which may also be used to change money at a bank. You must show your cheque guarantee card and your passport.

The most widely accepted card in Spain is the **VISA** card. **Diners Club**, **MasterCard** and **American Express** are also useful currency. The major banks will allow cash withdrawals on credit cards.

When you pay for goods or services with a card, cashiers will usually pass your card through a reading machine. Sometimes, however, you will be asked to punch your PIN into a small keypad attached to the machine.

Credit card reader with PIN keypad

24-hour cash dispenser (ATM)

CASH DISPENSERS

IF YOUR CARD is linked to your home bank account, you can use it with your PIN to withdraw money from cash dispensers. These are widespread and nearly all take MasterCard or VISA cards.

When you enter your PIN, instructions are displayed in English, French, German and Spanish. These days, many dispensers are inside buildings and to gain access you will have to swipe your card through a door-entry system.

Cards with Cirrus and Maestro logos can also be widely used to withdraw money from cash machines.

CURRENCY

THE CURRENCY OF Spain is the peseta, usually abbreviated to "pta", or "ptas". It is common to speak of *duros* in popular speech (1 *duro* is 5 pesetas). *Cinco* (5) *duros* equal 25 pesetas and *mil* (1,000) *duros* is 5,000 pesetas. Shop assistants giving change often round the figure up or down to the nearest 5 pesetas.

In the past, Spanish coins were rather confusing, with 58 different coins in circulation for only nine denominations. However, many of these coins have now been phased out; since January 1997 only coins minted after 1986 have been in use. The almost worthless 1-peseta and 2-peseta coins have been removed from circulation.

The seven denominations of coin currently in circulation are easy to distinguish by their shape and colour, but each year has a different design. A 200-peseta coin minted in 1992 shows King Juan Carlos and his son Prince Felipe on one side, and the statue of a bear in Madrid's Puerta del Sol on the other; paintings by Velázquez and Goya appear on the 1994 coin.

A 2,000-peseta coin, minted in silver to commemorate Spain's presidency of the EU Council of Ministers in 1996, is available as a collectors' item. One side shows the Palacio Real in Madrid and the other has the king's head.

1,000 pesetas

2,000 pesetas

Bank Notes
Spanish bank notes are in four denominations. The 1,000-peseta note (two designs, both in green), is the smallest, followed by the 2,000-peseta note (pink), the 5,000-peseta note (ochre with brown and purple) and the 10,000-peseta note (blue).

5,000 pesetas

10,000 pesetas

Coins
Spanish coins, shown here at actual size, are in denominations of 5 ptas, 10 ptas, 25 ptas, 50 ptas, 100 ptas, 200 ptas and 500 ptas. The 500-pta, 100-pta, 25-pta and 5-pta coins are all a dull gold colour. The 200-pta, 50-pta and 10-pta coins are all silvered.

5 pesetas

10 pesetas

25 pesetas

50 pesetas

100 pesetas

200 pesetas

500 pesetas

Communications

Sign for shops selling stamps

THE SPANISH TELECOMMUNICATIONS company, Telefónica, was digitized in 1995 and 1998 saw the end of the state monopoly. Public telephones are easy to find and most operate with a card or coins. International calls are expensive.

The postal service *(correos)* is identified by a crown insignia in red or white on a yellow background. Registered mail and telegrams can be sent from *correos* offices, but they have no public phones. They also sell stamps, as do state-run *estancos* (tobacconists).

Logo of the Spanish telecom system

USING A COIN AND CARD TELEPHONE

1 Lift the receiver, and wait for the dial tone and for the display to show *Inserte monedas o tarjeta*.

2 Insert either coins *(monedas)* or a card *(tarjeta)*.

3 Key in the number firmly, but not too fast – Spanish phones prefer you to pause between digits.

4 As you press the digits, the number you are dialling will appear on the display. You will also be able to see how much money or how many units are left and when to insert more coins.

5 When your call is finished, replace the receiver. The phonecard will then re-emerge automatically or any excess coins will be returned.

A 1,000-peseta phonecard

Denominations of pesetas accepted in coin-operated telephones

TELEPHONING IN SPAIN

AS WELL AS PUBLIC telephone boxes *(cabinas)*, there are nearly always payphones in bars. Both types take coins of 5, 25 and 100 pesetas. There will be a high minimum connection charge, especially for international calls. Phonecards can be bought at newsstands and *estancos*. Some phones are equipped with multilingual electronic instruction displays.

There are public telephone offices called *locutorios* where you can make a call and pay for it afterwards. The cheapest are those run by Telefónica; private *locutorios*, often found in shops, cost more. Calls from a *cabina* or a *locutorio* cost 35 per cent more than calls made from a private phone in someone's home. Calls from hotels can also be expensive.

There are four charge bands for international calls: EU countries; non-EU European countries and Northwest Africa; North and South America; and the rest of the world.

Collect calls within the EU may be dialled directly, but most others must be made through the operator.

USEFUL SPANISH DIALLING CODES

- To call another province, first dial the area code (beginning with 9, e.g. Barcelona 93). Area codes are listed in the A-K phone book or obtained from directory enquiries.
- Use area codes for calls within a province.
- To make an international call, dial 00, wait for the tone, then dial the country code, the area code and the number. Country codes are: UK 44; Eire 353; US and Canada 1; New Zealand 64; Australia 61; South Africa 27.
- If calling Spain from another country, dial that country's international access code, the code for Spain (34) and the full area code.

- For operator/directory service, dial 1003.
- For international directories, dial 025.
- To make a collect (reversed-charge) call within the EU, dial 900 99 00 followed by the country code; to the US or Canada, dial 900 99 00 followed by 11 or 15 respectively. Numbers for other countries can be found in the front of the A-K telephone directory under *Modalidades del Servicio Internacional*.
- To report technical faults, dial 1002.
- For the speaking clock dial 093, for the weather 094, for a wake-up call 096.

The first digit in each area code is 9. For example, Madrid's code is 91. To call Madrid from abroad, first dial your country's international access code, then Spain's country code (34), and then Madrid's area code (91).

City phone numbers generally have seven digits. Those in smaller towns have six.

MAIL (POSTAL SERVICE)

THE POSTAL SERVICE (*correos*) in Spain can be rather slow. Urgent or important items can be sent by *urgente* (express) or *certificado* (registered) mail, although to be sure of fast delivery it is wise to use a private courier.

Mail can be registered and telegrams sent from all *correos* offices. Stamps for letters and postcards can be bought from an *estanco* (tobacconist). Postal rates fall into four price bands: the EU; the rest of Europe; the USA; and the rest of the world. Parcels have to be weighed and stamped at a post office and must be securely tied with string or a charge may be made to have them sealed by a clerk.

The main *correos* offices open 8am–9pm from Monday to Friday and 9am–7pm on Saturday. Branches in the suburbs of cities and in smaller towns and villages open from 9am–2pm Monday to Friday and from 9am–1pm on Saturday.

Spanish mailbox

Standard issue postage stamps

ADDRESSES AND LETTERS

IN SPANISH ADDRESSES the house number follows the name of the street. The floor of an apartment block is indicated by the number which appears after the hyphen. Therefore, 4-2° means an apartment on the second floor of number

four. All postcodes have five digits, with the first two standing for the province.

If you mail your letters at a central post office they are usually likely to arrive more quickly than if you were to mail them in a local mailbox (*buzón*). Cities have yellow pillar boxes; towns and villages normally have small, wall-mounted mailboxes.

Poste restante letters should be addressed care of the *Lista de Correos* and the town. You will be able to collect them from main post offices.

To send and receive money by mail ask for a *giro postal*.

When dealing with businesses in Spain, it is always quicker and more convenient to phone or fax. The mail tends to be used only as a last resort. Fax facilities are available in some *locutorios*, in hotels and in many private shops. Look for a *telefax* sign.

TELEVISION AND RADIO

TELEVISIÓN ESPAÑOLA is Spain's state television company, which broadcasts two channels by the names of TVE1 and TVE2. Several of the autonomous regions have their own television stations. Madrid's is called Telemadrid and is a useful source of local news.

There are three national independent television stations in Spain: Antena 3, Tele-5 (Telecinco) and Canal+ (Canal Plus). Unfortunately, there are some Canal+ programmes which you will only be able to receive if you pay a subscription for a station decoder.

Most foreign films shown on Spanish television (and in cinemas) are dubbed. Subtitled films will appear in listings as *V.O. (versión original)*.

The Satellite channels CNN, Eurosport and Cinemanía can be received throughout Spain.

The state radio station, Radio Nacional de España, has four channels. Radio 2 and 3 play music, while Radio 1 and 5 broadcast news programmes.

NEWSPAPERS AND MAGAZINES

MOST OF THE KIOSKS around Puerta del Sol, Gran Vía, Calle de Alcalá and Paseo de la Castellana stock foreign newspapers and periodicals. English newspapers available on the day of publication are the *International Herald Tribune,* the *Financial Times* and *The Guardian Europe.* Many other English-language and European titles are sold, but usually not until a day after their publication.

The European newspaper and popular weekly current affairs magazines, such as *Time, Newsweek* and *The Economist,* are readily available throughout Madrid.

The most widely read of the Spanish newspapers, in descending number of sales, are *Marca, El País, El Mundo* and *ABC. Marca* is a sports newspaper while *El Mundo* is aimed at a younger market than the others, which cover international news in more depth.

The main weekly listings magazines for arts and events are the *Guía del Ocio*, which appears on Fridays; *Metrópoli,* free in *El Mundo* on Fridays; and *Tentaciones,* free with *El País,* on Fridays (*see p172*).

Local newspapers in Spanish can be a useful source of detailed information about events throughout the region.

Publications in English edited in Madrid are *Guidepost*, with business and general information; *In Madrid*, free each month and available in pubs, bookshops and record shops; and *Lookout*, with articles about Spanish life.

Spanish daily papers

TRAVEL INFORMATION

SPANISH ROAD AND RAIL LINKS were improved for the Expo in Seville and the Olympics in Barcelona in 1992, and Madrid, with its central location, is probably one of the easiest places in Spain to get to. The city is also a good starting point for trips to other destinations, whether Spanish, European or international.

Sign for the airport

While Barajas Airport, one of Europe's busiest, caters for domestic and European travel, it is also one of the main gateways to South America. By road, there are seven main points of entry to Madrid, and its train stations offer regular services to many European cities, as well as high-speed links with destinations all over Spain.

Travellers drawn by the duty-free goods on offer at Barajas Airport

FLYING TO MADRID

BARAJAS AIRPORT is served by dozens of international airlines and charter companies. **Iberia**, the national carrier, has daily flights linking all Western European capitals except Dublin, and once- or twice-weekly flights to the capitals of Eastern Europe. **Air Europa** and **Spanair** also fly between London and Madrid. **British Airways** and **EasyJet** are the only UK airlines to offer direct scheduled flights. **Virgin** offers a service via Brussels.

US airlines **Continental** and **Delta Air Lines** link Madrid to New York, while **American Airlines** links Madrid to Miami. Iberia now flies direct to New York, Montreal and Toronto.

GETTING TO AND FROM THE AIRPORT

IT TAKES ABOUT 20 minutes by taxi or bus to reach the city centre from Barajas Airport. The airport bus departs from International Terminal 1 and goes to Plaza de Colón. Taxis should cost no more than 3,000 pesetas and you can ask for a receipt. The Metro runs from the airport, giving fast and easy access to anywhere within Madrid.

Buses to the airport go from the Plaza de Colón via Calle de Velázquez (returning via Calle de Serrano) and Avenida de América. The airport buses run every 12 minutes between 4:45am and 1:50am and the journey costs 385 pesetas.

Self-ticketing machine

AIR FARES

AIR FARES TO MADRID vary throughout the year. They are generally at their highest in the summer months. Special deals for weekend breaks in the city are often offered during winter and may include a

number of nights at a hotel with vouchers to visit the sights. Iberia and British Airways invariably have some cheap return-flight deals on offer throughout the year. Air Europa and Spanair also have some very competitive deals.

DOMESTIC FLIGHTS

IBERIA OPERATES a shuttle service *(puente aéreo)* with numerous daily flights to Barcelona. Tickets can be purchased from machines as little as 15 minutes prior to departure.

Air Europa and Spanair also have scheduled services between Madrid and Barcelona. **Air Nostrum**, Spanair and Air Europa operate flights between Madrid and the regional capitals and, even though they are not quite as frequent as the *puente aéreo*, their prices tend to be slightly lower. As a rule, the earlier you can book a flight, the greater will be your discount. To benefit from the cheapest tickets, you must book at least one week in advance.

ARRIVING BY TRAIN

THE SPANISH national rail network, **RENFE** *(Red Nacional de Ferrocarriles Españoles)*, has two long-distance train stations in Madrid – Atocha *(see p85)* south of the centre and Chamartín in the northwest. Atocha receives trains from Portugal and the south and west of Spain, as well as the high-speed AVE trains from

National carrier, Iberia, connecting Spain with the rest of Europe

Atocha station, one of Madrid's first glass and wrought-iron structures

Seville and Córdoba. Those coming from France or northern and eastern Spain go to Chamartín station. Since the two stations are linked by a tunnel under the city, some trains stop at both stations.

There are TALGO expresses, which use both the AVE and European tracks, and slower, long-distance *(largo recorrido)* trains. The TALGO service operates between Madrid and the cities of Málaga, Valencia, Barcelona, San Sebastián and Santiago de Compostela.

Overnight sleeper trains arrive from Lisbon, Paris and distant parts of Spain. Cars can be loaded in advance to travel with the train. Bicycles can be carried only in the sleeping compartments of these trains and must be dismantled and packaged up, or otherwise taken unpackaged on regional trains, but only during non-peak periods.

ARRIVING BY CAR

MANY PEOPLE DRIVE to Spain via the French highways (motorways). From the UK there are also car ferries from Plymouth to Santander and from Portsmouth to Bilbao.

From whichever direction you approach Madrid, make sure you are able to identify your highway (motorway) turn-off by its street name. Madrid has two major ring roads, the outer M40 and the inner M30. If you need to cross the city, it is advisable

Typical road signs in Madrid

to take one of the two and get as close as possible to your destination before turning off. All highways (motorways) lead to the M30 but most do not continue into the city.

For information on Spanish driving law, see p195.

ARRIVING BY BUS

TRAVELLING BY BUS (coach) is usually a relatively cheap form of travel and, in Spain, it can quite often be a quicker way to get around than trains, especially from destinations such as the costas. These days, buses offer travellers a modern airline-style service on fast highways. **Eurolines** buses operate regular services throughout Europe.

There are three main long-distance bus stations in Madrid. The **Estación Sur de Autobuses**, situated just southeast of the city centre, serves the whole of Spain. The second is **Terminal Auto-Res**, which operates services to Valencia, eastern Spain, Lisbon and northwest Spain. And the third, **Terminal Continental Auto**, is located north of the city centre. Buses from this station serve towns in northern Spain and Toledo.

The transport interchange at Calle de Méndez Alvaro also provides convenient access to the city buses, the Metro and to regional trains.

DIRECTORY			

AIRPORT

Barajas Airport Information
📞 91 305 83 43.

IBERIA

Flights
📞 902 400 500 (Spain).

📞 (0870) 606 2032 (UK).

📞 (800) 772 4642 (US).

OTHER AIRLINES

Air Europa
📞 902 40 15 01.

Air Nostrum
📞 902 200.222.

American Airlines
📞 91 453 14 00.
📞 902 115 570.

British Airways
📞 902 111 333 (Spain).
📞 (0345) 222 111 (UK).

Continental
📞 91 559 27 10 (Spain).
📞 (800) 231 0856 (US).

Delta Air Lines
📞 91 577 06 50 (Spain).
📞 (800) 241 4141 (US).

EasyJet
📞 902 299 992 (Spain).
🌐 www.easyjet.com

Spanair
📞 902 131 415 (Spain).
🌐 www.spanair.com

Virgin
📞 900 467 612 (Spain).
📞 (0800) 891 199 (UK).

TRAIN STATIONS

RENFE
Calle de Alcalá 44.
Map 7 B1.
📞 902 24 02 02.

Chamartín
Calle de Agustin de Foxá
📞 902 24 02 02.

Atocha
Plaza del Emperador
Carlos V. **Map** 7 C5.
📞 902 24 02 02.

BUS STATIONS AND COMPANIES

Estación Sur de Autobuses
Calle de Méndez Alvaro,
Esquina Calle de la Retama.
📞 91 468 58 74.

Eurolines
📞 91 528 11 05 (Madrid).
📞 (0171) 730 8235 (UK).

Terminal Auto-Res
Calle Fernández Shaw 1.
📞 902 192 939.
📞 91 551 72 00.

Terminal Continental-Auto
Avenida de América.
📞 91 745 63 00.

Getting Around Madrid

MOST OF THE TOURIST SIGHTS are clustered together in the centre of Madrid within walking distance of each other. There are also other interesting attractions further afield, and you will have to decide how to get there. Plan your day in advance, bearing in mind that some museums and shops close between 2pm and 5pm, and try to cover one area at a time. The Metro is by far the best way to travel around Madrid because the trains are quick and clean. However, if you have more time and prefer to see where you are going, the city bus service is excellent, and there is no shortage of taxis in Madrid if you don't mind spending a bit extra.

Sightseeing in one of the city's bright red buses outside the Puerta de Toledo

GETTING AROUND BY BUS

BUSES ARE AN excellent way to see the city. If you plan to make a number of bus trips, it is best to buy a *Metrobus* – a ten-trip ticket good for buses and the Metro. It costs around 700 pesetas, so is better value than tickets bought individually. *Bonobuses* are available at *estancos* (tobacconists), news kiosks and the **EMT** booths in Plaza de Colón, Plaza de Cibeles, Plaza del Callao, Plaza de Manuel Becerra and Puerta del Sol. These booths and tourist information offices offer large maps and details of bus and Metro services and regional trains. Bus stop signs display the bus numbers and

also their basic routes. Either pay the driver or put your *Metrobus* ticket in the machine behind him or her. Request a stop by pressing a button next to the exit doors at the rear.

People in wheelchairs can board buses displaying the words *piso bajo* (low floor), which means that the rear exit is close to the ground and wheelchairs can enter and exit there.

Some useful bus routes: 2 crosses central Madrid east to west; 5 starts at Puerta del Sol, going northwest to Chamartín railway station via Plaza de Cibeles; 27 travels from north to south the length of the Paseo de la Castellana from Plaza de Castilla to Glorieta de Embajadores via Paseo del Prado and Calle de Atocha; C makes a circuit around Madrid via Calle de Atocha.

Day buses run from 6am until midnight. Twenty night buses, or *buhos* (owls), run every half an hour between midnight and 3am and then each hour until 6am. All leave from the Plaza de Cibeles.

THE METRO

THE METRO IS the quickest, cheapest and easiest way to travel around Madrid, avoiding the madness of the city's traffic at street level. Many of the main Metro stations have shops and bars, and Retiro station even boasts an art gallery.

The Metro is open from 6am to 1:30am and consists of over 125 stations which are linked by 11 colour-coded lines plus the Ópera-Príncipe Pío link. A *Metrobus* ticket for ten trips on either the Metro or bus can be bought at any of the stations. For a comprehensive map of the Metro system, see the inside back cover of this book.

New Metro extensions now provide fast and convenient links with the IFEMA Parque Ferial exhibition centre as well as Barajas Airport.

Sign for a Metro station

TAXIS

MADRID HAS some 15,000 taxis, identifiable by the red diagonal stripe on the door. If they are available, the green light on the roof will be illuminated and a card in the window will say *"libre"*.

Within Madrid's city limits, including the airport, taxis are obliged to turn on their meters once hired. The initial charge is 170 pesetas, but there are various additional charges, including fees for the airport, each piece of luggage, a dog (except guide dogs), IFEMA Parque Ferial and leaving from a train station between 11pm and 6am Saturdays, Sundays and public holidays.

You can order a cab by telephone through **Radio Taxi** or **Radioteléfono Taxi**. For a car specially adapted for the disabled, call Radioteléfono Taxi and ask for Eurotaxis.

City taxis with their logo and official numbers

Organized coach trips with Juliá Tours, one way to see the sights

BUS TOURS

A SIGHTSEEING SERVICE is operated by **Madrid Vision**, whose double-decker buses are equipped with multilingual headphone commentaries. There are 14 points along the route where you can get on or off, and it is possible to use the buses all day. The bus tours run all year round.

Juliá Tours also offers a variety of bus trips around the city, which can include visits to a *corrida* or bullfight *(see p111)* or an evening flamenco performance *(see p174)*.

DRIVING

I N SPAIN YOU MUST CARRY a valid driver's licence with you when driving, as well as your insurance documents. If you are not an EU citizen, it is essential to have an international driver's licence. In the United States, these are available through the AAA.

Driving around Madrid is quite an experience for the uninitiated as *Madrileños* tend to drive aggressively. Signs are often misleading or missing altogether, service stations are few and parking is usually difficult. Read the map before setting off, but watch out for one-way systems, tunnels and overpasses (flyovers). In rush hour, traffic hardly moves and the M30 inner ring road often comes to a standstill. If you get lost while driving, hail a taxi, shout the address and follow the driver.

In urban areas the speed limit is 50 km/h (31 mph), while it is 100 km/h (62 mph) on main roads and 120 km/h (75 mph) on highways (motorways).

CAR RENTAL (HIRE)

T O RENT A CAR in Spain you should have an international driver's licence (if you are an EU citizen your ordinary licence is usually sufficient) and be over 21 years of age. You can pay using cash, credit card or traveller's cheques.

On the ground floor of Barajas Airport's International Terminal 1 there are various car rental firms, including **Atesa**, **Avis**, **Budget**, **Europcar** and **Hertz**. Cars can also be rented at Atocha and Chamartín railway stations. You are strongly advised to take out full insurance, and air-conditioning is definitely a good idea.

In the city, your hotel or a travel agent will be able to arrange car rental for you.

Some of the leading car rental agencies operating in Spain

PARKING

P ARKING IN MADRID is difficult, so you may want to select a hotel with parking facilities. There are also underground parking garages (car parks) which charge by the hour. A green sign saying *"libre"* means that space is still available; a red sign saying *"completo"* means the car park is full.

Parking illegally can result in being towed away, with a fine of 30,000 pesetas to recover your vehicle. In the city centre, a special parking permit, available from newspaper kiosks and tobacconists, must be purchased and displayed between 8am and 8pm (3pm in summer). Tickets are priced according to the amount of time required and are colour coded.

When parking, lock your doors and do not leave anything of value in your car. If you must leave items in the car, stow them in the boot (trunk) before you set off.

No parking at any time of the day

CYCLING

R IDING A BICYCLE around Madrid in weekday traffic is dangerous. Only on Sundays and public holidays can cycling in Madrid be fun. **Karacol Sport SA** near Atocha train station rents bikes.

Travelling Outside Madrid

Logo of the Spanish national railways

THE MAIN SITES around Madrid can each be visited in a day but, if you plan to visit several, you might like to consider staying outside Madrid, at a hotel or at one of an increasing number of rural hostelries. The most convenient way to travel is by car, but trains are also very easy to use with services to all the main historic towns and cities. Even Córdoba, Seville and Valencia are accessible using the AVE and Alaris high-speed trains which afford superb views of the countryside. Tour companies offer coach trips to places such as Toledo, El Escorial and Segovia. A trip usually includes the main sites and a basic meal. If you intend to use a scheduled bus service, use the most direct, as some buses stop at every village.

TALGO trains at Atocha station

TRAIN SERVICES

MADRID IS SERVED by six types of train: *cercanías* (commuter), *regional* (local), *largo recorrido* (long-distance), TALGO (long-distance express), Alaris (from Madrid to Valencia) and AVE (high-speed link to Ciudad Real, Puertollano, Córdoba and Seville).

There are frequent services to Alcalá de Henares and Guadalajara on the *cercanía* C-2 from Chamartín, Nuevos Ministerios, Recoletos and Atocha. To reach Aranjuez, *cercanías* leave from Atocha every half an hour. During weekends from mid-April to mid-July and mid-September to mid-October, a special Strawberry Train *(Tren de las Fresas)*, pulled by a steam engine, serves Aranjuez from Atocha's AVE station. Strawberries are included and you must book in advance. To reach Puerto Navacerrada and

the ski resorts, take *cercanía* C-8b from Atocha station to Cercedilla and then change to *cercanía* C-9. Use C-8a for San Lorenzo de El Escorial, and C-8b or the *regional* from Atocha station for Segovia. Sigüenza is served by *regional* trains from Chamartín, with three or four trains a day. Toledo is served by *regional* trains from Atocha. Trains run every two hours.

TICKETS AND FARES

INFORMATION AND train tickets can be obtained at **RENFE** offices and stations, or from travel agents. Rail fares depend on the speed and quality of the train; obviously, therefore, TALGO, Alaris and AVE trains are the most expensive.

Bicycles can be taken only on *regional* trains on weekends and public holidays and

at specified non-peak times in the week. *Largo recorrido* and TALGO trains will take them if dismantled and kept in the sleeping compartments.

Fares rise on weekends and public holidays. Children, aged four to 11, get a 40 per cent discount, while students, aged 12 to 25, get a 20 per cent discount. Return tickets are valid for 15 days and carry the same discounts. For long journeys, RENFE may offer special rates on certain days. **Iberrail** also offers economical rail-plus-hotel deals. For a one-way journey, ask for *ida* and for a return, ask for *ida y vuelta*.

TAKING YOUR OWN CAR

A GREEN CARD and a bail bond from a motor insurance company are needed to extend your comprehensive cover to Spain. In the UK, the RAC, AA and Europ Assistance offer rescue and recovery policies with European coverage.

By law you must always carry with you your vehicle's registration document, a valid insurance certificate and your driving licence. Always be able to show a passport or a national ID card, and display a country of registration sticker on the rear of the vehicle.

The headlights of right-hand-drive vehicles must be adjusted. This can be done with stickers sold at ferry ports or on ferries. You risk on-the-spot fines if you do not carry a red warning triangle, spare light bulbs and a first-aid kit.

Driving along a mountain road through Spain's spectacular countryside

A filling station run by a leading chain with branches throughout Spain

In winter you should carry chains if you intend to drive in mountain areas. In summer, take drinking water if you are travelling in a remote area.

Spain's fastest roads are its *autopistas*, usually highways (motorways) with tolls *(peajes)*. *Autovías* are similar but have no tolls. The *carretera nacional* is Spain's network of main roads prefixed by "N".

Madrid is served by six main *autovías*, numbered NI to NVI, which fan out in different directions, and one *autopista*, N401, which goes to Toledo. In addition, there are two ring roads with links between the NI–NVI and the N401. The inner ring road is the M30 and the outer one, with direct access to and from the airport, is the M40.

For road and traffic information in Spanish call the toll-free number for **Información de Tráfico de Carreteras**.

BUYING FUEL

I N SPAIN *gasolina* (gas/petrol) and *gasóleo* (diesel) are sold by the litre. *Gasolina sin plomo* (unleaded gas/petrol) is available everywhere.

SPEED LIMITS AND FINES

S PEED LIMITS in Spain for cars without trailers are: 120 km/h (75 mph) on *autopistas* (toll highways/motorways); 100 km/h (62 mph) on *autovías* (non-toll highways/ motorways); 90 km/h (56 mph) on *carreteras nacionales* (main roads) and *carreteras comarcales* (secondary roads); 50 km/h (30 mph) in built-up areas. There are instant fines of 1,000 pesetas for every kilometre over the limit. Tests and fines for drinking and driving are increasingly common.

TOUR BUSES AND LOCAL BUSES

B Y FAR THE easiest and most relaxing way to visit the sights is by tour bus. Madrid's main tour bus company, **Juliá Tours** *(see p195)*, will take direct bookings. **Pullmantur** tours, on the other hand, have to be booked through a travel agency. **Mundo Joven** also gives guided tours but they tend to be in Spanish only.

Major towns and many villages are served by local buses. Buses for the following destinations depart from **Estación Sur de Autobuses**. Aranjuez is served by **Autocares Samar**, San Martín de Valdeiglesias by **Autocares Cevesa**, Segovia by **La Sepulvedana**, Sigüenza by **Floravilla** (6pm departure only) and Toledo by **Continental-Auto** and **Transporte Galiano Continental**.

Alcalá de Henares is served by **Continental-Auto** (corner of Calle de Cartagena/Avenida de América), Chinchón by **La Veloz** (Plaza de Conde Casal), Manzanares el Real by **Hijos de J Colmenarejo** (Plaza de Castilla), Puerto de Navacerrada by **Larrea SA** (Metro Moncloa), San Lorenzo de El Escorial by **Autocares Herranz** (Metro Moncloa).

Buses can be quicker than trains. **Enatcar** operates a competitively priced service from the costas, for example

Spanish touring bus, a quick and convenient way to see the sights

DIRECTORY

TRAIN SERVICES

Iberrail
☎ 91 571 66 92.
@ ibermad@iberrail.es

RENFE
☎ 902 24 02 01.
W www.renfe.es

TRAFFIC INFORMATION

Información de Tráfico de Carreteras
☎ 900 12 35 05.

CAR RESCUE SERVICE

RACE
Calle de José Abascal 10.
☎ 91 593 33 33.

TOUR BUSES AND LOCAL BUSES

Autocares Cevesa
☎ 91 539 31 32.

Autocares Herranz
☎ 91 890 41 22.

Autocares Samar
☎ 91 468 48 39.

Continental-Auto
☎ 91 745 63 00.

Enatcar
Estación Sur de Autobuses.
☎ 91 527 99 27 (national).
☎ 91 530 76 00 (international).
W www.enatcar.es

Floravilla
☎ 91 530 88 29.

Hijos de J Colmenarejo
☎ 91 845 00 51.

Larrea SA
☎ 91 530 48 00.

La Sepulvedana
☎ 91 530 48 00.
W www.lasepulvedana.es

La Veloz
☎ 91 409 76 02.

Mundo Joven
☎ 91 521 86 01.

Pullmantur
☎ 91 556 11 14.
@ Pullmantur@mad.servicom.es

Transporte Galiano Continental
☎ 91 527 29 61.

MADRID STREET FINDER

0 kilometres   1

0 miles   0.5

KEY TO STREET FINDER

▦ Major sight	🚕 Taxi	⊠ Post office	
▦ Place of interest	🅿 Parking	═ Railway line	
▦ Other building	ℹ Tourist attraction	→ One-way street	
🚆 Train station	✚ Hospital with emergency room	═ Pedestrianized street	
Ⓜ Metro station	🚓 Police station		
🚌 Main bus stop	✝ Church	**SCALE OF MAP PAGES**	
🚍 Bus station	⛪ Convent or monastery	0 metres 250	
		0 yards 250	

A

General Index

Acknowledgments

DORLING KINDERSLEY would like to thank the following people whose contributions and assistance have made the preparation of this book possible.

CONTRIBUTORS

ADAM HOPKINS is an indefatigable travel writer and author of *Spanish Journeys: A Portrait of Spain.*

MARK LITTLE, an American who grew up in Spain, is a freelance writer based in southern Spain. For many years he was the editor of *Lookout* magazine.

EDWARD OWEN has been, for many years, a foreign correspondent based in Madrid, contributing to *The Times* and *The Express* in London and *Time Magazine* among other publications.

JAMES RUSSO, a freelance journalist, is also a staff writer for Spain's state news agency, EFE. He has lived in Spain since the 1980s.

KATHY WHITE is a freelance journalist who has contributed to *The Christian Science Monitor* and *Newsweek.* She also worked for the French Service of the BBC and was foreign desk assistant at Channel 4 News.

DESIGN AND EDITORIAL ASSISTANCE

Special thanks to Hilary Bird for preparing the index, Juan Fernández for providing feedback on the content of the guide, Joy Fitzsimmons for visualizing the artworks, Elly King for the final design check, ERA Maptech for creating the maps, Graphical Innovations for outputting the text film, Barbara Minton for support from DK Publishing, Inc., Roberto Rama for fact checking, Mary Sutherland for providing feedback on the Survival Guide, Lynda Warrington for editorial assistance and Stewart Wild for proofreading. Project assistance given by Fay Franklin, Annette Jacobs, Vivien Crump, Gillian Allen, Douglas Amrine, Joanne Blackmore, Monica Allende and Pamela Shiels.

PHOTOGRAPHY PERMISSIONS

© Patrimonio Nacional, Madrid: Monasterio de las Descalzas Reales; El Escorial; La Granja de San Ildefonso; Palacio Real; Palacio Real Aranjuez; Palacio de Fernán Núñez propriedad de Renfe Sede de la Fundación de los Ferrocarriles Españoles.

Dorling Kindersley would like to thank all the cathedrals, churches, museums, restaurants, hotels, shops, galleries, and other sights too numerous to thank individually.

PICTURE CREDITS

t=top; tl=top left; tlc=top left centre; tc=top centre; trc= top right centre;
tr= top right; cla=centre left above;
ca=centre above; cra=centre right above;
cl=centre left; c=centre; cr=centre right;
clb=centre left below; cb=centre below;
crb=centre right below; bl=bottom left;
b=bottom; bc=bottom centre; bcl=bottom centre left; br=bottom right; d=detail

Works of art have been reproduced with the permission of the following copyright holders:

Gernika Picasso © Succession Picasso/DACS 1999 87br; *Lugar de Encument* Chillida © DACS 1999 99c; *Mosaic* Miró © ADAGP, PARIS and DACS, London 1999 107t, front cover c.

The publisher would like to thank the following individuals, companies and picture libraries for their kind permission to reproduce their photographs:

ACE PHOTO: Bill Wassman 172b; AISA, Barcelona: 7inset, 14cb, 17b, 21bl, 21bc, *Retrato de Camilo Jose Cela* Alvaro Delgado © DACS 1999 26t, 27t, 56c, 76b, 80t, 82t, 83b, *La Tertulia del Café de Pombo* Jose Gutiérrez Solana © DACS 1999 87t, 104b; MAX ALEXANDER: 118; MUSEO ARQUEOLOGICO NACIONAL, Madrid: 96, 97.

BRIDGEMAN PICTURE LIBRARY: *The Adoration of the Shepherds* El Greco 80ca, *The Annunciation* Fra Angelico 80cb, *The Clothed Maja* Goya 81t,
The Naked Maja Goya 81ca, *The Three Graces* Rubens 81cb, *The Martyrdom of St Philip* Jose Ribera 81b,
St Dominic of Silos Enthroned as Abbot Bermejo 82c, *Children at the Beach* Sorolla © DACS 1999 83t.

JOE CORNISH: 128c; COVER: Quim Llenas 27b; Matias Nieto 37c.

EL DESEO: 104tr.
AGENCIA EFE, Madrid: 35b, 36b.

MARY EVANS PICTURE LIBRARY: 14b, 117inset,
143inset, 183inset.

FUNDACIÓN LÁZARO GALDIANO: 25t, 100/101.

HULTON GETTY: 139b; GODO FOTOS: 131b.

ROBERT HARDING PICTURE LIBRARY: James
Strachan 53tr, 115t; P.Robinson 40

IMAGES COLOUR LIBRARY: A.G.E. Fotostock 23tr,
111cra; Horizon 111c; INDEX, Barcelona:
13b, 14c, 16b, 18b, 20ca, 20cbl, 21tl, 21tc,
21br, 26c, 26b, 27c; NICK INMAN: 187c, 193t.

ANTHONY KING: 76t.

ARXIU MAS, Barcelona: 10b.

NATURPRESS, Madrid: 178b; J.L. González
Grande 179b; A. Ibannez & Fco González
180c; Diana Kvaternik 23bc; W Kvaternik-
R. Olivas 2/3, 36c, 178c, 180t, 181t; Luis
Olivas 34b; Petro Retamar 180b; Carlos
Vegas 35c; Jaime Villanueva 1, 19c, 23ca,
34c, 113t, 178t; MUSEO NAVAL, Madrid: 65br.

ORONOZ, Madrid: 13t, 14t, 15t, 15c, 15b,
17c, 19t, 20tl, 20tr, 20cr, 24t, 24c, 24b, 47b,
56t, 56b, 57t, 57c, 57b, 67b, 75ca, 75b, 82b,
83c, *Portrait II* Miró © ADAGP, PARIS and
DACS, London 1999 86t, *Woman in Blue*
Picasso © Succession Picasso/DACS 1999
86ca, *El Espíritu de los Pájaros* Chillida ©
DACS 1999 87bl, 102b, 103b, 111cla, 124,
125.

MUSEO DEL PRADO, Madrid: 80b.
PRISMA, Barcelona: 12, 16t, 16c, 18t, 18c,

21tr, 21clb, 60b.
CENTRO DE ARTE REINA SOFIA, Madrid:
Retrato de Josette Juan Gris © ADAGP,
PARIS and DACS, London 1999 25b,
Landscape in Cadaqués Dalí © Salvador
Dalí – Foudation Gala – Salvador
Dalí/DACS 1999 86c, 86b, *Guitarra ante el
Mar* Juan Gris © ADAGP, PARIS and DACS,
London 1999 88t, *El Profeta* Pablo Gargallo
© ADAGP, PARIS and DACS, London 1999
88c, *Minotauromaquia* Picasso ©
Succession Picasso/DACS 1999 88b,
Muchacha en la Ventana Dalí © Salvador
Dalí – Foundation Gala – Salvador
Dalí/DACS 1999 89t, *Toda la Ciudad
Habla de Ello* Eduardo Arroyo © DACS
1999 89b.

6 TOROS 6 magazine: 111cr.

MUSEO THYSSEN BORNEMISZA, Madrid: 23cr,
70t, *Harlequin with Mirror* Picasso ©
Succession Picasso/DACS 1999 70c, 70bl,
Portrait of Baron Thyssen-Bornemisza ©
Lucian Freud 70br, 71t, 71ca, 71c, *Autumn
Landscape in Oldenburg* Karl Schmidt-
Rottluff
© DACS 1999 71b, 72, 73.

M ANGELES SANCHEZ: 35t, 105b; Juan Carlos
Martínez Zafra 52b; ARCHIVO DEL SENADO:
Oronoz 53b; SCIENCE PHOTO LIBRARY:
Geospace 8; STOCKPHOTOS: Marcelo Brodsky
34t; TONY STONE: 164b.

PETER WILSON: 38; WORLD PICTURES: 165c.

JACKET: All special photography except
PRISMA front t.

FRONT END PAPER: All special photography
except MAX ALEXANDER tr.

DORLING KINDERSLEY SPECIAL EDITIONS

Dorling Kindersley books can be purchased
in bulk quantities at discounted prices for
use in promotions or as premiums. We are
also able to offer special editions and
personalized jackets, corporate imprints,
and excerpts from all of our books, tailored
specifically to meet your own needs.

To find out more, please contact:
(in the United Kingdom) – SPECIAL SALES,
DORLING KINDERSLEY LIMITED, 9 HENRIETTA
STREET, COVENT GARDEN, LONDON WC2E 8PS;
TEL. 020 7753 3572;

(in the United States) – SPECIAL MARKETS
DEPARTMENT, DORLING KINDERSLEY PUBLISHING, INC.,
95 MADISON AVENUE, NEW YORK, NY 10016.

Phrase Book

IN AN EMERGENCY

Help!	¡Socorro!	soh-**koh**-roh
Stop!	¡Pare!	**pah**-reh
Call a doctor!	¡Llame a un médico!	**yah**-meh ah oon **meh**-dee-koh
Call an ambulance!	¡Llame a una ambulancia!	**yah**-meh ah **oonah** ahm-boo-**lahn**-thee-ah
Call the police!	¡Llame a la policía!	**yah**-meh ah lah poh-lee-**thee**-ah
Call the fire brigade!	¡Llame a los bomberos!	**yah**-meh ah lohs bohm-**beh**-rohs
Where is the nearest telephone?	¿Dónde está el teléfono más próximo?	**dohn**-deh ehs-**tah** ehl teh-**leh**-foh-noh mahs **prohx**-ee-moh
Where is the nearest hospital?	¿Dónde está el hospital más próximo?	**dohn**-deh ehs-**tah** ehl ohs-pee-**tahl** mahs **prohx**-ee-moh

COMMUNICATION ESSENTIALS

Yes	Sí	see
No	No	noh
Please	Por favor	pohr fah-**vohr**
Thank you	Gracias	**grah**-thee-ahs
Excuse me	Perdone	pehr-**doh**-neh
Hello	Hola	**oh**-lah
Goodbye	Adiós	ah-dee-**ohs**
Good night	Buenas noches	**bweh**-nahs **noh**-chehs
Morning	La mañana	lah mah-**nyah**-nah
Afternoon	La tarde	lah **tahr**-deh
Evening	La tarde	lah **tahr**-deh
Yesterday	Ayer	ah-**yehr**
Today	Hoy	oy
Tomorrow	Mañana	mah-**nya**-nah
Here	Aquí	ah-**kee**
There	Allí	ah-**yee**
What?	¿Qué?	keh
When?	¿Cuándo?	**kwahn**-doh
Why?	¿Por qué?	pohr-**keh**
Where?	¿Dónde?	**dohn**-deh

USEFUL PHRASES

How are you?	¿Cómo está usted?	**koh**-moh ehs-**tah** oos-**tehd**
Very well, thank you.	Muy bien, gracias.	mwee bee-**ehn** **grah**-thee-ahs
Pleased to meet you.	Encantado de conocerle.	ehn-kahn-**tah**-doh deh koh-noh-**thehr**-leh
See you soon.	Hasta pronto.	ahs-tah **prohn**-toh
That's fine.	Está bien.	ehs-**tah** bee-**ehn**
Where is/are . . . ?	¿Dónde está/están . . . ?	**dohn**-deh ehs-**tah**/ehs-**tahn**
How far is it to . . . ?	¿Cuántos metros/ kilómetros hay de aquí a . . . ?	**kwahn**-tohs **meh**-trohs/kee-**loh**-meh-trohs **eye** deh ah-**kee** ah
Which way to . . . ?	¿Por dónde se va a . . . ?	pohr **dohn**-deh seh **bah** ah
Do you speak English?	¿Habla inglés?	**ah**-blah een-**glehs**
I don't understand	No comprendo	noh kohm-**prehn**-doh
Could you speak more slowly please?	¿Puede hablar más despacio por favor?	pweh-deh ah-**blahr** mahs dehs-pah-thee-oh pohr fah-**vohr**
I'm sorry.	Lo siento.	loh see-**ehn**-toh

USEFUL WORDS

big	grande	**grahn**-deh
small	pequeño	peh-**keh**-nyoh
hot	caliente	kah-lee-**ehn**-teh
cold	frío	**free**-oh
good	bueno	**bweh**-noh
bad	malo	**mah**-loh
enough	bastante	bahs-**tahn**-teh
well	bien	bee-**ehn**
open	abierto	ah-bee-**ehr**-toh
closed	cerrado	thehr-**rah**-doh
left	izquierda	eeth-key-**ehr**-dah
right	derecha	deh-**reh**-chah
straight on	todo recto	toh-doh **rehk**-toh
near	cerca	**thehr**-kah
far	lejos	**leh**-hohs
up	arriba	ah-**ree**-bah
down	abajo	ah-**bah**-hoh
early	temprano	tehm-**prah**-noh

late	tarde	**tahr**-deh
entrance	entrada	ehn-**trah**-dah
exit	salida	sah-**lee**-dah
toilet	lavabos, servicios	lah-**vah**-bohs sehr-**bee**-thee-ohs
more	más	mahs
less	menos	**meh**-nohs

SHOPPING

How much does this cost?	¿Cuánto cuesta esto?	**kwahn**-toh kwehs-tah **ehs**-toh
I would like . . .	Me gustaría . . .	meh goos-ta-**ree**-ah
Do you have?	¿Tienen?	tee-**yeh**-nehn
I'm just looking.	Sólo estoy mirando, gracias.	soh-loh ehs-**toy** mee-**rahn**-doh **grah**-thee-ahs
Do you take credit cards?	¿Aceptan tarjetas de crédito?	ah-**thehp**-tahn tahr-**heh**-tahs deh **kreh**-dee-toh
What time do you open?	¿A qué hora abren?	ah **keh** oh-rah **ah**-brehn
What time do you close?	¿A qué hora cierran?	ah keh oh-rah thee-**ehr**-rahn
This one.	Éste	**ehs**-teh
That one.	Ése	**eh**-seh
expensive	caro	**kahr**-oh
cheap	barato	bah-**rah**-toh
size, clothes	talla	**tah**-yah
size, shoes	número	**noo**-mehr-oh
white	blanco	**blahn**-koh
black	negro	**neh**-groh
red	rojo	**roh**-hoh
yellow	amarillo	ah-mah-**ree**-yoh
green	verde	**behr**-deh
blue	azul	ah-**thool**
antiques shop	la tienda de antigüedades	lah tee-**ehn**-dah deh ahn-tee-gweh-**dah**-dehs
bakery	la panadería	lah pah-nah-deh-**ree**-ah
bank	el banco	ehl **bahn**-koh
book shop	la librería	lah lee-breh-**ree**-ah
butcher's	la carnicería	lah kahr-nee-theh-**ree**-ah
cake shop	la pastelería	lah pahs-teh-leh-**ree**-ah
chemist's	la farmacia	lah fahr-**mah**-thee-ah
fishmonger's	la pescadería	lah pehs-kah-deh-**ree**-ah
greengrocer's	la frutería	lah froo-teh-**ree**-ah
grocer's	la tienda de comestibles	lah tee-**yehn**-dah deh koh-mehs-**tee**-blehs
hairdresser's	la peluquería	lah peh-loo-keh-**ree**-ah
market	el mercado	ehl mehr-**kah**-doh
newsagent's	el kiosko de prensa	ehl kee-**ohs**-koh deh **prehn**-sah
post office	la oficina de correos	lah oh-fee-**thee**-nah deh kohr-**reh**-ohs
shoe shop	la zapatería	lah thah-pah-teh-**ree**-ah
supermarket	el supermercado	ehl soo-pehr-mehr-**kah**-doh
tobacconist	el estanco	ehl ehs-**tahn**-koh
travel agency	la agencia de viajes	lah ah-**hehn**-thee-ah deh bee-**ah**-hehs

SIGHTSEEING

art gallery	el museo de arte	ehl moo-**seh**-oh deh **ahr**-teh
cathedral	la catedral	lah kah-teh-**drahl**
church	la iglesia la basílica	lah ee-**gleh**-see-ah lah bah-**see**-lee-kah
garden	el jardín	ehl hahr-**deen**
library	la biblioteca	lah bee-blee-oh-**teh**-kah
museum	el museo	ehl moo-**seh**-oh
tourist information office	la oficina de turismo	lah oh-fee-**thee**-nah deh too-**rees**-moh
town hall	el ayuntamiento	ehl ah-yoon-tah-mee-**ehn**-toh
closed for holiday	cerrado por vacaciones	thehr-**rah**-doh pohr bah-kah-thee-**oh**-nehs
bus station	la estación de autobuses	lah ehs-tah-thee-**ohn** deh owtoh-**boo**-sehs
railway station	la estación de trenes	lah ehs-tah-thee-**ohn** deh **treh**-nehs

STAYING IN A HOTEL

Do you have a vacant room?	¿Tiene una habitación libre?	tee-**eh**-neh **oo**-nah ah-bee-tah-thee-**ohn** lee-breh
double room	habitación doble	ah-bee-tah-thee-**ohn** doh-bleh
with double bed	con cama de matrimonio	kohn **kah**-mah deh mah-tree-**moh**-nee-oh
twin room	habitación con dos camas	ah-bee-tah-thee-**ohn** kohn dohs **kah**-mahs
single room	habitación individual	ah-bee-tah-thee-**ohn** een-dee-vee-doo-**ahl**
room with a bath	habitación con baño	ah-bee-tah-thee-**ohn** kohn bah-nyoh
shower	ducha	**doo**-chah
porter	el botones	ehl boh-**toh**-nehs
key	la llave	lah **yah**-veh
I have a reservation.	Tengo una habitación reservada.	tehn-goh **oo**-na ah-bee-tah-thee-**ohn** reh-sehr-**bah**-dah

EATING OUT

Have you got a table for . . .?	¿Tiene mesa para . . .?	tee-**eh**-neh meh-sah pah-**rah**
I want to reserve a table.	Quiero reservar una mesa.	kee-eh-roh reh-sehr-**bahr** **oo**-nah **meh**-sah
The bill please.	La cuenta por favor.	lah **kwehn**-tah pohr fah-**vohr**
I am a vegetarian	Soy vegetariano/a	soy beh-heh-tah-ree-**ah**-no/na
waitress/ waiter	camarera/ camarero	kah-mah-**reh**-rah kah-mah-**reh**-roh
menu	la carta	lah **kahr**-tah
fixed-price menu	menú del día	meh-**noo** dehl **dee**-ah
wine list	la carta de vinos	lah **kahr**-tah deh **bee**-nohs
glass	un vaso	oon **bah**-soh
bottle	una botella	oo-nah boh-**teh**-yah
knife	un cuchillo	oon koo-**chee**-yoh
fork	un tenedor	oon teh-neh-**dohr**
spoon	una cuchara	oo-nah koo-**chah**-rah
breakfast	el desayuno	ehl deh-sah-**yoo**-noh
lunch	la comida/ el almuerzo	lah koh-**mee**-dah/ ehl ahl-**mwehr**-thoh
dinner	la cena	lah **theh**-nah
main course	el primer plato	ehl pree-**mehr plah**-toh
starters	los entremeses	lohs ehn-treh-**meh**-sehs
dish of the day	el plato del día	ehl **plah**-toh dehl **dee**-ah
coffee	el café	ehl kah-**feh**
rare (meat)	poco hecho	**poh**-koh **eh**-choh
medium	medio hecho	**meh**-dee-oh **eh**-choh
well done	muy hecho	mwee **eh**-choh

MENU DECODER

al horno	ahl **ohr**-noh	baked
asado	ah-**sah**-doh	roast
el aceite	ah-**thee-eh**-teh	oil
las aceitunas	ah-theh-**toon**-ahs	olives
el agua mineral	**ah**-gwa mee-neh-**rahl**	mineral water
sin gas/con gas	seen gas/kohn gas	still/sparkling
el ajo	**ah**-hoh	garlic
el arroz	ahr-**rohth**	rice
el azúcar	ah-**thoo**-kahr	sugar
la carne	**kahr**-neh	meat
la cebolla	theh-**boh**-yah	onion
el cerdo	**therh**-doh	pork
la cerveza	thehr-**beh**-thah	beer
el chocolate	choh-koh-**lah**-teh	chocolate
el chorizo	choh-**ree**-thoh	spicy sausage
el cordero	kohr-**deh**-roh	lamb
el fiambre	fee-**ahm**-breh	cold meat
frito	**free**-toh	fried
la fruta	**froo**-tah	fruit
los frutos secos	froo-tohs **seh**-kohs	nuts
las gambas	**gahm**-bahs	prawns
el helado	eh-**lah**-doh	ice cream
el huevo	oo-**eh**-voh	egg
el jamón serrano	hah-**mohn** sehr-**rah**-noh	cured ham
el jerez	heh-**rehz**	sherry

la langosta	lahn-**gohs**-tah	lobster
la leche	**leh**-cheh	milk
el limón	lee-**mohn**	lemon
la limonada	lee-moh-**nah**-dah	lemonade
la mantequilla	mahn-teh-**kee**-yah	butter
la manzana	mahn-**thah**-nah	apple
los mariscos	mah-**rees**-kohs	seafood
la menestra	meh-**nehs**-trah	vegetable stew
la naranja	nah-**rahn**-hah	orange
el pan	pahn	bread
el pastel	pahs-**tehl**	cake
las patatas	pah-**tah**-tahs	potatoes
el pescado	pehs-**kah**-doh	fish
la pimienta	pee-mee-**yehn**-tah	pepper
el plátano	**plah**-tah-noh	banana
el pollo	**poh**-yoh	chicken
el postre	**pohs**-treh	dessert
el queso	**keh**-soh	cheese
la sal	sahl	salt
las salchichas	sahl-**chee**-chahs	sausages
la salsa	**sahl**-sah	sauce
seco	**seh**-koh	dry
el solomillo	soh-loh-**mee**-yoh	sirloin
la sopa	**soh**-pah	soup
la tarta	**tahr**-tah	pie/cake
el té	teh	tea
la ternera	tehr-**neh**-rah	beef
las tostadas	tohs-**tah**-dahs	toast
el vinagre	bee-**nah**-greh	vinegar
el vino blanco	**bee**-noh **blahn**-koh	white wine
el vino rosado	**bee**-noh roh-**sah**-doh	rosé wine
el vino tinto	**bee**-noh **teen**-toh	red wine

NUMBERS

0	cero	**theh**-roh
1	uno	**oo**-noh
2	dos	dohs
3	tres	trehs
4	cuatro	**kwa**-troh
5	cinco	**theen**-koh
6	seis	says
7	siete	**see**-eh-teh
8	ocho	**oh**-choh
9	nueve	**nweh**-veh
10	diez	dee-**ehth**
11	once	**ohn**-theh
12	doce	**doh**-theh
13	trece	**treh**-theh
14	catorce	kah-**tohr**-theh
15	quince	**keen**-theh
16	dieciséis	dee-eh-thee-**seh-ees**
17	diecisiete	dee-eh-thee-see-**eh**-teh
18	dieciocho	dee-eh-thee-**oh**-choh
19	diecinueve	dee-eh-thee-**nweh**-veh
20	veinte	**beh**-een-teh
21	veintiuno	beh-een-tee-**oo**-noh
22	veintidós	beh-een-tee-**dohs**
30	treinta	**treh**-een-tah
31	treinta y uno	treh-een-tah ee **oo**-noh
40	cuarenta	kwah-**rehn**-tah
50	cincuenta	theen-**kwehn**-tah
60	sesenta	seh-**sehn**-tah
70	setenta	seh-**tehn**-tah
80	ochenta	oh-**chehn**-tah
90	noventa	noh-**vehn**-tah
100	cien	thee-**ehn**
101	ciento uno	thee-**ehn**-toh **oo**-noh
102	ciento dos	thee-**ehn**-toh dohs
200	doscientos	dohs-thee-**ehn**-tohs
500	quinientos	khee-nee-**ehn**-tohs
700	setecientos	seh-teh-thee-**ehn**-tohs
900	novecientos	noh-veh-thee-**ehn** tohs
1,000	mil	meel
1,001	mil uno	meel **oo**-noh

TIME

one minute	un minuto	oon mee-**noo**-toh
one hour	una hora	oo-na **oh**-rah
half an hour	media hora	**meh**-dee-a **oh**-rah
Monday	lunes	**loo**-nehs
Tuesday	martes	**mahr**-tehs
Wednesday	miércoles	mee-**ehr**-koh-lehs
Thursday	jueves	hoo-**weh**-vehs
Friday	viernes	bee-**ehr**-nehs
Saturday	sábado	**sah**-bah-doh
Sunday	domingo	doh-**meen**-goh

MADRID TRANSPORT MAP

Madrid's metro runs from 6am–1:30am daily. Its 11 lines are identified by number and colour, both in the stations and on the trains. Platform signs display the time elapsed since the last train, not how long to the next train. A fixed-price ticket *(billete)* will take you anywhere on the system, although a ten-trip ticket *(metrobus)* is much better value for money.

The metro lines are linked with the RENFE train stations: Chamartín, Atocha and Norte (Príncipe Pío), which has a fast line from Ópera. *Largo recorrido* (long-distance) and *cercanías* (suburban) trains leave from these stations. A monthly travel pass can be used on the metro, on suburban trains and on buses. A long period of major construction work has created several extensions to existing metro lines, including line 8 to Barajas Airport.